The United States and Decolonization

Also by David Ryan

THE HISTORICAL ATLAS OF NORTH AMERICA (*with Philip Davies, Ronald Mendell and David Brown*)

US–SANDINISTA DIPLOMATIC RELATIONS

The United States and Decolonization

Power and Freedom

Edited by

David Ryan
Department of Historical and International Studies
De Montfort University
Leicester

and

Victor Pungong
The Commonwealth Secretariat
London

Foreword by Warren Kimball

148899

First published in Great Britain 2000 by
MACMILLAN PRESS LTD
Houndmills, Basingstoke, Hampshire RG21 6XS and London
Companies and representatives throughout the world

A catalogue record for this book is available from the British Library.

ISBN 0–333–73055–0

 First published in the United States of America 2000 by
ST. MARTIN'S PRESS, INC.,
Scholarly and Reference Division,
175 Fifth Avenue, New York, N.Y. 10010

ISBN 0–312–23158–X

Library of Congress Cataloging-in-Publication Data
The United States and decolonization : power and freedom / edited by David Ryan
and Victor Pungong.
    p.   cm.
Includes bibliographical references and index.
ISBN 0–312–23158–X (cloth)
1. Decolonization. 2. United States—Foreign relations—20th century. I. Ryan,
David, 1965– II. Pungong, Victor, 1966–

JV151 .U55   2000
327.73—dc21
                                                                        99–059274

This book is printed on paper suitable for recycling and made from fully managed and sustained
forest sources.

10   9   8   7   6   5   4   3   2   1
09   08   07   06   05   04   03   02   01   00

Printed and bound in Great Britain by
Antony Rowe Ltd, Chippenham, Wiltshire

For Daniel and Heidi
&
Jessie, Amah & Solomon Jr

Contents

Acknowledgements

Primarily the editors would like to thank the authors in this collection for their contributions, their encouragement and support throughout the process. In addition they would like to acknowledge the support and understanding provided by their partners Heidi and Jessie. At Macmillan, thanks are due to all the people involved in the process, particularly: Tim Farmiloe, Melanie Blair, Aruna Vasudevan, John Smith and Sue Neville. David Ryan would like to acknowledge the time De Montfort University provided to complete the project. And Victor Pungong would like to acknowledge the inspiration provided by Dr Davidson Nicol over the years.

Notes on the Contributors

Cary Fraser is an historian of international relations who currently teaches in the Department of African and African-American Studies at the Penn State University – University Park. He is the author of *Ambivalent Anticolonialism: the United States and the Genesis of West Indian Independence, 1940–1964* and is currently writing a book which explores the international and domestic dimensions of race in American politics over the period 1941–65.

Lloyd C. Gardner is Charles and Mary Beard Professor of History at Rutgers University, where he has taught since 1963. He is the author of numerous books on US foreign relations. His most recent book is *Pay Any Price: Lyndon Johnson and the Wars for Vietnam*. He is currently working on a book on the Korean War.

Michael H. Hunt, Everett H. Emerson Professor of History at the University of North Carolina at Chapel Hill, writes and teaches in the general field of international history. His most recent works include *Crises in U.S. Foreign Policy: an International History Reader*; *The Genesis of Chinese Communist Foreign Policy*; and *Lyndon Johnson's War: America's Cold War Crusade in Vietnam, 1945–1968*. He is currently engaged in exploring interpretive frameworks for post-1945 global history.

Laurie Johnston teaches Latin American and Caribbean History at University College London and Latin American Economic History at the London School of Economics. She has researched and published on pre-Revolutionary Cuba. In addition to her interest in political economy, she has worked on social policy, particularly education, ideology and nationalism and national identity.

John Kent is Reader in International Relations at the London School of Economics. He has recently completed a three-volume documentary study of Egypt and the defence of the Middle East, 1945–1965, as part of the Documents on the End of Empire project. His publications also include *British Imperial Strategy and the Origins of the Cold War 1944–1949* and *The Internationalization of Colonialism: Britain, France and Black Africa 1939–1956*. He is currently writing a book with John Young on international politics after 1945 and has begun research on the Cold War and the end of Empire in Africa in the 1950s and 1960s.

Warren F. Kimball, the Robert Treat Professor of History at Rutgers University – Newark, was Pitt Professor of American History at Cambridge University, 1988–89, president of the Society for Historians of American Foreign Relations in 1993, and chair of the State Department Historical Advisory Committee, 1991–98. He has written extensively on Roosevelt's foreign policy and Anglo-American relations during the Second World War. He is the author of *The Juggler: Franklin Roosevelt as Wartime Statesman*. His latest book is *Forged in War: Roosevelt, Churchill, and the Second World War* (1997). He is presently working on Reagan, Thatcher and the 'special relationship'.

Walter LaFeber is the Noll Professor of History at Cornell University. His recent publications include *Michael Jordan and the New Global Capitalism* (1999); *The Clash: U.S.–Japan Relations throughout History* (1997); and *America, Russia and the Cold War, 1945–1996* (1997).

Scott Lucas is Head of American and Canadian Studies at the University of Birmingham. He is the author of numerous books and articles on British and US foreign policy, including *Divided We Stand: Britain, the US, and the Suez Crisis* and *Freedom's War: the US Crusade against the Soviet Union, 1945–1956*.

Dennis Merrill, a professor of history at the University of Missouri-Kansas City, is author of *Bread and the Ballot: the United States and India's Economic Development, 1947–1963* (1990). He is also co-editor of *Major Problems in American Foreign Relations* (1994), and general editor of the 25-volume series *A Documentary History of the Truman Presidency* (1995–98). The Society for Historians of American Foreign Relations honoured him with its Stuart L. Bernath Article Prize, and he has received two Fulbright awards to India. His current research interests focus on US–Third World relations during the Cold War, and the history of international tourism.

Paul Orders was until recently a research student at Downing College, Cambridge, where he was awarded a doctorate for his thesis on American–Commonwealth relations in the Pacific during the Second World War. His first book, *Britain, Australia, New Zealand and the Expansion of American Power in the South-West Pacific, 1940–46*, will be published shortly by Macmillan. He currently works as a senior officer in the corporate policy unit of Cardiff City Council.

Victor Pungong is currently a Senior Political Officer at the Commonwealth Secretariat in London. He was previously a lecturer in international relations and comparative politics at De Montfort University, Leicester. He has published on the political and diplomatic aspects of decolonization, government and politics in Africa, and on United Nations peacekeeping.

David Ryan is Principal Lecturer in the Department of Historical and International Studies, De Montfort University, England. He is the author of *US–Sandinista Diplomacy: Voice of Intolerance* (1995) and *US Foreign Relations in World History* (2000) and a co-author of *Historical Atlas of North America* (1998). His current research interests focus on US–Third World issues.

A. J. Stockwell is Professor of Imperial and Commonwealth History and Head of the History Department at Royal Holloway, University of London. His publications include *British Policy and Malay Politics during the Malayan Union Experiment* (1979); *British Imperial Policy and Decolonization, 1938–64* (edited with A. N. Porter, vol. I, 1987, and vol. II, 1989); and *British Documents on End of Empire: Malaya* (editor, 1995). He is joint editor of the *Journal of Imperial and Commonwealth History*.

Foreword

Colonialism. The word brings an automatic frown and shake of the head among Americans. Historical memory is part of what nations are all about, and a visceral dislike of colonialism is part of the American self-image. The conventional wisdom in the United States has long been that colonialism, with its suppression of political freedom, has generated discontent, conflict and eventually revolution. That self-definition began 250 ago when the United States was a small, undeveloped, weak nation. Whatever its potential, the European powers unanimously predicted, a bit wishfully, that the new nation would disintegrate into a babble of little states. As English colonies they had quarrelled as much with each other as with England. Why should that change?

Revolutionary-era Americans also condemned colonialism for its closed economic systems, since those closed doors threatened 'freedom' for the United States to grow and prosper in a world of empires. In fact, political and economic freedom have remained, for Americans, inseparable. Nearly two centuries after the American Revolution, Franklin Roosevelt asserted in his Four Freedoms speech in January 1941, that 'freedom from want' was a prerequisite to political freedom. American leaders during the Cold War justified aid programs to the Third World on the grounds that poverty bred communism and revolution.

Even while post-revolutionary Americans, fearing the power of European empires, were still sharpening their anti-colonial rhetoric, they were acquiring an empire to the West. The American Indians, the oppressed native population that went with 'traditional' European colonialism, disappeared – either further west or into the ground – allowing 'expansion' instead of colonialism to describe the process. Then, after a civil war that insured and enhanced centralised national authority, the Americans indulged in the creation of formal, territorial (what is routinely called European-style) colonialism, acquiring the Philippines, Puerto Rico, Hawaii, and a few other tinier pieces of property – in the process changing both the colonized and the colonizer. Claims that this was but a limited and brief 'experiment' hold up only in comparison to the vast and long-lasting British Empire. And how 'colonial' was the American relationship with Cuba after 1900?

The two twentieth-century world wars accelerated the real and relative growth of American economic and political power, ushering in a period of 'informal empire', which allowed the exercise of power without formal political control. In the eyes of some, that ploy allowed Americans to indulge in self-deceptive anti-colonial rhetoric and to avoid the 'responsibilities' of colonialism, all the while accruing the benefits of hegemony. For others, American economic and political power, which translated into cultural influence, was a natural part of history – an attitude captured in the remark of one adviser to Prime Minister Margaret Thatcher who noted that neither she nor President Ronald Reagan felt any guilt about redistribution of wealth, at home or abroad.[1]

For historians, neither colonialism, imperialism, nor hegemony should carry a specific moral/ethical coding. Results as well as motives are part of any 'cost–benefit' analysis. Are, for example, American claims to have preserved the 'free world' from the Soviet empire offset, even made hypocritical, by US hegemony? Colonialism and imperialism, both forms of empire whatever their differences, require near full control. But 'control' is the wrong word to describe the US world role during and since the Second World War. The United States either could not or would not (perhaps both) exercise control. Other nations could be pressured and coerced, but not consistently commanded. 'Informal empire' was coined to describe that relationship, but perhaps 'hegemony' is a less loaded phrase, in its meaning of a looser, more flexible structure of predominant power rather than empire.[2]

But academic debates do not diminish the American concern, even preoccupation, with territorial (European and Japanese) colonialism; a preoccupation that helped generate change. (One might ask whether or not for a powerful nation to support and promote decolonization is not, in essence, just another form of imperialistic intervention in the affairs of both the colonized and the colonizer – but let us cast that academic debate aside.) Decolonization is the unifying thread of this volume.

The most identifiable beginning of that American policy is the ambivalent episode of the decolonization of Cuba from Spain in the last half of the nineteenth century. However that turned out for Cubans, the elimination of European empires was a major factor. Two decades later, Woodrow Wilson confronted colonialism from the perspective of 'self-determination'. His own racist assumptions worked against that concept, as did awareness of the increasing political/economic imbalance created by Western technology. Time, education, experience, and training were needed in most places, went the argument, before self-determination could become a reality. Stability had to be maintained. But for Wilson, as for most Americans, colonialism was both unethical and destabilizing. When his Secretary of State, Robert Lansing, complained that his president had 'let the genie out of the bottle' by proposing self-determination, Lansing missed the point. As Wilson sensed, and Franklin Roosevelt understood, self-determination was endemic to all cultures. Nationalism, in its uniting of culture and state, was the signal feature of the era, in the East, the West, and all parts in between. The impulse came from the inside, from the colonized, not from external influences. Like the child playing hide-and-seek, nationalists cried, 'Ready or not, here we come.'

But it was Franklin Roosevelt who made decolonization (a word he would not have recognized) part of American foreign policy. He believed adamantly that colonialism fomented violence and revolution, making it the greatest single threat to immediate postwar peace. Churchill and the British, as well as the French mumbled and rumbled about FDR's malign influence on their relationships with their empires, but that was a self-deception. Hitler, the Japanese, and even Vladimir Lenin were more important stimulants. Yet Roosevelt's advocacy of decolonization did inspire and galvanize nationalism in the colonial world (as many of these essays demonstrate). He alone among the Big Three – Churchill, Roosevelt and Stalin – believed that the end of colonial empires was near, although even FDR never expected it to come as swiftly as it did. He placed great-power cooperation ahead of decolonization, believing his European allies had perhaps thirty years in which to educate the 'natives' and prepare their colonies for independence. Roosevelt did not even try to reconcile the contradiction of his condemnations of European colonialism with his passive acceptance of Soviet absorption of the Baltic States. Whatever the practical effect of FDR's public statements and his compromises with his European allies, the issue was joined. It would not go away.

Yet, with the arrival of the Cold War, paradox appeared. American leaders faced what they saw as a dilemma. Great Britain and France in particular held empires with economic resources and strategic positions that seemed essential to success in the confrontation with both the Soviet Union and the spectre of communism (revolution?). Yet colonialism had quickly become a chink in the West's armour. In the struggle for the 'hearts and minds' of the peoples of the world,

Soviet/communist leaders argued that colonialism was part of the very nature of Western, capitalist society. Only we can make you free, proclaimed the Kremlin. (Western leaders quickly hurled the epithet back, arguing that the Soviet Union had an informal empire in Eastern Europe, and a formal one at home.)

The American solution was, in the phrase of two historians, 'The Imperialism of Decolonization'.[3] Support the preservation of economic and political ties between ex-colonial powers and new nations; maintain the military bases and the intelligence assets; continue to train and arm the native military forces that had once been used to control the colony; keep the ex-colony in the 'system'. But divest yourselves of direct political control, they told the Europeans. No more the Union Jack flying over Government House; no more the imposition of a colonial governor; no more British or French forces trooping the streets in a display of who's in charge. As Vietnam and Iran demonstrated, that path had its dangers. As the collapse of the Cold War demonstrated, that path had its successes.

The debate over definitions never leaves us, and colonialism is no exception. I recall an impassioned discussion with one British historian over my insistence that, when he wrote about these matters, he had to recognize that, rightly or wrongly, Americans perceived a great difference between 'colonialism' and 'imperialism'. His response was that 'they were wrong!' The juxtaposition of the title and subtitle of this book seems to argue, implicitly, that the distinctions lack precision and thus are only marginally useful. Accordingly, this is all about a nation's power, economic and political, and the exercise of that power. Power is both the temptation and the prerequisite to colonialism. Thus the paradox that the United States stands accused and found guilty of being a colonial power, today and in the past, despite its own history of anti-colonialism.

But conflating colonialism, expansionism, neo-colonialism (whatever that means), imperialism and hegemony threatens to eliminate ideas from the analysis. Is American colonialism an inevitable product of the nation's political economy, or is it a natural impulse of nations to expand and, in one form or another, colonize? Does that leave to capitalism only the shaping of style rather than the substance of America's exercise of power – be it colonialism, imperialism, or hegemony? Those questions offer intersections of agreement and disagreement in these essays, and in the ongoing debate.

WARREN F. KIMBALL

Notes

1 Interview, Dame Pauline Neville-Jones, 15 May 1998 (London).
2 See the perceptive recent work of Bruce Cumings on this; for example, 'Global Realm with No Limit, Global Realm with No Name', RHR/MARHO Imperialism Roundtable, American Historical Association Meeting, Dec. 1992, posted on the internet at http://chnm.gmu.edu/rhr/cumings.htm.
3 See Wm Roger Louis and Ronald Robinson, 'The Imperialism of Decolonization', *The Journal of Imperial and Commonwealth History*, vol. 22, no. 3 (September, 1994), pp. 462–511.

By Way of Introduction: the United States, Decolonization and the World System

David Ryan

The collapse of the Soviet imperial system increased the tendency to look at the period since 1945 through paradigms other than those that centralized the Cold War. Though the Cold War exerted considerable influence, greater attention is being paid to the dynamics of the US–European relationship, their colonial systems, the independence movements and later to the nations that were identified collectively as the Third World. The international system struggled with the centralizing tendencies of the superpowers and the de-centring challenges of other states trying to assert a more independent role. Similarly analysts of the period struggled within a charged atmosphere that hung over the development of the historiography. Warren Kimball commented that the historical imperialism of the Cold War had colonized much of the history of the Second World War, because many of the scholars writing about the war were in part fighting the Cold War. Even though the bipolar paradigm may be useful to analyse the US–Soviet confrontation, Fraser contends that it 'has consistently proved itself inadequate as an analytical tool in studying the forces of change that have reshaped the international order' since 1945.[1]

The essays here on the United States and decolonization[2] advance the post-Cold War writing on the important formative relationships and the systems within which they operate. While the Cold War added a new layer on to the international system, much of the political and economic structures were derivative of processes erected in the nineteenth century.[3] Ironically, the various independence movements, the United States and the Soviet Union, though all were agents of decolonization[4] of the European empires in the twentieth century, clashed with each other on numerous occasions. The first section looks at the emergence of the system and US views on decolonization. This essay concentrates on decolonization and the US interests in the world system; Walter LaFeber traces the historical evolution of US views on colonialism and decolonization as an 'irony of American history'; and Laurie Johnston examines Washington's informal imperialism in the Western Hemisphere. The two contributions by Orders and Pungong specifically look at Franklin Roosevelt's approach to decolonization and his ideas on Trusteeship. Five further studies examine specific regions. Beginning with, in roughly chronological development, Dennis Merrill on the successful decolonization of India, and Lloyd C. Gardner on the frustrations of Vietnam. Stockwell, Lucas and Kent treat the evolution of US policies towards Malaya, the Middle East and Black Africa respectively. The US response was rarely consistent, either from region to region, or between its traditions, rhetoric and its policies. Michael H. Hunt concludes the main part of the volume by dissecting these arguments, and using his work on ideology to explain the apparent gaps and inconsistencies. Cary Fraser provides a few thoughts on the transformation of the United States as colony to that of empire, with suggestions of where further research might lead.

Moving beyond the Cold War, this contribution traces the US relationship with decolonization situated within a broader history of integration and the advancing dominance of the United States in the world system which it increasingly shaped through the twentieth century. I end the discussion in the early postwar period from when most of the contributions begin.

This essay moves back in both time and space, which facilitates an interpretation of the US policies on decolonization set within the increasing tendency towards integration within the world system. David Reynolds argues that in the 'long run, the most important fact of twentieth century world history lies in the nineteenth century, in the failure of secession and the triumph of federal unionism'. This permitted the construction of a vast continental empire whose various powers could be effectively used in the twentieth, 'American century'. The impetus towards integration, of course, began long before, in the colonization of the western parts of the continent. Stephanson makes a distinction between the 'empire of liberty' and the 'empire for liberty', noting that in the early formulation, typical in Jefferson's thinking, there was no contradiction between the creation of an empire and the promotion of self-determination. The 'empire for liberty' is perpetuated precisely to serve the purposes of liberty, sovereignty and self-determination as a compound set. Self-determination that did not serve the empire for liberty was often not tolerated. This sort of empire was 'a perpetually growing space for the demonstration of the higher historical purposes of humankind as such, all in the name of self-determination and autonomy. It is a timeless, physically indeterminate space of movement and colonization.' In the early post-Second World War period the US was at the core of an 'empire by integration'.[5]

In the collective US mind, nurtured on the formal and informal ideologies and traditions of its society, there was perhaps little contradiction between empire and liberty. The bridge between the apparent gap between an imperial system and self-determination can be crossed through an understanding of the legitimizing ideologies of the people accorded citizenship within the United States. For these people empire enhanced and secured their self-determination. And in so far as the empire for liberty enhanced the sovereign opportunities for its realm this statement can generally be held. The process was active in the Monroe Doctrine, the open-door notes, Wilson's Fourteen Points, and in the formulations of 'free world' politics during the Cold War. These landmark symbols of US foreign policy reinforce the formulation within the culture. But at each point of expansion there was also considerable disagreement within the US culture, which tended after time towards reconciliation and consensus and the reconstruction of the narrative of US foreign relations with the discourse of the benevolent mission.

Thus empire served the self-determination of those within the Union after periods of social or civil conflicts. Self-determination was enhanced as a concept in US foreign relations with the prohibition of acquiring new territory in the Teller amendment, through to Wilson's encouragement for nationalist movements in the Fourteen Points. Great traditions in US history enhanced these ideas. The thirteen states were realized through the process of decolonization; Monroe, McKinley, Wilson, and Roosevelt's policies all enhanced self-determination against other empires: against the Spanish, the Russians or the Holy Alliance, against the European and Japanese powers in China, against the collapsing and yet-to-collapse European empires between Versailles and Yalta. All of these formulations supported the 'empire for liberty'. But where nationalism or self-determination resisted the political or economic forces of the US empire, Washington was often swift to undermine expressions of autonomy. Within the world system, autarky was intolerable precisely because it limited the sphere in which the empire for liberty could operate. Pluralism in the economic realm was not encouraged within the visions of integration and global economy that advanced through the twentieth century. The anti-colonial traditions enhanced political self-determination against other empires, yet in the sphere of economy Washington was often described as neo-colonial. The contradictions between the essentially political international system and the transnational global economic forces have been overcome through the exercise of hegemony, especially in the period since 1945.[6]

Viewed from afar one can see in the US experience colonial, anti-colonial, post-colonial and neo-colonial facets, which successively move towards economic integration, towards a globalizing economy. The expansion moved in several directions at different times: across to the western coasts of North America, further west across the ocean highway to the East, south through the Caribbean and the Central American republics, back to engage with the old world to prise open their empires, and finally to confront the Soviet empire and extend the western economy into Eastern Europe and the former Soviet Union. This left Clinton the task of directing the *Strategy for Engagement and Enlargement*, and of confronting the 'backlash states' which do not seem to conform to accepting 'empire as a way of life'.[7]

Moving the centre in the world system

The United States was born with a declaration and a war of independence from 1776 in the first wave of decolonization. Almost immediately it began a colonial project which imposed a system in which citizens could pursue the right of life, liberty and happiness. The empire was justified through reference to the higher purposes of liberty. Coupled with their worldview on the hierarchy of race, the voices of dissent and the resistance of the colonized were largely not troublesome. Through colonialism[8] the empire for liberty spread across the continent. In 1853 the contiguous expansion had been completed, by which point rival European powers had been displaced, Native American populations had been removed, cleared or eliminated, and the Mexicans had lost half their territory. This expansion, legitimized through ideologies of 'manifest destiny' and eventual incorporation on an equal basis, removed the idea of colonialism from the predominant discourse of US history. Even after this the United States exhibited another form of colonialism in their acquisition of the Philippines and Puerto Rico, and their extensive control over Cuba and an array of Pacific islands in the twentieth century. Despite this the anti-colonial sentiment endured because the non-contiguous colonization was identified as an 'aberration'.

Even though reconciliation may occur and produce ideological consensus within the United States, a tension exists temporarily within US society during expansive periods and more permanently in the histories of the colonized, the tension again basically between empire and liberty. Fuelled by nationalism it first served US self-determination, which through hegemonic processes of inclusion later served such concepts as 'the empire for civilization',[9] the 'West' and so forth. It did not serve to create an 'empire of liberty' in which pluralism and a tolerance of difference was acceptable. The tension is evident in the symbols US history throws up, often the foundations of various ideologies and political agendas. Jefferson can be seen as both the author of the Declaration of Independence and as that of the treaties of the Louisiana Purchase. The symbolism remains pertinent to the various discussions on the United States and decolonization, because as Americans tended to absolutize their culture the Jefferson of 1803 was often forgotten. The pursuit of 'life, liberty, and happiness' was seen as 'self-evident'. The pursuit of territory or 'property' facilitated that purpose for some.[10] The essentially Enlightenment project envisioned no 'life expectancy' on such self-evident truths. The end of history would bring about the realization of the 'American dream' in an open world economy characterized by liberal democracy.[11]

Expansion was a constant in US history. The United States at once claimed to be an exceptionalist power, and yet their project was, according to Thomas Paine, 'the cause of all mankind'. For Ricard the expansive republicanism 'rested on an irreducible contradiction that would forever vitiate U.S. foreign policy: the basic incompatibility of the exceptionalist claim with political messianism, of singularity with universalism'.[12] Empire and liberty, conquest and freedom, democracy and self-determination were all concepts which were retrospectively merged through the workings of the national ideology, though at almost every point of US expansion there was some opposition and protest, not only from the victims in the process. So, Manifest Destiny eased the passage to the conquest and settlement of the west; Progressivism that of US colonialism and neo-colonialism in the Philippines, in Central America and the Caribbean.[13] There were enough references in the baggage of US ideologies to first justify its colonialism and then to oppose that of others.

The symbolic landmarks of US foreign relations – the Monroe Doctrine, the Open Door notes, and Wilsonian internationalism – established traditions in US diplomacy. Monroe told Congress in 1823, following a wave of decolonization in Latin America, that 'the American continents, by the free and independent condition which they have assumed and maintain, are henceforth not to be considered as subjects for future colonization by any European powers'. John Hay ostensibly sought to 'preserve Chinese territorial and administrative entity', to stop the potential consolidation of European 'spheres of influence' in the region. And Woodrow Wilson at once advocated the Monroe Doctrine for the world and in the Fourteen Points of 1918 sought a: 'free, open-minded, and absolutely impartial adjustment of all colonial claims'.[14] The United States had a certain political self-consciousness that they were a new force in world history. Theirs in a sense was an evangelical foreign policy to begin with (still echoed in current speeches), but then the religious overtones gave way to secular rhetoric based on progress, efficiency and improvement.[15] But with this quest for perfectibility, assuming in many ways that it was the end point of ideological evolution, as Stephanson puts it, 'History could not conceivably evolve a better system of sustaining the liberty of man to permit the unfettered pursuit of his desires. Indeed, there could be nothing 'higher,' only more of the same.'[16] The progressive logic coupled with beliefs in the hierarchy of race resulted in incalculable misery for countless people.

As LaFeber argues, while Americans often presented themselves as the leaders of the global process of decolonization, these principles have often been sacrificed 'for the practices of imperial conquest and global hegemony'.[17] Despite all of this it should be borne in mind that ideologies and worldviews often have a very loose relationship to consistency, and that it is not that surprising that apparent contradictions could be advanced simultaneously. The United States had created for itself (because others did not see it this way) a more or less coherent identity associated with the champion of decolonization, the well-wisher of them all, as John Quincy Adams put it.[18]

These traditions also had a great deal to do with the world system. In President Monroe's injunction that the Western Hemisphere should not be considered as an area for future colonization by the European powers there was also a calculated strategy that facilitated contemporary US opportunities. At that point in time the United States had little naval power and had to rely on the commercial interests of the British to inhibit any inclinations the Spanish had to recolonize territories in Latin America. Largely as a result of the political manoeuvring of Monroe's Secretary of State, John Quincy Adams, the United States had rejected a similar proposal from the British precisely because one objective was to remove rival powers from the hemisphere. This would facilitate the process of westward expansion and colonization, still incomplete in 1823. The British Foreign Secretary, George Canning, saw the policy as self-interested, associated with commercial gain, and devoid of altruism. Later, Robert Lansing, soon Wilson's Secretary of State, wrote that the Monroe Doctrine was based on 'selfishness alone'. The 'integrity of the other American nations is an incident, not an end'.[19] In 1823 there was no contradiction between US national interests in exclusion of European empires and the political self-determination of the Latin American nations. By the turn of the century, however, the expressions of self-determination in Central America and the Caribbean and US opportunities clashed precisely because the world system had integrated these areas more comprehensively. Roosevelt's civilizing discourse turned Monroe's formulation from an ostensible support of self-determination into a corollary that undermined the sovereignty of many a Caribbean island or Central American nation. The vital aspect here is the continued economic integration of the region, echoed in Lodge and Wilson's additions to the doctrine and through their multiple interventions.

Similarly, the Open Door notes were presented as enhancing Chinese territorial integrity and national self-determination. They were designed to prevent further European colonialism in the region and facilitate equal access to the markets. Despite this, the Chinese complained that they were not consulted by the United States and that they had very limited ability to determine their own fate.[20] The arguments relating to colonialism seemed again more an incident than an end in US policy; they were an attempt to frame the desire for economic access around some more palatable concept. This was especially important after the Anti-Imperialist League in the United States had been so vocal in their condemnation of US colonialism in the Philippines.[21] They did not object to expansion *per se*.

Access was required, if not in actuality, at least in the financial imagination of policy-makers at the time. In the winter of 1884–85 Washington had watched the European colonial powers settle their differences on Africa around a conference-table in Berlin. The resulting partition, first on paper through agreements before the actual partition in Africa, had an enduring impact in the shape of the current African states. US commerce was largely excluded from these areas. Such an outcome had to be prevented, as Germany and Russia, the losers in the 'scramble for Africa', threatened to expand their spheres in China.[22]

US decision-makers were caught between several competing forces. The Teller amendment and the Anti-Imperialist League made further territorial acquisition difficult. The closing of the frontier, domestic recession, a sevenfold increase in US exports, all necessitated the guarantee of continued US expansion. The open-door policy was, according to Zinn, 'a more sophisticated approach to imperialism than the traditional empire-building of Europe'.[23]

The US anti-colonial inclination in the twentieth century was born from the assumed traditions of the nation and the continued search for opportunities. Though the United States did not add further major colonies to its jurisdiction after the Philippines, which eventually was granted independence in July 1946, it continues to hold jurisdiction over several Pacific islands, and it rarely shied away from operating an imperial system during the twentieth century. Imperialism here must be understood as something more than the operation of a colonial system alone. Said suggests that it should include the theory and practice, and 'attitudes of a dominating metropolitan centre ruling a distant territory'.[24] Attitudes of superiority are thoroughly ingrained in the ideologies associated with US foreign policy.[25] The ability to exercise economic or military muscle varied according to time and place. By the twentieth century US foreign policy could be characterised as both anti-colonial in some spheres, yet still imperial.

Establishing the centre

Depending on one's view, this more sophisticated approach to imperialism can be wrapped up in the discourse of exploitation and degradation or in that of progress and further contributions to civilization. The apparent contradictions exist in one discourse but not in the other. So in 1904 when Theodore Roosevelt provided his corollary to the Monroe Doctrine he was, from his perspective, furthering the progressive ideals:

> If a nation shows that it knows how to act with reasonable efficiency and decency in social and political matters, if it keeps order and pays its obligations, it need fear no interference from the United States. Chronic wrongdoing, or an impotence which results in a general loosening of the ties of civilized society, may in America, ultimately require intervention by some civilized nation, and in the western Hemisphere the adherence of the United States to the Monroe Doctrine may force the United States, however reluctantly, in flagrant cases of such wrongdoing or impotence, to the exercise of an international police power.

Ultimately access was required. The US wanted the Europeans out of the Western Hemisphere, and so collected their debts. Americans went in search of markets and to promote an understanding of 'civilization'; and as Roosevelt put it, 'They have great riches, and if within their borders the reign of law and justice obtains, prosperity is sure to come to them. While they thus obey the primary laws of civilized society they may rest assured that they will be treated by us in a spirit of cordial and helpful sympathy.'[26] While Roosevelt no doubt saw himself and the United States as the engine of history and civilization, the bearer of the 'white man's burden', there was awareness of another narrative and opposition to these assumptions from both within and outside the United States. As Laurie Johnston's essay demonstrates, José Martí had forecast the emerging relationships in the Western Hemisphere and how commercial dominance compromised political liberty.[27] Even though Martí railed against the US system in the 1890s, the substantial and popular protests against European colonialism accelerated in the 1930s and the collapse in the world economy demonstrated the interconnections between the colony and the colonial power. Only when these economic ties were more extensive did Third World leaders protest at what they considered US neo-imperialism.

Between the 1890s and the 1960s the world passed through the 'apogee of nationalism'. National self-determination became particularly attractive to the European empires so long as it was merely applied to the empires that collapsed in the First World War, which areas soon became 'mandates', mainly of the British and the French. But as the Russian revolution presented an alternative that was far more radical, Wilson's national self-determination became more palatable. Many Third World leaders lobbied the victorious powers at Versailles to recognize their national self-determination, but their tactical or sincere requests fell largely on deaf ears. However, a nationalism of a more threatening sort to the US empire for liberty also emerged in the inter-war period. Various national economies prevailed over the aspirations to return to the international economy of 1913. The crisis of the late 1920s and the depression of the 1930s compounded the process. World capitalism 'retreated into the igloos of its nation-state economies and their associated empires'.[28]

The Wilsonian self-determination at the political level was an uncomfortable partner to the vision of the open door world economy that the US promoted in that the liberal values were always applied selectively and, as Rosenberg has demonstrated, the values put forward were at odds with the experience of US history. The US formulae of progress, for the advancement of civilization, or modernization, were at odds with their own practices of using protective tariffs and import quotas, by subsidizing the export sector through promotional state activities. They warned foreigners not to operate tactics which had frequently been used in the development of the US economy.[29]

The imperialism and the economic activity that were seen as progress in metropolitan centres, perhaps necessary to maintain a type of liberty within the United States, and certainly necessary to protect their way of life, simultaneously changed forever the structure of the international order and lifestyles around the world. Barraclough has described the process as a revolution in world history:

> From the heart of the new industrial societies forces went out which encompassed and transformed the whole world, without respect for persons or for established institutions. Both for the inhabitants of the industrialised nations and for those outside conditions of living changed in fundamental ways; new tensions were set up and new centres of gravity were in process of formation.

Even earlier, Karl Marx recognized the effects of the emerging system of capitalism, describing it as contributing to the 'uninterrupted disturbance of all social conditions, everlasting uncertainty and agitation [that] distinguish the bourgeois epoch from earlier ones'.[30] Capitalism, colonial or not, thoroughly disrupted and disturbed traditional life. And 'empire of liberty' it certainly was not. From the ethnocentric perspectives of the policy-makers in the metropolitan centres, these disturbances represented progress; progress against the older ways of life; progress towards a global civilization; progress towards further economic integration. Now, for the United States, only European empires, Soviet power and national economic autarky stood in the way of continued economic expansion and the avoidance of further and subsequent depression.

Economic multilateralism emerged as a staple tradition, perhaps invented tradition, of US diplomacy. While countries already firmly within the international financial system could attract US loans, countries on the periphery, less attractive to investment bankers without government assistance had to accept what President Taft called 'dollar diplomacy . . . the process of arranging loans in exchange for some kind of financial supervision'. Rosenberg explains that 'the architects of dollar diplomacy – foreign policy-makers, investment bankers, and professional economists – tended to equated the spread of American bank loans and financial expertise with the spread of "civilization" generally'. Through these practices the US 'government sought to enlarge its economic and strategic presence by measures short of outright colonialism'.[31] Apart from the interruption of the Great Depression, the Taftian practice continued from his presidency, through Wilson's and the 1920s, and was resumed in the postwar period through the prescriptive packages associated with the IMF and the World Bank, as they both 'bail out' and westernize Third World economies.

Even then the practices associated with this type of exercise of power produced debate. Rosenberg relates the story of one Samuel Guy Inman who wrote a piece in the *Atlantic Monthly* arguing that an imperial America 'cannot go on destroying with impunity the sovereignty of other peoples . . . cutting across the principles for which our fathers fought'. None other than the State Department's Sumner Welles provided the response, repositioning dollar diplomacy within a progressive framework, arguing that contact and commercial exchange inculcate better understanding between nations, distancing the ideas of commercial exchange and 'economic domination'.[32] These days, it is not difficult to see which narrative holds greater sway in the policy-making circles filled with neo-liberal economists in Washington at the IMF and the World Bank and in Geneva at the World Trade Organization. Still, various echoes of Inman's narrative have been heard from around the world from the Zapatistas to the Sandinistas, from Nkrumah, Nehru, and Ho Chi Minh, to the liberation theologians.

Whatever the ends of the issue, the process of economic integration proceeded through these decades backed by Wilson's Fourteen Points, on the removal of colonialism and the 'removal . . . of all economic barriers and the establishment of an equality of trade conditions among all the nations'.[33] The process was not linear, however. The 1930s depression forced Americans to concentrate on domestic issues. In retreat the global economy fragmented. The economies of central and eastern Europe resorted to barter in an unpredictable international environment. Japan's invasion of Manchuria closed a further area of China, and ultimately its economy moved towards autonomous recovery. The British closed the trade of its colonies through the introduction of the Imperial Preference System in Ottawa (1932), creating the Sterling Area. The United States formalized the process of repatriating capital that had begun in 1928. Roosevelt placed the importance of the domestic economy above all in his inauguration speech, before retreating into relative economic isolationism. Nazi Germany removed itself from the international system, creating a sphere of influence in central Europe, which preceded a formal policy of autarky from 1936.[34] By the end of the decade businessmen and policy-makers in the United States wondered whether capitalism could survive in such restricted circumstances.[35]

Notwithstanding their own closure, Secretary Hull equated prosperity with peace and increasingly sought agreement on international economic matters. In 1934 Hull envisaged a worldwide peace brought about through the Reciprocal Trade Agreements Act. Economic warfare created internal strife, and much of this could be avoided through international trade. The system of a liberalized world trade would eventually find its way into the Bretton Woods agreements in 1944, after the punctuation of the war.[36]

For its part Washington sought to avoid war through what Gardner calls 'multilateral appeasement'. Hull sought agreements between the large industrialized powers to halt and reverse the process of economic fragmentation. The economic multilateralism envisaged in Washington by the end of the 1930s was seen, however, in London as an attempt to break up the British Empire. Neville Chamberlain did not want to give up the British Imperial Preference system and thought that 'appeasement . . . might rescue Britain from unwanted entanglements across the Atlantic'. Chamberlain was willing to reconsider the adjustment of the colonial system with German inclusion. British power would still be backed by empire, but the US economic system would mean an eventual end to Empire. Gardner writes:

> After failing to enlist British support for his 'multilateral appeasement' proposal, Roosevelt stood aside while Chamberlain pursued 'bilateral appeasement' to its unhappy conclusion. He wished the prime minister well at the time of Munich while doubting the outcome. But the Roosevelt proposal never really disappeared, for it became the basis of various statements of American war aims throughout World War II, all of them designed to avoid American participation in a spheres-of-influence 'deal' that the other great powers might arrange among them.[37]

The major sites of disagreement on the issue of the postwar international economy and colonialism were in Article VII of the Lend-Lease agreement and in the Atlantic Charter of 1941. Through both, Washington had made its assistance during the war conditional. As it made clear to Keynes, they expected the British to open up their Imperial Preference system. Dean Acheson made it clear Americans would not tolerate their government providing the British with aid without some reciprocity. This did not necessarily involve repayment, but did at least involve removing trade barriers. Sumner Welles brought up the issue at the Atlantic Conference, indicating that the closed systems had been fatal in the past. Churchill bitterly complained that it seemed as though Washington was expecting concessions on the part of the British without reducing its own trade barriers.[38] Such, however, was the power of the United States, which sought full opportunity from the effects of the war on Europe. The hegemonic advantage had particular attraction. As McCormick put it, 'World War II . . . would be the means by which the United States asserted and assumed hegemony in the world-system; it would become global workshop and banker, umpire and policeman, preacher and teacher.'[39] Decolonization was not necessarily expected in the late 1930s but the shift in global power through the war made all the difference.[40]

The Atlantic Charter too had advanced the prospects for decolonization. The overriding objective was to defeat the Axis powers, which meant that in the process various compromises were made. But defeating the Axis powers was not the only agenda item on the minds of the European powers and the US. Throughout the war they made policies and decisions with eyes cast both on the Axis and on each other. Hence, Reynolds suggests there is a double image of the alliance, captured in the titles of various books: 'ambiguous partnership', 'competitive co-operation', and 'allies of a kind'. The *status quo ante bellum* would not return. Decolonization and the future shape of the world economy were clearly on the agenda with the strength of nationalist movements and US pressure.[41]

While there was considerable agreement on the European sphere the major disagreements concerned the colonial world. Washington saw an opportunity to gain access to areas previously denied to its economic reach. The process of decolonization was advanced in the Atlantic Charter when the powers agreed to 'respect the right of all peoples to choose the form of government under which they will live'. Though the British were able to insert an exception for their empire, nationalist leaders around the world used the language to advance their cause. This time it was more effective than at Versailles. Holland suspects that though historians have 'probably exaggerated the significance of this piece of windbaggery, it did play a part in stimulating nationalist ideas in the non-European world by giving them the touch of Anglo-American acceptability'. Apart from everything else, the language of the Charter was probably necessary for domestic political reasons.[42]

The United States moderated its anti-colonial stance during the war, not least because of Churchill's reactions. While Washington intended to integrate the economies of the colonial areas and extend the open door, it became increasingly aware that the European powers would be useful in controlling the 'volatility' of nationalists during the transitionary period. Washington preferred a gradual move towards independence, in some cases advocating a period of western tutelage under the trusteeship system.[43] These potential new nations would not be under immediate US influence and so not immediately susceptible to its pressure. Nationalist leaders were often critical of the United States because in many ways they had been 'allies of a kind' with the imperial powers. Moreover, since 1917 the Soviet model of national development offered an alternative.

In 1944 the Swedish economist Gunnar Myrdal had identified a sort of panic in Washington's rhetoric on the new world order. Their incessant search for foreign markets was not only concerned with a healthy economy, but also linked to an attempt to prevent the spread of radical ideas.[44] Prosperity in Hull's thinking was intertwined with peace, and it seemed according to this formula that peace could only be maintained through the application of the open door. Thus Washington was at once trying to transcend the Old World powers, contain Soviet-centred power, and those of radical nationalism. Given that Washington could not openly oppose national self-determination, such movements were often labelled 'communist'. The threat of communism, apart from the ideological formulas, also included the propensity of nationalist regimes to move towards greater control of their resources through various forms of autarky or import substitution, in later years. The threat of such 'communist' powers included their unwillingness to 'complement the industrial economies of the West'.[45]

Both economy and ideology challenged Washington where the Soviets exercised influence. Ideologically, all the successful independence movements prior to the 1970s had subscribed to 'western' formulas of either the left or the right. States rarely sought independence on a traditionalist basis. Ideologies of universal progress had supplemented more traditional and particular forms of autonomy, democracy and development. The myth of 1776, Jefferson and Paine had been compromised by the US occupation of the Philippines and because the open door was in many ways regarded as imperial. The Soviet Union, however, provided models for planned industrialization and their anti-imperial ideas were both more recent and seemingly more relevant. Nationalists all over the world had read the writings of Paine and

Jefferson, the addresses of Lincoln and had taken comfort in these visions. Ho Chi Minh had actually declared Vietnamese independence by borrowing heavily the words and the structure of the US Declaration of Independence. Clearly he and other leaders looked to the United States of Jefferson of 1776, or 1801, but not the Jefferson of 1803, imperial president, colonist, slaveholder. Gardner writes, 'How crushing, then, that so many Asians and Africans held up to America after World War II a new image in which Uncle Sam had become corroded and evil.' For one group, he points out, 'this was part of the Irony of American History: there never was an America (or any nation of mortals) so pure or so innocent'.[46]

US engagement with the process of decolonization involved far more than the traditions of self-determination and liberty. While it could echo many traditions from its past, the compromises that it made were also thoroughly traditional. Theirs was a vision in which Americans would serve others by serving themselves.[47] In the brief period of hegemony over the global economy Acheson indicated that there was the opportunity to 'grab hold of history and make it conform'.[48] European competitors rescued their nation-states through the formation of a defensive economic union,[49] even though US culture and ideologies increasingly penetrated them.[50] Washington was in a unique position to advance its interests in both the colonial and independent worlds. In short, it could move forward the process of globalization through economic integration. The motivations and effects were varied, as the essays in this book attest. The processes met with various obstacles and forms of resistance. But nevertheless, there was a determination: a sort of imperialism of decolonization.[51]

From World War to Cold War

Franklin Roosevelt was divided on the issue. Many point to his genuine interest in and inclination to push for decolonization where and when he could. They also recognized that the United States, powerful though it was, was not omnipotent. The British and the French, weakened though they were, were not completely pliable. Kimball considers Roosevelt as tireless in his attempts to bring the issue on to the agenda at the wartime conferences and in his communications especially with Churchill. Nevertheless, he had still inherited the paternalism that went with the culture of great-power politics and the ideologies with which he had grown up. He wanted both the concepts of the Four Policemen and gradual self-determination for the colonial areas. Above all, the process had to be orderly. 'Roosevelt consistently used his vast presidential powers to push for a faze out of colonial empires, although he sometimes side tracked his anti-colonial initiatives when such moves conflicted with immediate wartime or post-war military and geopolitical objectives.'[52] He was constantly torn between constructing a system of great-power collaboration and promoting decolonization. His approach represented a blend of idealism and self-interest, self-determination and the open door.[53]

Crucially, the US support for decolonization was not a zero-sum game. While often presented as such in the totalizing or universalistic visions of US policy-makers, the pragmatic approach to global affairs has brought about compromise and concession. In the postwar period, when the demands for decolonization became even more acute, Washington found itself in an extremely difficult position. It viewed itself as the 'honest broker' between the imperial powers and the colonies, though neither viewed Washington as such. In the emerging Cold War context Washington viewed both the move towards independence and the maintenance of the colonial system as agents for stability. Similarly, if the independence movement was seen to be heavily influenced by socialist ideas or the Soviet Union, Washington viewed self-determination and decolonization as incompatible.[54] The horrors of European colonialism were one thing, those of Soviet communism quite another. In many ways the Soviet Union was not only being portrayed as the new fascist power, Red Fascism, but also the new form of colonialism.[55]

This sort of reductionism was attractive to policy-makers. Throughout his influential period in the Truman administration, George Kennan complained about the tendency to use an all-encompassing universal language to promote US foreign policy. He wrote in his Policy Planning Studies: 'This universalistic approach has a strong appeal to U.S. public opinion; for it appears to obviate the necessity of dealing with the national peculiarities and diverging political philosophies of foreign peoples; which many of our people find confusing and irritating. In this sense, it contains a strong vein of escapism.' And, 'instead of being compelled to make the sordid and involved political choices inherent in traditional diplomacy, we could make decisions on the lofty but simple plane of moral principle and under the protecting cover of majority decision'.[56] The tendency both simplified and complicated the US situation.

The US promotion of economic integration was particularly concerned with avoiding the autarky that descended on the 1930s. Containment was in this sense not only limited to the Soviet Union, but also extended to containing rival forms of national capitalist development. Crucially it sought to maintain the American way of life, necessitating maintenance of 'a position of disparity' in the wealth distribution of the world.[57] The language of the Truman Doctrine made it difficult for Washington to appear in a position of supporting colonial powers, and yet they needed the revival of a healthy European economy in part for their own prosperity, and to contain the Soviet Union. As Kennan saw it, an integrated Europe needed Britain. In turn, Britain needed either North America or Africa, or a 'second possible solution would lie in arrangements whereby a union of Western European nations would undertake jointly the economic development and exploitation of the colonial and dependent areas of the African Continent'.[58]

The dollar gap forced European powers to increasingly earn dollars through their colonial possessions. Thus the links between the United States, Europe and the Third World became vital to the health of the western economy. The Cold War and US power spread to the Third World because these economic links were so important to all concerned. Robert Wood writes: 'The European Recovery Program was not simply about either Europe or recovery; it was much more ambitious than that.' Secretary Marshall's plan addressed the economic problems of the 1930s with a vision of a global integrated economy. The Soviet sphere lay outside this structure. East European food supplies had been 'lost' to Soviet domination; colonial dollars may be lost if the independence movement was too nationalistic or pro-Soviet; Europe had lost significant earning from Latin America which were used to pay for their wartime debts; the terms of trade worked against the Europeans and their colonies; and the European dependency left the economies somewhat vulnerable and susceptible to changes in the US economy.[59] Hence Washington collaborated with the European colonial powers, the rhetoric of their foreign policy notwithstanding, to foreclose opportunities for the Soviet Union and to bolster the western economic system. Rapid decolonization might both undermine the European economies, and cause instability in the Third World, which could only benefit Moscow.[60] While Europe came first, the two spheres should not be separated. Leffler demonstrates the 'periphery had to be held or the Eurasian industrial core would be weakened. To simplify, Japan needed Southeast Asia; Western Europe needed the Middle East; and the American rearmament effort required raw materials from throughout the Third World.'[61]

The political stability of the periphery was of vital importance because political unrest or economic instability in these areas directly affected the economic rehabilitation of the European countries. By adding the Cold War layer to the dynamics on the emerging Third World, US policy-makers 'hopelessly distorted US perceptions of the revolutionary forces that were rapidly transforming those regions'. In failing to deal successfully with the aspirations for self-determination, development, and the much deeper historical roots of the decolonization process, Washington ultimately belittled the efforts of the nationalists, failing to treat them as equals in the political sense. The resulting instability in both South and Southeast Asia had lasting consequences for US relations with the Third World, and US foreign policy in general.[62]

The irony of the period is that as the United States had to deal increasingly with the national aspirations of Third World countries which moved against US interests, this period can also be viewed in a wider historical context. The integration of the Third World, with emerging independent nations, 'ensured the universalization of Western political practice through the institutional spread of the nation-state which now progressively enveloped the globe'.[63] The further irony may be that just as these states were achieving the formal recognition they had sought, the open door with its transnational basis was simultaneously eroding their new power.

When the American colonies existed at the periphery of essentially a European system decolonization and self-determination made perfect sense. The national ideologies that developed through the subsequent decades reinforced the idea of a different identity. The European empires were troublesome, exclusive and dangerous. But when the United States increasingly became the centre of a global system, their opportunities and 'national interests' became entangled with their traditional beliefs. They could not return to disengagement. The open door coupled with the destinarian thought was in many ways both anti-colonial and imperial. Self-determination was compromised by its compatibility with the 'empire for liberty'. It was promoted most when the economy in question was sufficiently integrated into the US-centred economic system. And still, the logic of the open door was compromised by an assertive nationalism founded on both material interests and national ideologies. Walter Lippmann caught the resulting tensions well in 1927:

> the rest of the world will continue to think of us as an empire. Foreigners pay little attention to what we say. They observe what we do. We on the other hand think of what we feel. And the result is that

we go on creating what mankind calls an empire while we continue to believe quite sincerely that it is not an empire because it does not feel to us the way we imagine an empire ought to feel.[64]

Notes

1 Cary Fraser, 'A Requiem for the Cold War: Reviewing the History of International Relations since 1945,' in Allen Hunter, *Rethinking the Cold War* (Philadelphia, 1998), pp. 94, 111; Warren Kimball, paper delivered at the Callum McDonald Commemorative Conference, Warwick University, 23 May 1998. See also Thomas McCormick, ' "Every System Needs a Center Sometimes", an essay on Hegemony and Modern American Foreign Policy', in Lloyd C. Gardner, *Redefining the Past: Essays in Diplomatic History in Honor of William Appleman Williams* (Corvallis, 1986), and his 'World Systems' in Michael J. Hogan and Thomas G. Paterson, *Explaining the History of American Foreign Relations* (Cambridge, 1991) for a paradigm that influences this argument.

2 Decolonization is the process through which there is a change in sovereignty over a given territory. The colonial state withdraws its rule either voluntarily or involuntarily. See Tony Smith's definition in note 1 to Walter LaFeber's chapter in this volume. Neo-colonialism refers to the process through which that political sovereignty is undermined through undue economic predominance, leaving the state little ability to exercise self-determination. The distinction between formal and informal imperialism is also relevant. As Osterhammel indicates, 'imperialism presupposes the will and the ability of an imperial centre to *define* as imperial its own national interests and enforce them world-wide . . . [it] implies not only *colonial* politics, but *international* politics for which colonies are not just ends in themselves, but also pawns in global power games.' Jürgen Osterhammel, *Colonialism: a Theoretical Overview* (Princeton, 1997), p. 21. See also Joseph A. Fry, 'Imperialism, American Style, 1890–1916', in Gordon Martel (ed.), *American Foreign Relations Reconsidered, 1890–1993* (London, 1994), pp. 52–67.

3 See, for instance, the chapter on 'End of Empires' in Eric Hobsbawm, *Age of Extremes: the Short Twentieth Century, 1914–1991* (London, 1994), especially p. 200.

4 The suggestion does not stand universally as both Washington and Moscow exercised imperial systems of different sorts during the century. The process in what became the United States was characterized by 'constantly renewed sameness. Such a settlement which endlessly reproduces the original moment and principle of liberty in an agrarian setting is surely colonization in the strongest meaning of the word; but it is not a conventional empire.' Anders Stephanson, 'A Most Interesting Empire', paper delivered to the symposium, 'Reviewing the Cold War: Interpretation, Approaches, Theory', Norwegian Nobel Institute, 1998.

5 David Reynolds, 'Beyond Bipolarity in Space and Time', in Michael J. Hogan,

The End of the Cold War: Its Meaning and Implications (Cambridge, 1992), p. 256; Stephanson, 'A Most Interesting Empire', Nobel Symposium paper; Geir Lundestad, ' "Empire" by Integration: the United States and European Integration, 1945–1997* (Oxford, 1998).

6 Thomas McCormick, ' "Every System Needs a Center Sometimes"', an essay on Hegemony and Modern American Foreign Policy', in Lloyd C. Gardner, *Redefining the Past: Essays in Diplomatic History in Honor of William Appleman Williams* (Corvallis, 1986), p. 198.

7 The White House, *A National Security Strategy of Engagement and Enlargement*, July 1994; William Appleman Williams traced the process of enlargement through an understanding of hegemony in *Empire as a Way of Life* (New York, 1980).

8 Osterhammel, *Colonialism*, pp. 25–38. This analysis situates US colonialism within the category of 'Border colonization' though in the United States the discourse on the Frontier and its significance is better known. The term refers to the extensive opening up of land for agricultural use or the acquisition of resources. Other examples include the Han Chinese expansion into inner Asia and the Russian expansion eastward also into Asia (pp. 5–6).

9 Stephanson, 'A Most Interesting Empire', Nobel Symposium paper.

10 Merrill D. Peterson, *The Jefferson Image in the American Mind* (New York, 1962), p. 266; Ernest Gellner, *Postmodernism, Reason and Religion* (London, 1992), p. 52. For more elaboration on these ideas, see David Ryan, 'US Expansionism: from the Monroe Doctrine to the Open Door', in Philip John Davies (ed.), *Representing and Imagining America* (Keele, 1996), pp. 181–90.

11 Cropsey draws a distinction between the meanings of the word 'end' in terms of its application to 'History'. The end as 'termination' is opposed to the search for the 'end' as in 'perfectible'. If the end of history was characterized in Fukuyama's terms as the perfectible political and economic form of liberal capitalist democracy, then that necessitated the destruction of all forms of other empires and alternative ideologies. See Joseph Cropsey, 'The End of History in the Open-ended Age? The Life Expectancy of Self-Evident Truths', in Arthur M. Melzer *et al.* (eds), *History and the Idea of Progress* (Ithaca, 1995), p. 97; Francis Fukuyama, *The End of History and the Last Man* (Harmondsworth, 1992); for a good review of the destinarian thinking in the formation of US foreign policy, see Anders Stephanson, *Manifest Destiny: American Expansionism and the Empire of Right* (New York, 1995).

12 Thomas Paine, *Common Sense* (ed.) Isaac Kramnick (1776, Harmondsworth, 1986), p. 63; Serge Ricard, 'The Exceptionalist Syndrome in U.S. Continental and Overseas Expansionism', in David K. Adams and Cornelis A. van Minnen (eds), *Reflections on American Exceptionalism* (Keele, 1994), p. 73.

13 See the chapters by LaFeber and Johnston in this volume.

14 President Monroe's Seventh Annual Message to Congress, 2 December 1823, Secretary of State Hay's circular letter of 3 July 1900, and President Wilson's address to Congress, 8 January 1918, in Henry Steele Commager (ed.), *Documents of American History* (New York, 1963), vol. I, p. 236, & vol. II, pp. 11, 138.

15 Ricard, 'The Exceptionalist Syndrome,' p. 76. Even though US diplomacy explicitly added the language of the Enlightenment, Hobsbawm suggests

that capitalism provided the only model till 1917 for 'those who did not want to be devoured or swept aside by the juggernaut of history'. The twentieth-century process of decolonization was 'essentially determined by its relations with the countries which had established themselves in the late nineteenth century as the lords of human kind'. Eric Hobsbawm, *Age of Extremes: the Short Twentieth Century* (London, 1994), p. 200. See also for comparative reasons Anthony Pagden, *Lords of All the World: Ideologies of Empire in Spain, Britain and France, c. 1500–c. 1800* (New Haven, 1995).

16 Stephanson, *Manifest Destiny*, p. 18.

17 Walter LaFeber, 'The American View of Decolonization,' in this volume, pp. 24–40; see p. 24.

18 Terry Eagleton, *Ideology: an Introduction* (London, 1991), pp. 18–19, 15. The reference is of course to John Quincy Adams, Address, 4 July 1821, in Walter LaFeber (ed.), *John Quincy Adams and the American Continental Empire: Letters, Papers and Speeches* (Chicago, 1965), p. 45. See also Warren Kimball, 'In Search of Monsters to Destroy' in *The Juggler: Franklin Roosevelt as Wartime Statesman* (Princeton, 1991).

19 Ryan, 'US Expansionism', pp. 183–4; Harold Temperley, *The Foreign Policy of Canning, 1822–1827* (London, 1966), pp. 123–4; Robert Lansing, memorandum, 11 June 1914, *Foreign Relations of the United States: the Lansing Papers 1914–1920*, vol. 2 (Washington, DC, 1940), p. 462. President Wilson sought to apply a rather different Monroe Doctrine to the world.

20 Cohen cited in Cecil V. Crabb, *The Doctrines of American Foreign Policy: Their Meaning, Role, and Future* (Baton Rouge, 1983), p. 72 n. 33. See also Warren I. Cohen, *America's Response to China: a History of Sino-American Relations* (New York, 1990), pp. 26–54.

21 Carl Schurz, for instance, vocally condemned US imperialism. In the Anti-Imperialist platform he argued, 'We maintain that governments derive their just powers from the consent of the governed. We insist that the subjugation of any people is "criminal aggression" and open disloyalty to the distinctive principles of our government.' 18 October 1899 in Commager, *Documents*, vol. II, p. 11. See also, Carl Schurz, *Speeches, Correspondence and Political Papers of Carl Schurz* (New York, 1969).

22 Emily Rosenberg, *Spreading the American Dream: American Economic and Cultural Expansion, 1890–1945* (New York, 1982), p. 39; Osterhammel, *Colonialism*, pp. 33–4.

23 Paul Kennedy, *The Rise and Fall of Great Powers: Economic Change and Military Conflict from 1500 to 2000* (London, 1989), p. 317; Howard Zinn, *A People's History of the United States* (London, 1980), p. 294.

24 Edward Said, *Culture and Imperialism* (London, 1993), p. 8.

25 Hunt, *Ideology*, pp. 19–45.

26 President Roosevelt's Annual Message, 6 December 1904, in Commager (ed.), *Documents of American History*, vol. II, p. 33.

27 See Johnston's chapter in this volume.

28 Eric Hobsbawm, *Nations and Nationalism since 1780: Programme, Myth, Reality* (Cambridge, 1990), pp. 131–6.

29 Rosenberg, *Spreading the American Dream*, pp. 231–2.

30 Geoffrey Barraclough, *An Introduction to Contemporary History* (Harmondsworth, 1964), p. 64; Karl Marx cited in John Cassidy, 'The Next Big

Thinker', *The Independent on Sunday* (London), 7 December 1997. (It is an irony that Marx viewed some aspects of capitalism as a progressive force in world history, in that with its pervasive effects throughout the globe it was one of the major contributors to the erosion of local traditions and particularities.)

31   Emily S. Rosenberg, 'Revisiting Dollar Diplomacy: Narratives of Money and Manliness', *Diplomatic History* 22, no. 2 (Spring 1998), pp. 158–61.

32   Rosenberg, ibid., pp. 163–5.

33   President Wilson's Address to Congress, 8 January 1918, in Commager (ed.), *Documents of American History*, vol. II, p. 138.

34   Ian Clark, *Globalization and Fragmentation: International Relations in the Twentieth Century* (Oxford, 1997), pp. 92–3.

35   Thomas J. McCormick, *America's Half-Century: United States Foreign Policy in the Cold War* (Baltimore, 1989), p. 32.

36   Tony Smith, *America's Mission: the United States and the Worldwide Struggle for Democracy in the Twentieth Century* (Princeton, 1994), p. 115.

37   Lloyd C. Gardner, *Spheres of Influence: the Partition of Europe, from Munich to Yalta* (London, 1993), pp. 18–26.

38   Lloyd C. Gardner, *Economic Aspects of New Deal Diplomacy* (Madison, 1964), pp. 276–80.

39   McCormick, *America's Half Century*, p. 33.

40   Hobsbawm, *Age of Extremes*, p. 216.

41   David Reynolds, 'Roosevelt, Churchill, and the Wartime Anglo-American Alliance, 1939–1945: Towards a New Synthesis,' in W. R. Louis and Hedley Bull (eds), *The 'Special Relationship': Anglo-American Relations since 1945* (Oxford, 1989), p. 18.

42   R. F. Holland, *European Decolonization 1918–1981: an Introductory Survey* (London, 1985), pp. 52–3; Kimball, *The Juggler*, p. 54.

43   Clark, *Globalization and Fragmentation*, p. 119.

44   Myrdal cited by Gardner, *Economic Aspects of New Deal Diplomacy*, p. 283.

45   Noam Chomsky, *On Power and Ideology* (Boston, 1987), p. 10.

46   Eric Hobsbawm, *The Age of Extremes* (London, 1994), pp. 200–3; Gardner, *Economic Aspects of New Deal Diplomacy*, pp. 175–6.

47   Hunt, *Ideology*, pp. 19–20.

48   Acheson cited by Benjamin Schwarz, 'Why America Thinks it Has to Run the World', *Atlantic Monthly* (June 1996), p. 94.

49   Alan S. Milward, *The European Rescue of the Nation-State* (London, 1992).

50   Michael J. Hogan, *The Marshall Plan: America, Britain, and the Reconstruction of Western Europe, 1947–1952* (Cambridge, 1987).

51   See for instance, Wm Roger Louis and Ronald Robinson, 'The Imperialism of Decolonization', *Journal of Imperial and Commonwealth History*, vol. 22, no. 3 (September 1994).

52   Kimball, *The Juggler*, p. 131.

53   Robert J. McMahon, 'Toward a Post-Colonial Order: Truman Administration Policies toward South and Southeast Asia', in Michael Lacey, *The Truman Presidency* (Cambridge, 1989), p. 340.

54   Cary Fraser, 'Understanding American Policy towards the Decolonization of European Empires, 1945–64', *Diplomacy and Statecraft*, vol. 3, no. 1 (1992), pp. 105–7.

55 See John Kent in this volume and Thomas G. Paterson, *On Every Front: the Making and Unmaking of the Cold War* (New York, 1992), p. 103.
56 Report by the Policy Planning Staff, PPS/23, Review of Current Trends in U.S. Foreign Policy, 24 February 1948, *FRUS*, vol. 1, 1948, p. 526.
57 PPS 23, ibid., p. 524.
58 PPS 23, ibid., p. 511.
59 Robert E. Wood, 'From The Marshall Plan to the Third World', in Melvyn Leffler and David Painter, *Origins of the Cold War: an International History*, pp. 202–5.
60 Gabriel Kolko, *Confronting the Third World: United States Foreign Policy 1945–1980*, pp. 17–19.
61 Melvyn P. Leffler, *A Preponderance of Power: National Security, the Truman Administration, and the Cold War*, pp. 18–19.
62 McMahaon, pp. 263–5.
63 Clark, *Globalization and Fragmentation*, p. 144.
64 Walter Lippmann, *Men of Destiny*, extracted in Robert S. Leiken and Barry Rubin (eds), *The Central American Crisis Reader* (New York, 1987), p. 82.

1

The American View of Decolonization, 1776–1920: an Ironic Legacy

Walter LaFeber

Since 1776, when their Declaration of Independence listed their lengthy grievances against British colonial rule and argued eloquently for self-government based on 'the Laws of Nature and of Nature's God', Americans have professed to lead the world's decolonization struggle.[1] They have professed to do so, and sometimes have actually done so, but at critical junctures in the past two centuries, they have easily sacrificed the principles of decolonization for the practices of imperial conquest and global hegemony. Americans, to paraphrase St Augustine's famous prayer, have often demanded decolonization, but then added they do not want it quite yet.

This ambiguity blending into irony during the centuries of US policy and practices comes directly from the policies and practices of the Founders who set the system, and the nation's foreign policies, into motion during its first generation. One Virginian, Thomas Jefferson, sounded the original blast with 'Facts . . . submitted to a candid world' that detailed the 'absolute Despotism' of London's colonial government. These 'facts' included imposing 'absolute rule into these colonies', most notably by 'taking away our Charters, abolishing our most valuable laws', and allowing faraway officials to declare 'themselves invested with Power to legislate for us in all cases whatsoever'.

A decade later, however, another Virginian, James Monroe, confronted a potentially lethal problem and dealt with it by sacrificing Jefferson's principles to practices that promised to work. The problem was how to govern new lands stretching from the Appalachian Mountain chain to the Mississippi River, the region won from the British in the 1783 peace treaty. The area was as large as Western Europe and filled with ne'er-do-wells and escapees from eastern courts, as well as more governable types such as Revolutionary War veterans, but few tolerated outside interference in their frontier individualism. These restless settlers, moreover, were willing to work with anyone to survive and prosper, especially with the powerful British across the Great Lakes in Canada and the Spanish officials who tried to control the Mississippi and beyond. Monroe was convinced it was only a matter of time before some of the larger settlements, such as Kentucky, 'petition . . . for a separation' from the rest of the United States.[2] Monroe devised a solution that became the Northwest Ordinance of 1787. This law governed the development of US settlement across much of the continent over the next century.

The measure required newly settled territory to pass through three stages before becoming a full state in the Union. In the first two stages, a governor, appointed by the national government which sat a virtual world away across the mountains, enjoyed virtually complete control, including authority over the military. Monroe was honest when he began drafting the legislation. 'Shall it be upon colonial principles, under a governor, council, and judges of the United States . . . or shall they be left to themselves' until admitted as states?[3] Monroe had no hesitation: Jefferson's famous words about everyone having 'certain inalienable rights' were temporarily set aside as 'colonial principles' were imposed. Otherwise, the western settlements might become independent nations or extensions of London or Madrid, rather than of Philadelphia. As Monroe and a number of his colleagues in the new US government viewed it, only the right kind of colonialism could lead to happy decolonization at some future, undetermined time. It was not the last time US officials accepted that approach to governing difficult areas whose control was, they believed, indispensable to the nation's survival.

Indeed, just 17 years later, Jefferson himself took this approach. In 1803 his diplomacy in the vital New Orleans-trans-Mississippi region, claimed by Napoleon in 1801–3, was so successful that the President suddenly found himself the beneficiary of a seemingly infinite land stretching from the Mississippi to the Rocky Mountains and, perhaps, even to the Pacific Ocean. Jefferson's immediate problem was how to maintain control of such a vast region in an era when it took a month to get a message from Washington to New Orleans. As with Monroe, Jefferson's problem was made worse by anti-US groups of Roman Catholics, renegades from American justice, and Creoles whose property rested on Spanish law. Jefferson concluded such groups 'as yet as incapable of self-government as children'.[4]

His solution was to guarantee the inhabitants their 'liberty, property, and religion', as his treaty with Napoleon required the President to do. But Jefferson then conveniently forgot his 1776 language that governments derived 'their just powers from the consent of the governed'. He appointed a military governor who was to rule in the iron-fisted manner of the former Spanish governor and was to be responsible only to the President himself, not the local citizens, until enough people (preferably Anglo-Saxon) who knew how to govern themselves moved in from the east to outvote the original inhabitants. In the meantime the huge territory, divided into Orleans and Louisiana, was to be ruled by presidentially appointed governors and a legislative body, which the governor would choose. Critics cried that the author of the Declaration of Independence had established a regime 'about as despotic as that of Turkey in Asia'. But the regime remained until Orleans became the state of Louisiana in 1811. Jefferson's colonization policy had worked until it finally produced decolonization and statehood on an equal basis with the original states.

The Founders generation did not shy away from colonizing policies if they promised to work. But in both Monroe's 1787 Ordinance and Jefferson's Louisiana system decolonization was viewed as necessary, if placed in an indefinite future as far as its termination was concerned. When US officials next encountered such problems, however, they bitterly divided over the virtues of decolonization itself. This moment of truth arrived in 1820 to 1823 when Latin America rebelled against Spanish colonial control.

Powerful US leaders, headed by Senator Henry Clay of Kentucky, pushed now-President Monroe to recognise the Latin American independence movements and help them whenever possible. The most experienced diplomat of the time (indeed, the figure still viewed as the greatest Secretary of State in the nation's history), strongly opposed Clay. John Quincy Adams, lusting after the presidency in 1824, vividly recalled how his father, John Adams, had lost re-election to the presidency in 1800 to Jefferson because he had been hurt by the political fallout from the French Revolution. John Quincy had no intention of allowing Latin American decolonization movements to do the same to him.

But his reservations went far deeper. He believed the United States should not become involved in this particular decolonization because, although 'I wished well to their cause', such Roman Catholic, Spanish-influenced regions could not 'establish free or liberal institutions of government. . . . They have not the first elements of good or free government', the Secretary of State preached to Henry Clay directly in early

1821. 'Arbitrary power, military and ecclesiastical, was stamped upon their education, upon their habits, and upon all their institutions . . . I had little expectation of any beneficial result to this country from any future connection with them, political or commercial.' Clay, Adams wrote with satisfaction in his diary, 'did not pursue the discussion'.[5]

Adams's view of why the Latin Americans were incapable of governing themselves, as well as Jefferson's view of the New Orleans inhabitants in 1803, anticipated the arguments used in a different cultural context by Franklin D. Roosevelt in 1945. Roosevelt, who had hoped that French colonialism in Southeast Asia could somehow be replaced by a more human and efficient system, changed his mind and allowed the French to reoccupy the region in February. His rationale included the belief that the Vietnamese, Cambodians, and Laotians lacked the experience and virtues required for self-government. Colonization was preferable to probable anarchy and possible Communist penetration.[6]

In 1812, however, Monroe overruled his Secretary of State. Domestic political pressures, especially from merchants who feared losing potentially rich markets to the British (who worked with many of the southern revolutionaries), forced Adams finally to move toward recognition of these decolonization movements in 1812–22. He did so with great reluctance. It was in this context that the President's historic message of December 1823, later known as the Monroe Doctrine, has to be understood. Adams was the major author of the Doctrine's three principles: that the New and Old world had distinct, separate systems; that 'we should consider any attempt' by the monarchical systems of Europe 'to extend their system to any portion of this hemisphere as dangerous to our peace and safety'; and – of special importance to Adams and Monroe – 'that the American continents, by the free and independent conditions which they have assumed and maintain, are henceforth not to be considered as subjects for future colonization by any European power'.[7]

Adams had carefully developed the non-colonization principle since he had entered office in 1817, while believing that its roots reached back to his father's and Jefferson's actions in the 1770s. For the Secretary of State, however, non-colonization had two sides. The first was to keep, at all costs, decadent European colonial rule from further infecting the New World. 'In the theories of the Crown and the Mitre man had no rights', he announced in a remarkable Fourth of July Address in 1821. 'Neither the body nor the soul of the individual was his own. From the impenetrable gloom of this intellectual darkness, and the deep degradation of their servitude, the British nation had partially emerged' before trying to colonize the Americans permanently. He doubted the British or Spanish had evolved much since that time.[8]

The second side of non-colonization, however, was that by keeping the Europeans out of the hemisphere, the United States had an opportunity to get into new parts of it. Adams was the greatest expansionist in an era surfeited with expansionists (or, at least he was until he began to fear in the 1830s that his doctrines would lead to the expansion of the American slavery system). He believed it to be only a matter of time, and not much of it, before the Russians, Spanish, French, and British would lose all their New World possessions. In a heated argument with British Minister Stratford Canning, Adams staked out claims south and west, then declared bluntly that the British should understand 'that there would be neither policy nor profit in caviling with us about territory on this North American continent'. Oh, Canning replied, 'you include our northern provinces [Canada] on this continent?' 'No', Adams responded with notable reluctance. 'Keep what is yours, but leave the rest of this continent to us.'[9] The Secretary of State had not only parts of Mexico, especially California, and Oregon in view, but at least Cuba in the Caribbean.

Each one of these areas was claimed in one or (in the case of Oregon), by several European powers down to the 1820s. Adams, along with most other Americans, intended to decolonize them, while, as the Monroe Doctrine announced, opposing further European colonization in the New World. Then, with decolonization, the United States could pull these regions into its own Union. In Oregon and California the decolonization job would be done by what became known as the American multiplication table – that is, young families with numerous children who generation after generation became more acquisitive in their search for land. American settlement in Oregon after the early 1830s undermined British and Russian claims until the United States annexed the region in 1846. The same process could have been repeated in California, but Mexico broke free from Spain's colonialism and then the United States, impatient with Mexican rejections of Washington's demands for California, declared war and seized California and the rest of northern Mexico in 1848. As for Cuba, Adams again believed it was only a matter of time before Americans decolonized the island: 'There are laws of political as well as physical gravitation,' he instructed the US Minister to Spain in 1823, 'and if an apple severed by the tempest from its native tree cannot choose but to fall to the ground, Cuba, forcibly disjoined from its own unnatural connection with Spain, and incapable of self-support, can gravitate only towards the North American Union.'[10]

In Adams's hands, decolonization became an almost automatic, unstoppable natural act, comparable to the laws of gravity. In his eyes, the history of Oregon, California, Cuba, and other European-claimed land had to end with decolonization. For decolonization in North America was a transitional step to annexation by the United States.

Decolonization was not some abstract principle leading, as it did later in Africa and Asia, to the creation of sovereign, self-governing states. Decolonization was, among other things, a device for conquering a continental empire. In nineteenth-century US foreign policy, decolonization became less an act of altruism or the working-out of what Jefferson had called 'Nature's laws' than an integral and successful part of the nation's most aggressive self-interest.

The Indians, or Native Americans, tragically provide a case-study of the problem. Since the early days of European settlement, Great Britain had made treaties with the Indians – that is, they were considered separate nations. The US government began to change this approach in the early nineteenth century, most notably during the 1830s when President Andrew Jackson's administration broke earlier treaties and forced tribes in Florida and Georgia to trek west in poorly prepared journeys that cost thousands of lives. The survivors received lands beyond the Mississippi where they were essentially colonized on US territory. Their peace, such as it was, proved to be short-lived. The conquests obtained from the Mexican War drew a flood of white settlers into the Indians' region. In 1851, an Indian Appropriation Act announced a new set of policies. The Native Americans' holdings were slashed in area while the tribes were restricted to reservations of a specific size. In traditional colonial style, the Federal Government not only exercised political control, but through treaty provisions reached into the reservations in an attempt to change Indian culture.

The next step came in 1871 when, in the aftermath of the Civil War, another flood of white settlers streamed into the Great Plains of the trans-Mississippi. Congress declared that no Indian nation or tribe was henceforth to be considered independent. Washington would no longer deal with the Indian by treaty, but by *fiat*. Congressional and presidential orders determined the nature of colonization. Indians were 'wards of the United States'. This amounted to 'internal colonialism', as later analysts styled the relationship. It has been compared to the White South African government's brutal 'black homelands' policy of the twentieth century.[11] The process climaxed with the 1887 Dawes Act that empowered the President to break up reservations into private plots of 160 acres, the same acreage as the laws for white settlement provided. Whites enjoyed access to any land designated to be surplus. The colonization effort was nearly complete. Many Indian tribes became wracked by isolation, poverty, horrible educational facilities and alcoholism.

A deadly combination of greed and racism had shaped the colonial policies toward the tribes. As the bitter fruits of these policies became apparent after the First World War, and as decolonization accelerated globally after the Second World War, US officials began haltingly and reluctantly to give more authority back to the Native Americans. But for a century those officials had believed the colonization of the Indians to be in the national interest, albeit hardly in the interest of the tribes themselves. They found that white Americans willingly placed severe limits on who might enjoy Jefferson's 'inalienable rights'.

The colonization of Indians by the 1880s led inextricably to colonization of Filipinos and, in slightly varying forms, Cubans and Puerto Ricans in the late 1890s.[12] Decolonization or non-colonization had little place in the world of 1880 to 1914, a world dominated by powerful European colonial powers soon joined by their American and Japanese counterparts. The post-1860 wave of colonialism arose from many causes, most importantly the industrial revolution that rearranged western societies and global relationships. The coin of empire was less gold and silver, as in earlier centuries of colonization, than steel and oil. Whoever could most efficiently process and sell these new goods could not only create great capital surpluses, but build large battleship fleets to protect the evolving empires.

In the industrial revolution's new era, successful colonial powers had three basic requirements: raw materials for the making of the new goods, above all steel; expanded markets, especially in the potentially immense marketplaces of Asia, Africa and Latin America; and naval bases where the steel-plated, increasingly oil-driven battleships could obtain provisions, fuel and strategic control of surrounding waters. In much rarer instances (as Japan), colonies could also act as safety-valves for a crowded population.

The United States did not need colonies for either raw materials or surplus population. The North American continent was both incredibly abundant with basic items needed by new industry and sufficiently spacious for many future generations of immigrants from the east or overseas. By the 1890s, however, a consensus developed among national leaders that the nation required the other two essentials of empire: overseas markets and naval bases. Actually the process had begun in the 1860s when Secretary of State William Henry Seward obtained the Midway Islands in the Pacific and then, more importantly, acquired Alaska, the 'drawbridge to Asia' as it was known, from Russia in 1867. Resembling his hero John Quincy Adams, Seward turned the decolonization of Alaska into a pivotal imperial possession that waited nearly a century before it became a full-fledged state.

A long, post-1873 depression that worsened in the mid-1890s forcefully drove home the need for markets and bases. Social and political upheavals, including bloody labour strikes, pockmarked the country. Most observers agreed that these horrors had been caused by, ironically, the tremendous success of American industry and agriculture. Overproduction had led to depression. The obvious solution was to obtain overseas markets. To protect these markets, a battleship fleet, the first recognisable ancestor of the modern US Navy, began to be built between 1886 and 1895. This fleet fought the major battles in 1898 that decolonized the Spanish holdings of Cuba, Puerto Rico, and the Philippines, while turning them, along with the annexation of Hawaii and Guam in 1898, into the main parts of a US colonial empire.

Americans, the first modern decolonizers, joined the scramble for overseas colonies. They soon claimed that this urge was a temporary aberration; Cuba and the Philippines were put on the road to self-government, while Hawaii entered the process for statehood. Americans also believed that, in any event, their colonialism was not nearly as bad or as extensive in terms of territory as the European and Japanese brand. Something can be said about this obvious bad conscience that Americans developed, but not as much as they believed.

Until the 1950s, the textbooks and more historically minded US citizens believed the country went to war in 1898 primarily to free Cuba from brutal Spanish rule. President William McKinley, the story went, hated the idea of war, but was pushed into waging it by an angry public opinion that damned colonial rule and demanded it finally be evicted from the Caribbean. That somehow the United States ended up with Puerto Rico (which was not given self-government after the Spanish were driven out), and the Philippines (which was actually annexed to the United States), had to be explained as accidents or a kind of collective but temporary insanity cured by returning to the tenets of Jefferson.[13]

Newly opened documents and fresh perspectives in the 1950s and 1960s put together a more accurate and interesting story.[14] President William McKinley indeed did not at first want to go to war. He feared a conflict might drain the treasury and throw the country back into the worst days of economic depression. Between the autumn of 1897 and

March of 1898, however, two events changed his mind. The first was the scramble for colonies that erupted during 1897 when Germany, then other powers, threatened to carve off and colonize strategic pieces of China. The scramble directly threatened one of the most sacrosanct and important US foreign policy principles, the open door. Evolved since the 1830s and 1840s, the open-door policy was a quintessential statement of Americans' belief in non- or decolonization. The open-door principle aimed at keeping China whole, with its political and territorial integrity intact, and with European colonizers prevented from seizing parts of this ancient country as they were taking over Africa and other parts of Asia. This American demand for no colonization had, as usual, its highly realistic side: only by keeping China whole and free from colonization could Americans sell their growing surplus of goods to all 400 000 000 Chinese.[15]

In late 1897, therefore, McKinley supported decolonization because he hoped to roll back European incursions and regain the entire China market. Words, however, had little impact on rampant colonialism. He needed a navy and a base from which that fleet and US troops could, if necessary, be projected into Asia. The Spanish-held Philippines seemed to be the answer. In September 1897, McKinley and his hyperactive Assistant Secretary of the Navy, Theodore Roosevelt, discussed in detail the importance of striking the Philippines once war broke out with Spain over Cuba.[16]

The Cuban crisis was the second event that changed McKinley's mind about not going to war. The crisis was not that Spain was overpowering the Cubans. To the contrary, the crisis arose in March and April of 1898 when observers, including McKinley and his advisers, began to see that the Cuban revolutionary troops were going to succeed in decolonizing the island then, as Jefferson's principles advocated, self-govern themselves. For decades, Americans had believed Cuba was vital for their own interests. McKinley further believed that only a US-controlled island could adequately protect American security interests in the Caribbean.[17] Those interests increasingly revolved around the building of a future isthmian canal which could put producers in the eastern half of the United States thousands of miles closer to Asian markets, as well as expedite passage of the new battleship fleet from ocean to ocean. In April 1898, McKinley thus went to war not primarily to decolonize Cuba, but to prevent the Cubans from decolonizing themselves and to obtain at least the Philippine port of Manila. Not coincidentally, the first military action in a war supposedly declared to remove Spain from Cuba occurred on 1 May 1898 when a US fleet easily demolished a Spanish flotilla and decolonized the Philippines. After a triumphal war that lasted less than three months, McKinley was faced with fashioning a government for his new acquisitions. Convinced by advisers that Manila could not be defended without annexing the rest of the country, he moved to take all the islands. In early February 1899, the Filipinos, who had thought Americans took Jefferson's 1776 language seriously, fought back. A brutal three-year war followed that took the lives of 200 000 Filipinos and 4000 US soldiers. In reality, the war lingered on for years thereafter. But McKinley had his colony from which US power could be dispatched into Asia to prevent Europeans from obtaining more areas of China. The President used Manila exactly for this purpose in mid-1900 when he dispatched 5000 troops from the port to protect US citizens in Peking, then besieged by the anti-foreign Boxers, and to ensure that the other imperial powers who had also landed to protect their nationals did not remain to seize parts of China.

McKinley had an easier time in Cuba and Puerto Rico. Cuba was close enough (90 miles) so US power could easily move on to the island if necessary. Moreover, given the bloody racial episodes in the United States during the 1890s, the last thing Americans needed was annexation of, and possible statehood for, the multi-racial Cuban society. In 1901, McKinley therefore imposed the Platt Amendment that allowed Cubans to govern themselves under certain stringent conditions, including the right of the United States to intervene whenever Washington considered it to be necessary. Limits were placed on Cuba's financial dealings. One part of the island, Guantanamo, was taken to become a US naval base. Thus Cuba was decolonized from Spanish rule and turned into an informal colony of the United States.[18] Puerto Rico became a more formal colony, stripped of the political rights the Spanish had begun reluctantly to grant before the war, and ruled by the US Congress and President as a commonwealth. Again, especially for racial reasons, there was no intention of giving Puerto Rico statehood. (Hawaii was put on the road to statehood because, regardless of its racial composition, the archipelago had been ruled by white, pro-US planters who had overthrown the Hawaiian Queen in 1893.)

The costs of creating such a formal and informal colonial empire were building. President Theodore Roosevelt concluded he had to send troops into Cuba to restore order in 1906. They remained three years, as even sceptical Cubans began to understand they had only the trappings of self-government. They therefore easily began to blame the United States for their problems.

The Philippine dilemma was much worse. Not only did war erupt, but also in 1898–99 the Boston-based Anti-Imperialist League recruited hundreds of thousands of Americans. A two-year debate exposed the beliefs underlying US policy. Senator Albert Beveridge of Indiana lectured the Anti-Imperialists: 'You, who say the Declaration [of Independence] applies to all men, how dare you deny its application to the American Indian? And if you deny it to the Indian at home, how dare you grant it to the Malay abroad . . . ? There are people in the world who do not understand any form of government . . . [and] must be governed. . . . And so the Authors of the Declaration themselves governed the Indian without his consent.'[19]

McKinley beat back the anti-imperialist challenge to win re-election in 1900, but the Philippine revolt was not as easily put down. Even after the fighting finally lessened after 1902, another danger emerged. Japan, fresh from its surprise victory over Russia in the war of 1904–5, became the rising power in Asia. Japan, as President Roosevelt fully realised by 1907, could make demands on the United States (such as demanding that Washington forget its open-door policy while Japan colonized what it wanted in Manchuria and North China), and could threaten to hold the Philippines hostage until the Americans gave in. Roosevelt knew he could never defend the islands in such a crisis. By 1907 he considered the Philippines 'our heel of Achilles'.[20] The once ardent and outspoken colonizer was quietly beginning to think about decolonization. As colonization had been in the US interest during 1898 to 1903, so after 1907 decolonization became the interest. By 1916, the Philippines were finally, if tentatively, put on the path to independence.

A most interesting result of the War of 1898 was not merely that Americans gained a colonial empire, but that responsible leaders began to believe there must be better methods for expanding their new global power. It was not that colonization was un-American, but that it was too costly. As this debate's intensity rose, however, in 1903 Roosevelt created another type of colony.

Panama was a province of Colombia, but solidly separated from the mother country by impenetrable jungle. The province's inhabitants, moreover, knew they stood astride one of the potentially most lucrative sites in the world, once a canal was built on it to link the Atlantic and Pacific oceans. Since the 1880s a Panamanian nationalism had developed that urged separation from the faraway Colombian government. On the basis of an 1846 treaty in which the United States obtained transit rights on the isthmus in return for promising to help maintain free transit (a provision aimed to prevent British seizure of Panama), Washington officials could play a dominant role. Under this provision, US naval officers repeatedly intervened in Panama between 1850 and 1902 to maintain peace between Colombia and an increasingly restless Panama.[21]

In mid-1903, President Roosevelt offered to buy a strip of Panama to build a US-controlled canal. Considering the financial offer inadequate, Colombia rejected the deal. A bitterly disappointed and angry Roosevelt then worked with Panamanian nationalists and, more importantly, their French and US representatives, to instigate a revolution. The President landed US sailors to prevent Colombia from smashing the uprising. Roosevelt took Panama away from Colombia, created a new country, then negotiated a treaty with Panamanian agents that gave the United States a six-mile-wide area through the centre of the country in which to build the canal. In return, he gave Panama $10 million plus $250 000 rent each year, while guaranteeing the country's independence.

The Canal Zone was a US-controlled enclave in a supposedly sovereign country. Secretary of State John Hay strained to define the US right to the area as 'titular sovereignty'.[22] The vagueness of the term ultimately undermined the US claim when Panamanian nationalists turned on Washington after the 1950s. In the meantime, Panamanians working (and the many fewer who lived) in the Canal Zone fell under complete US control. The surrounding country was itself an informal colony. Its currency and economy totally depended on the United States, its political leaders followed Washington's wishes, and the American military used Panama as a base. In the eyes of early Panamanian nationalists, their country had been decolonized with the indispensable help of US sailors. In the eyes of later Panamanian nationalists and their sympathizers in the United States and elsewhere, Roosevelt had then recolonized the country.

The canal opened in 1914. The first ships passed through just as the First World War erupted. The war had many causes, but primary was the growing contest among Great Britain, France, Germany and Russia over who would control affairs in southern and south-eastern Europe, where the Austro-Hungarian Empire was collapsing, and in parts of the eastern Mediterranean and the Middle East as the Ottoman Empire began to break apart: Britain and France's vulnerabilities became apparent when they had problems dealing with powerful anti-colonial movements in Africa and Southeast Asia respectively. In China, anti-foreign troops led by the Chinese Rights Recovery Movement concluded that their country was being formally colonized in the north-east with the seizure of territory by Germans, Japanese and Russians, while being informally colonized in the interior by powerful railroad-builders and bankers led by British, American and Japanese entrepreneurs. With the fall of the Manchu dynasty in early 1912, opposing Chinese nationalist forces manoeuvred for power.

President Woodrow Wilson thus had good evidence to support his belief that the age of colonialism was rapidly passing. He fervently held to the idea that he and his country, given its anti-colonial tradition and principles of self-government, were perfectly positioned to take the world into a new era. But the President encountered problems. Despite his avowals that all peoples were capable of self-government, he compromised this belief for other more compelling interests. Wilson dispatched US troops into Haiti, the Dominican Republic, and Mexico, while maintaining them in Nicaragua, in order to create the kind of order he deemed necessary if these peoples were to learn self-government. Despite these setbacks, as a generation of young men began to lose their lives on European battlefields, Wilson grew even more convinced that he had to be involved in the conflict so that after it was over he could lead the world into the light.

Wilson's conviction about his mission heightened in 1916–17 when he learned of secret deals the allied powers (Great Britain, France, Russia, Japan and Italy) had concluded among themselves. In one set of agreements, they set up tariff and subsidy policies to protect themselves against the rapidly rising US economic power that was fattening on Europe's growing bankruptcy. They also agreed to parcel out Germany's colonies among themselves after the war. Wilson bitterly opposed these deals. They struck at his determination to create an open world of self-governing nations and free-enterprise markets. That kind of world best suited US interests, especially its now unmatched economic capacity. In the 1917 message that finally took the United States into the war, the President's words used to describe his overriding goal were not well-chosen, given the past century of US activities in the Western Hemisphere: 'I am proposing . . . that the nations should with one accord adopt the doctrine of President Monroe as the doctrine of the world: that no nation should seek to extend its polity over another nation or people.'[23]

Wilson took the nation into war in large part so he could sit at the postwar peace table rather than, as he told a friend, having to 'shout' at the other powers 'through a crack in the door'. High on his agenda, as he declared in his famous Fourteen Points speech that outlined his peace programme in early 1918, was the 'absolutely impartial adjustment of all colonial claims' so that 'the interest of the populations concerned must have equal weight' with the claims of the powers and their secret treaties.[24] These promises of justice to large portions of the world became even more urgent after V. I. Lenin and Leon Trotsky imposed a Bolshevik regime on Russia, took the country out of the war in March 1918, then began calling for revolution against the capitalist nations. Wilson entered into direct competition with Lenin and Trotsky for the souls of the colonized, revolutionary, and near-revolutionary peoples around the globe. The President travelled to the Paris Peace Conferernce in early 1919 full of the belief that unless he could realize his liberal programme, including a fair adjustment of colonial claims and an effective League of Nations to enforce the adjustment, the world would race off in one of two directions: back into more big-power competition resulting in another world war, or forward into a series of radical revolutions spawned by colonized and other peoples who saw Lenin, not Wilson, as the answer.[25]

His vision was not shared by the other victors. Great Britain, Italy, and especially France and Japan, insisted that their secret agreements took precedence over Wilson's Fourteen Points. Worn out physically, outvoted on crucial issues, weakened by outspoken congressional criticism back in Washington, and compromised by his own military interventionism and his country's own history of conquest, the President repeatedly gave way.[26]

In the end, a mandate system was set up to deal with the former German colonies and the after-effects of the Ottoman Empire's break-up. Lebanon, Syria, Iraq, and part of the Cameroons were to be supervised by France; Palestine, Transjordan, Togoland, Cameroons, and Tanganyika by Great Britain; and Rwandi-Urundi by Belgium. In the Pacific, the once-German-controlled colonies of the Mariana and the Caroline and Marshall Islands were placed under the Japanese, while the British Empire took over German holdings south of the equator. A fig-leaf was thrown over this distribution of spoils with the provision that the League of Nations would oversee and ultimately be responsible for the conditions of the mandates. The provision proved to be largely meaningless. Nearly all the mandated areas (Iraq was a notable exception when it obtained independence in 1932), remained under *de facto* European or Japanese control through the interwar years.[27]

The cynicism accompanying much of the mandate plan became evident when French Prime Minister Georges Clemenceau convinced

Wilson that the President could best watch over the system by joining it and making a divided, bloody Armenia a US mandate. 'When you cease to be President,' Clemenceau taunted Wilson, 'we will make you Grand Turk.'[28] The US Congress, not the President, finally and emphatically rejected the mandate over Armenia and, with less emphasis, voted down Wilson's entire postwar plan that revolved around his Fourteen Points and a League of Nations.

The mandate system developed into the United Nations trusteeship system that, with the crucial push from post-1945 nationalisms, finally carried out a historic process of decolonization. In some of those tests, as during the Indonesian revolt against the Dutch, the United States largely sided with the decolonialists. In other critical moments, as in the Vietnamese war against the French, Americans provided massive support to the colonizer. Such a record was consistent with the previous two centuries of US policy and experience. The line from Monroe's and Jefferson's political necessities of 1786–1803; to McKinley's and Roosevelt's requirements of 1899–1903; to Wilson's agonising compromises of 1913 to 1920; to Eisenhower's, Kennedy's, and Johnson's dilemmas in Algeria, Africa and Vietnam in the 1950s and 1960s – the line may not be straight, but it is direct enough so that the history of the pre-1920 era helps us understand the events after 1945.

Born to the principles of self-government in 1776, Americans often proved to be an indispensable partner in the decolonization movement over the next 150 years. But they also repeatedly supported decolonization so they could acquire territory. They established informal and formal colonies themselves. Unlike most other powers, Americans professed decolonization, and like all other nations, the United States followed its self-interest.

Notes

1 In this chapter, a colony, as the dictionary phrases it, is considered to be a group of people who form a settlement subject to a mother state, or as any people or area separated but subject to a ruling power. 'American' is used in the essay interchangeably with United States for purposes of word variation. 'Irony' is used in the title for one of its dictionary definitions: an outcome of events contrary to what was, or might have been, expected. These definitions are from *Random House College Dictionary* (New York, 1984). A working definition of decolonization is given by Tony Smith, 'Decolonization', in Joel Krieger (ed.), *The Oxford Companion to Politics of the World* (New York, 1993),

p. 217. Smith states that it 'is commonly defined as a change in sovereignty, in which a state recognises the independence of a segment of the people formerly under its rule and their right to government formed according to procedures determined by them'. This definition needs the qualification that a colonizer often does not voluntarily recognize such 'independence', but is brought to do so by force.

2   Monroe to Jefferson, 25 August 1785, in Edmund C. Barnett (ed.). *Letters of Members of the Continental Congress*, 8 vols (Washington, DC, 1921–36), VII, p. 203.

3   Quoted in Merrill Jensen, *The New Nation* (New York, 1950), p. 358.

4   The quotes and interpretation in this and the following paragraph are drawn from Walter LaFeber, 'An Expansionist's Dilemma', *Constitution*, V (Fall 1993): esp. pp. 10–11.

5   Charles Francis Adams (ed.), *Memoirs of John Quincy Adams*, 12 vols (Philadelphia, PA, 1874–7), V, pp. 323–6.

6   FDR's view and the citations can be found in Walter LaFeber, 'Roosevelt, Churchill, and Indochina, 1942–1945', *American Historical Review*, LXXX (Fall 1975): pp. 1277–95.

7   J. D. Richardson (ed.), *Messages and Papers of the Presidents*, 10 vols (Washington, DC, 1896), II, pp. 209, 218–19.

8   The text, taken from the original Adams speech, can be found in Walter LaFeber (ed.), *John Quincy Adams and American Continental Empire* (Chicago, IL, 1965), pp. 42–6.

9   Adams (ed.), *Memoirs of John Quincy Adams*, V, pp. 251–3.

10   Adams to Hugh Nelson, 28 April 1823, in Worthington C. Ford (ed.), *Writings of John Quincy Adams*, 7 vols (New York, 1913–17), pp. 371–81.

11   The quotes and analysis can be found in Michael K. Donoghue, 'Colonialism', in Bruce W. Jentleson and Thomas G. Paterson (eds), *Encyclopedia of US Foreign Relations*, 4 vols (New York, 1997), I, p. 291; and Philip Weeks, 'Native Americans', ibid., III, pp. 217–25.

12   This story, and the links, can be found in the important analysis by Walter L. Williams, 'US Indian Policy and the Debate over Philippine Annexation', *Journal of American History*, LXVI (March 1980), pp. 819–31.

13   An influential account that stresses US decolonization and well represents pre-1950s interpretations is Thomas A. Bailey, *A Diplomatic History of the American People*, 7th edn (New York, 1964), esp. pp. 456–64.

14   Breakthrough accounts were Margaret Leech, *In the Days of McKinley* (New York, 1959), that first exploited the papers of McKinley's personal secretary, George Cortelyou; William Appleman Williams, *The Tragedy of American Diplomacy* (Cleveland, OH, 1959); and H. Wayne Morgan, *William McKinley and His America* (Syracuse, NY, 1963).

15   The story of the open door and its application to China in the 1893 to 1901 years is told in Thomas J. McCormick, *China Market* (Chicago, IL, 1967).

16   Elting E. Morison (ed.), *The Letters of Theodore Roosevelt*, 8 vols (Cambridge, MA, 1951), I, pp. 685–6.

17   Louis Perez, Jr, *Cuba: between Reform and Revolution*, 2nd edn (New York, 1995), esp. pp. 161–5.

18   The story was detailed initially by David Healy in *The United States in Cuba, 1898–1902* (Madison, WI, 1963).

19   Williams, 'US Indian Policy and the Debate over Philippine Annexation', pp. 819–20.

20   James Chace and Caleb Carr, *America Invulnerable* (New York, 1988), pp. 138–40; Henry Pringle, *Theodore Roosevelt, a Biography* (New York, 1931), pp. 684–5.

21   Michael L. Conniff, *Panama and the United States* (Athens, GA, 1992), esp. pp. 32–5.

22   Different perspectives, and the quotations, can be found in Dana G. Munro, *Intervention and Dollar Diplomacy in the Caribbean, 1900–1921* (Princeton, NJ, 1964), pp. 57–8; and David S. Patterson, *Toward a Warless World: the Turmoil of the American Peace Movement, 1887–1914* (Bloomington, IN, 1976), pp. 124–5.

23   Arthur S. Link, *Wilson*, 5 vols (Princeton, NJ, 1947), V, pp. 265–74.

24   The quote and a succinct discussion are in Lloyd Gardner, *et al.*, *The Creation of the American Empire*, 2nd edn (Chicago, IL, 1976), p. 340.

25   The crucial contexts for the debate over colonialism at Paris are spelled out in Arno Mayer, *Political Origins of the New Diplomacy, 1917–1918* (New Haven, CN, 1959); Lloyd Gardner, *Safe for Democracy* (New York, 1984), esp. chapters 10–12; and Thomas J. Knock, *To End All Wars* (New York, 1992).

26   A classic British account by a conference participant that emphasizes these specific constraints on Wilson is Harold Nicolson, *Peacemaking, 1919* (Boston, 1933).

27   A fine succinct account from which these lists and part of the interpretation are drawn is Harold K. Jacobson, 'Mandates', in Jentleson and Paterson, (eds) *Encyclopedia of US Foreign Relations*, III, pp. 99–103.

28   Thomas A. Bailey, *Woodrow Wilson and the Lost Peace* (New York, 1944), p. 170.

2
The Road to Our America: the United States in Latin America and the Caribbean

Laurie Johnston

At the end of the nineteenth century, Cuban patriot José Martí warned the Latin American nations – 'our America', as he referred to them, to distinguish them from the United States – that their northern neighbour posed a serious threat to their independence. 'It is essential to say,' he argued, 'for it is true, that the time has come for Spanish America to declare its second independence' against US expansionism.[1] Martí did not fear anything so crude as invasion and conquest. Rather, he recognized the dangers posed by an unequal economic relationship. 'The nation that buys, commands', he cautioned. 'The nation that sells, serves. It is necessary to balance trade in order to guarantee liberty. The nation eager to die sells to a single nation, and the one eager to save itself sells to more than one. A country's excessive influence over the commerce of another becomes political influence.'[2] Martí rightly feared that the United States would intervene in the Cuban struggle for independence, to Cuba's detriment, and from there expand throughout the Antilles. The Latin American nations, he argued, should be 'vitally concerned with preventing the opening in Cuba . . . of the road that must be closed, and we are closing with our blood, the annexation of the peoples of our America to the brutal and turbulent North which despises them'.[3]

Although the United States had already extended its reach into the Caribbean and Central America through private US business ventures and its interest in securing an isthmian canal in Central America, it was with the end of the Spanish–Cuban-American war in 1898 that, as Martí had feared, its power became manifest. With the military occupations of Cuba and Puerto Rico, US capital, business and culture accelerated their march southward, embarking on programmes of 'Americanization' and the infiltration and transformation of the local economies that would enhance US influence in the region.[4] US investment often brought employment, higher wages, and improved infrastructure, education and healthcare facilities to impoverished regions, but at a price. Access to benefits was confined to those connected with corporate capital, dividing the wider community. US corporate culture stressed individualism, competition and consumerism over community and social responsibility.[5] Workers' needs were entirely subject to corporate interests and their benefits were by no means guaranteed. National advantage was deemed to be coterminous with corporate well-being, which demonstrably operated to the disadvantage of the Latin American nations. As Eduardo Galeano has argued:

> the new model does not make its colonies more prosperous, although it enriches their poles of development; it does not ease social and regional tensions, but aggravates them; it spreads poverty even more widely and concentrates wealth even more narrowly; it pays wages twenty times lower than in Detroit and charges prices three times higher than in New York: it takes over the internal market and the mainsprings of the productive apparatus; it assumes proprietary rights to chart the course and fix the frontiers of progress; it controls national credit and orients external trade at its whim; it denationalizes not only industry but the profits earned by industry; it fosters the waste of resources by diverting a large part of the economic surplus abroad; it does not bring in capital for development but takes it out.[6]

At a time when neo-liberalism is often mistaken for the natural order of the world, rather than a specific ideology which benefits some and disadvantages many, it has become unfashionable to argue that the form of Latin America's insertion into world capitalism lies at the centre of the region's poverty and inequality. For the historian, however, Galeano's argument retains force; the fact remains that while US capitalists and their local allies saw a handsome return on their Latin American investments, the majority of Latin Americans did not. Explaining this condition does not, however, lead to the argument that US government and business interests were always homogeneous and that every US intervention, however undertaken, arose from the need to protect those interests. Nor does it imply that Latin Americans never benefited from US involvement in the region. While the strength and coherence, or otherwise, of indigenous elites always proved to be a critical factor in the extent of US penetration, Washington could be a generous suitor and ally to those sectors within Latin America whose interests it believed to be sympathetic. In fact, over the century US and Latin American commercial, strategic and political interests have intertwined, coincided and diverged, and become overlaid with ideological justification and belief, leading to an historical relationship that cannot be explained by economics, ideology or politics alone. Nonetheless, the relationship has been and remains unequal; at its centre lies the assertion by the United States of its exclusive right to define its interests in Latin America and how best they might be defended.

The imperatives of US expansion at the turn of the century ensured that US interest in the Americas extended far beyond Cuba and Puerto Rico. Domestic capitalist development drove the actuality of US expansionism in Latin America, already asserted ideologically by the Monroe Doctrine of 1823. By the end of the nineteenth century US westward expansion had reached its limits, and both industrial and agricultural output were growing. The business community commanded an excess of goods and capital and looked abroad for investment and marketing opportunities. Economic depression in the 1890s convinced policy-markers and business alike that the United States required secure foreign markets to maintain economic stability at home. At the same time, the US needed raw materials to fuel its economic growth. Secretary of State James G. Blaine argued in 1890 that 'our great demand is expansion. I mean expansion of trade with countries where we can find profitable exchanges. We are not seeking annexation of territory. . . . At the same time I think we should be unwisely content if we did not seek to engage in what the younger Pitt so well termed annexation of trade.'[7] The European powers dominated trade with Asia and Africa. The Americas were closer to home, and had already been audaciously declared a US sphere of influence, from which European powers were to be excluded except where they still held colonies, by the Monroe Doctrine. The construction of the US Navy made enforcement of the Monroe Doctrine, particularly against the competing powers of Great Britain and Germany, a realistic possibility.

Although the economic motivation for expansion was recognized within the United States, and openly discussed, political and racial ideologies were used to distinguish US action from anything so crude as naked imperialism. From the beginning, US policy-makers took the moral high ground, preferring to present their actions as those undertaken by a nation on a civilizing mission. They argued that the United States was uniquely able, by virtue both of its superior system of government and its Anglo-Saxon racial composition, to set an example for those of lesser ability and had a responsibility, however, reluctantly undertaken, to do so. Political cartoons frequently portrayed Latin Americans as children, usually black, often in the schoolroom, being instructed or reprimanded by Uncle Sam.[8] The programme of moral and civic training introduced to Cuban schools by the US military government in 1901 succinctly informed organizers that 'the United States is the most successful of all human governments'. Cubans, on the other hand, were assured that they could not govern themselves, as they had no experience of doing so. Such experience took 'decades and centuries' to acquire, or could possibly be learned by emulating 'successful republics', i.e. the United States. Hispanic American republics, on the other hand, had failed at self-government, led as they were by 'chronic revolutionists . . . where the people are impulsive and easily led by hotheaded orators' who 'collect exorbitant taxes and blackmail from the people so they can live in ease and luxury without doing much work'. These orators 'make fiery speeches and incite a lot of men to get out their machetes and guns and kill or drive away the other orators. In Colombia this sometimes happens as often as four times a year. . . .'[9] The United States took upon itself the responsibility of defining good government, and then policing its execution in Latin America.

Different definitions of the former were provided over the years but tended to follow the rules laid down for Cuba and the Dominican Republic by Theodore Roosevelt. Those two countries, he promised, could 'remain independent always if only they will not be too foolish, will not contract debts they cannot pay, and will not indulge in revolutions'.[10] In practice, a warm welcome for US capital; firm control of local labour; containment of popular mobilization and any potential resistance to the *status quo*; repayment of debts; and acceptance of US definitions of its security needs, became basic requirements to avoid US hostility.

In the period up to the First World War, US interest focused primarily, although not exclusively, on the Caribbean and Central America. Concerned to establish mastery of Caribbean sea-lanes and its own naval power in the face of German and British competition, the United States built the Panama Canal after engineering Panama's secession from Colombia. It then established a permanent occupation of the Panama Canal Zone.[11] Close, small and economically and militarily weak, the Central American and Caribbean nations were easy targets for US action. The pattern of occupation and the penetration of US capital established in Cuba and Puerto Rico occurred throughout the Caribbean region, under the aegis of the Roosevelt Corollary to the Monroe Doctrine, which argued that 'in the western hemisphere the adherence of the United States to the Monroe Doctrine may force the United States, however reluctantly, in flagrant cases of such wrongdoing or impotence, to the exercise of an international police power'.[12] At various times before, during and after the First World War, US troops occupied, often more than once, Cuba, Haiti, Panama, Honduras, Nicaragua and the Dominican Republic and made repeated incursions on to Mexican soil.[13] The terms on which the United States withdrew often compromised the national sovereignty and development of the invaded nation. Perhaps the most famous and extreme example is the imposition of the Platt Amendment on Cuba in 1901, but others abound.[14] Panama had been forced to grant the US similar rights to intervention as had Cuba.[15] US occupations fostered the development of the national guards in Nicaragua and the Dominican Republic from which emerged enduring US client regimes. The United States took control of the customs revenues and national finances of Nicaragua, Haiti and the Dominican Republic. Agreements to lower duty on US goods were reached with Cuba, Haiti and the Dominican Republic, undermining the local manufacturing base in each country. Additionally, these countries borrowed from their northern neighbour, their indebtedness leaving them vulnerable to further political and economic pressure from the United States.[16]

By the 1920s, US fruit companies, led by United Fruit, dominated banana production and marketing in Central America. Hispanic Caribbean sugar production was controlled by US capital, as was mining rubber and oil production in Mexico. US money poured into ranching, railways, utilities, banking. The US requirements of a compliant labour force and the economic and political freedom to maximize profits made the elites of Latin America its normal allies, provided they received some economic benefit and assistance in suppressing popular movements. Factionalism within the elites complicated matters; one group might use US support to buttress its power against rival groups, or US intervention might be invoked to that end. Latin Americans had always to take the precaution of calculating possible US responses, whether or not they wished for one, although political infighting among the elite was not normally sufficient on its own to stir US interest.

Nationalist feeling also proved to be a variable in the response to US capital penetration and any alliance with the elite or factions of the elite. The issue of national sovereignty could unite normally diverse interests within a country in opposition to US presence and control. In the 1930s, economic contraction forced the issue. Although the 1929 economic collapse and subsequent depression may have facilitated the growth of US influence, particularly at the expense of Great Britain, labour organization, populist alliances, rival ideologies such as fascism and communism, and economic nationalism militated against US dominance.[17] Workers protested against US corporations in Peru, Chile, Cuba, Central America and Mexico, with Cuban workers occupying sugar mills and setting up soviets.[18] The Good Neighbour Policy then in favour in Washington, designed to minimize costly military interventions and improve the US image in Latin America, made military intervention an undesirable option in the Caribbean region, while it was simply not feasible in South America. Nonetheless, US warships sat off the coast of Cuba until the crisis there had been resolved.[19]

In the Mexican case, time and a diversion of interests between Washington and US business operated in Mexico's favour. The 1917 constitution had claimed Mexico's resources for the nation, and on this basis President Lázaro Cárdenas began a programme of nationalization in 1934. Repeated strikes by Mexican oil workers, culminating in 1937, led to the appointment of a commission which ultimately supported the workers' claims. The oil companies responded by initiating a propaganda campaign, launching a legal action and attempting to undermine Mexico's financial stability. When the Mexican courts also ruled against them, the companies refused to accept the judgement. This defiance of Mexican sovereignty generated such powerful feeling against the oil companies that the government nationalized the industry. In spite of intense company lobbying, Washington resisted pressure to settle the issue forcefully. In this case, government and corporate interests diverged: the Good Neighbour Policy and impending war outweighed corporate political pressure. In much the same way that the build-up to the First World War prompted the US to restrain its interference in the Mexican Revolution in order not to foster a Mexican–German alliance, the military build-up in Germany and Japan and the importance of Latin America as a supplier of strategic raw materials in the imminent confrontation preoccupied Washington in 1938. It was this larger concern which allowed a financial settlement between the Mexican government and the oil companies in 1942.[20]

The end of the Second World War left the United States in a position of undisputed hegemony in the Americas; the European nations, devastated by war, no longer remained serious rivals. Latin American resistance, most notably in Argentina under Juan Perón, affected the depth and extent of US power, but the power was incontrovertible. The expansion of US military bases to the British Caribbean during the war reflected increased US influence there, although the islands remained British colonies. The ratification of the Rio Treaty in 1947 and the formation of the Organization of American States in 1948 gave the appearance of collective decision-making on the continent, but the extent of US power subverted any notion of equal partnership.[21] Even when Latin Americans did not feature significantly in the global concerns of the United States, the United States continued to be influential in Latin America.

With the advent of the Cold War, the ideological battle with communism, although not new, took on increased significance in the US response to developments in Latin America and superseded instruction in good government as the reasoning for intervention. Washington regularly elevated internal Latin American conflicts to the status of battles in a global war. However, whether the United States ignored, accepted or opposed the direction taken by Latin American governments depended not on the reality of communist influence, but rather on assertions of economic nationalism; whether policy maintained a capitalist direction; the extent of the redistribution of wealth proposed; whether any perceived threat could be contained internally; whether a viable internal alternative existed; and how feasible or likely to succeed US military intervention might be.

This analysis explains the seemingly anomalous behaviour of Washington towards the apparent revolutionary process in Bolivia in 1952. Washington accepted the nationalization of some Bolivian tin-mines and supported the government of the Movimiento Nacional Revolucionario (MNR) throughout an agrarian reform process. A number of points must be considered in this regard. First, the MNR was a factional, middle-class party with its origins in right-wing and nationalist politics, which had a relationship of mutual distrust with the tin-workers. Second, the MNR used the peasants and agrarian reform as a means of undermining labour's political power. Third, not all US investors were affected, those that were received generous compensation packages, and investors retained control both of tin-refining and the price of tin within Bolivia. Fourth, no credible alternative remained to the MNR, the elite and military having been seriously undermined by the events of 1952. Finally, a military operation was simply unfeasible. Instead, having little other alternative, the United States used a combination of support and pressure to bend the MNR to its desired policies, which it succeeded in doing by 1956, in the meanwhile gaining some approbation for supporting a process of social reform at little cost to itself.[22]

The first major postwar intervention occurred in 1954 on the familiar ground of Central America, specifically Guatemala, when the reformist government of Jacobo Arbenz nationalized idle landholdings in the implementation of an agrarian reform policy, arousing the hostility of Guatemalan landowners and the United Fruit Company. The government offered United Fruit compensation based on the value of the land given in the company's tax declarations. In this instance, the interests of Washington, United Fruit and Guatemalan landowners coincided, not least because members of the US government were major shareholders in or otherwise connected with the company. Washington chose to frame the conflict as one between communism and freedom, however, although there is no serious evidence to support claims of communist control of the Guatemalan government or a threat to the Panama Canal, as Washington also alleged. In fact, the United States took advantage of the split within Guatemala's elite, and used Guatemalan exiles, funded and trained by the CIA, to overthrow Arbenz. By eliminating the move for reform in Guatemala, Washington bolstered the right in the country and laid the grounds for the reactionary violence that would plague it for more than thirty years.[23]

In 1959, the Cuban Revolution changed the entire perception of political possibility on the continent. The *fidelistas* swept to power on a wave of popular support for meaningful national sovereignty and social and economic justice. Ultimately, the years 1959–61 made perfectly clear – as indeed had the previous history of the Cuban republic – that the fulfilment of Cuban nationalist aspirations required Cuba to break free from US hegemony. It could not be otherwise when so much of Cuba's distorted development arose directly from its relationship with the United States. Although Washington quickly recognized Cuba's new government, it embarked almost as quickly on strategies designed to overthrow it. Meanwhile, the revolutionary government implemented policies intended to fulfil its promises and consolidate support. These policies brought the Cuban government into direct conflict with US capital and its allies within Cuba, whose profits and ownership were affected by the policy decisions. Detailing Cuba's high unemployment and illiteracy, its lack of medical services for the poor, the unequal distribution of land, political corruption and the loss to Cuba's treasury of income taken to the United States, Fidel Castro demanded, 'what alternative was there for the Revolutionary government? To betray the people?' This question went to the heart of the antagonism between Washington and Havana. Castro put the alternative: 'Of course, as far as the President of the United States is concerned, we have betrayed our people. But this would certainly not have been considered so, if, instead of the Revolutionary government being true to its people, it had been loyal to the big American monopolies that exploited the economy of our country.'[24]

In his first State of the Union address in January 1961, President John F. Kennedy declared that 'Cuban social and economic reform should be encouraged. Questions of economics and trade policy can always be negotiated. But Communist domination in this hemisphere can never be negotiated.'[25] Castro responded on the occasion of the victory celebration following the US defeat at the Bay of Pigs. 'If Mr. Kennedy does not like socialism,' he rejoined, 'well, we do not like imperialism! We do not like capitalism! We have as much right to protest over the existence of an imperialist-capitalist regime ninety miles from our coast as he feels he has to protest over the existence of a socialist regime ninety miles from his coast.' Nonetheless, Castro went on, 'it would be absurd for us to try to tell the people of the United States what system of government they must have, for in that case we would be considering that the United States is not a sovereign nation and that we have rights over the domestic life of the United States'.[26] Castro thus signalled that the issue of national sovereignty remained live. The United States responded by economically blockading the island, and making every effort to isolate it politically.

The Bay of Pigs invasion proved to be the crucial turning-point for the Cuban Revolution. As in Guatemala, Washington hoped to take advantage of a disaffected elite to overthrow the new government. The invasion failed due to the overwhelming support which the Revolution commanded, but nonetheless provided a bloody illustration of the lengths to which Washington would go in order to prevent an assertion of national sovereignty contrary to the interests of US capital in a country it expected to control. The message that any attempts at implementing meaningful change would be countered, ultimately, with direct force, left the revolutionary government, regardless of what its wishes might otherwise have been, with little room for manoeuvre if it wished to continue with the revolutionary project. The lines of battle became much more clearly drawn and the language of revolution altered to reflect this state. Faced with the choice of radicalizing or turning back, the Cubans chose the former. Cuba secured its freedom to pursue socialist policies unimpeded by US military intervention only at the extraordinary cost of nuclear confrontation between the United States and the Soviet Union.

In 1962, the United States succeeded in having Cuba expelled from the Organization of American States. Castro responded with the Second Declaration of Havana, a searing condemnation of US imperialism, particularly in Latin America. The Declaration opened with reference to the death of José Martí, and quoted at length from Martí's celebrated last letter in which he declared that his aim was to prevent the extension of US control over Cuba and the other nations of 'our America'. The quote closed with perhaps the best known and most frequently used of Martí's images. 'I have lived in the monster,' Martí wrote, 'and I know its entrails – and my sling is that of David.'[27] The Declaration emphasized the ways in which Washington undermined national sovereignty in Latin America and suggested that sovereignty was incompatible with US interests in the region. Castro argued that, at the OAS meeting, which expelled Cuba, the United States and Cuba had spoken for different principles, which he noted at length. 'Cuba represented the people, the United States represented the monopolies', he began. 'Cuba spoke for America's exploited masses; the United States for the exploiting, oligarchic, and imperialist interests', he went on; 'Cuba for sovereignty; the United States for intervention . . . Cuba for bread; the United States for hunger. Cuba for equality; the United States for privilege and discrimination . . . Cuba for liberation; the United States for oppression. Cuba for the bright future of humanity; the United States for the past without hope.' 'Cuba [spoke] for socialism,' he concluded, 'the United States for capitalism.'[28]

The Cuban Revolution redefined the issues at the heart of the US–Latin American relationship, forcing the Latin American perspective to the forefront, highlighting poverty and inequality and their human cost in the region. At the very least, it demonstrated that the United States ignored the destitution in Latin America at its peril. Even as the US military prepared for the Bay of Pigs invasion with his approval, Kennedy announced a new initiative to combat poverty in Latin America, known as the Alliance for Progress. The aims of the Alliance included improved economic performance, through regional integration, increased production, sustained growth, economic diversification, stable prices and more equitable distribution of wealth; land reform; and representative democracy, thereby conceding some of the issues at the core of inequality in the region. It also targeted adult illiteracy, poor housing conditions and low life-expectancy, thus acknowledging the social problems arising from poverty and their explosive potential.

The Alliance for Progress provided another example of conflicting views over US motivation in its policy towards Latin America. The Kennedy administration sold the initiative to Latin Americans as a means to eliminate poverty, and backed this claim with a huge injection of dollars. Yet, whenever Congress resisted budget approval, both Kennedy and his successor, Lyndon Johnson, stressed the benefits which the initiative brought the US economy, by providing funds for Latin American nations to purchase goods manufactured in the United States. Latin Americans at all levels of society voiced concerns that the Alliance would prove to be another means of perpetuating US hegemony. Opponents generally argued that it would be used to stave off meaningful change in the region and restore business confidence in the wake of the Cuban Revolution. Certainly it operated in no one's clear interest, neither radical enough to achieve a genuine transformation of economic relationships in the region, and thereby attack poverty, nor toothless enough to avoid resistance from the Latin American elites. Ultimately it withered away; leaving little imprint on the region it was designed to help, other than stronger militaries, which had benefited from US loans and training.

Nor did the Alliance for Progress put an end to US intervention, either indirect or military. The Cuban Revolution heightened US anxiety about alternative regimes. In the 1964 election in British Guiana, the CIA took advantage of a split among the nationalists, providing assistance and funding which ensured the victory of Forbes Burnham and prevented the return of Cheddi Jagan and the Marxist People's Progressive Party to power.[29] In the Dominican Republic in 1965, the United States landed over 20000 marines, ostensibly to prevent a communist take-over, a possibility for which there was and is little evidence. Washington did, however, wish to support the expansion of US capital in the country's sugar industry. Through the long dictatorship of Rafael Trujillo, US capital had lost ground as Trujillo increasingly dominated the nation's resources. Following the loss of investments in Cuba, his greed became unacceptable and in 1961 the CIA connived in his assassination. Division among the elite allowed a nationalist government to take power following Trujillo's death. A right-wing faction which favoured US interests overthrew the government (the new leader was nicknamed 'el americanito'); the nationalist government's attempt to regain control prompted the marine landing. As previously in the Caribbean, US capital followed the marines, and Washington successfully assisted the fulfilment of the presidential ambitions of one of Trujillo's advisers.[30]

The reformist, anti-communist military regime of Juan Velasco in Peru arose in 1968 in part from a concern within the military that Peru's worsening economic situation and the entrenchment of the oligarchy against reform would lead to a radical revolution which might alter the country's development from a capitalist path. Organisation of marginalized groups occurred from the top down, with the emphasis on the elimination of class struggle, in a model closer to corporatism than socialism. Consequently, from the beginning the regime represented an attempt to contain rather than promote radical change. Deeply influenced by theories of dependence emanating from the Economic Commission for Latin America, the government nationalized foreign-owned companies in an attempt to redress the balance between foreign capital penetration and state control of the economy. In response to US pressure, specifically a block of international loans, it paid generous compensation for thriving concerns and reinvigorated others which had neglected investment, while continuing to work with foreign capital. The military regime itself was divided and the United States remained on good terms with the right-wing faction. Given these factors, even Peru's purchase of arms from the Soviet Union did not signal a threat to Washington. When the regime's policies led to the point where it had to choose between deeper radicalization against elite opposition or a return to orthodox economics, it chose the latter course, thereby nullifying any possible threat it might once have posed.[31]

The overthrow of President Salvador Allende of Chile by the Chilean military in 1973 has become one of the more controversial cases of US involvement in Latin America. The absence of military intervention, either direct or by proxy, has led to the presentation of the argument that internal chaos destroyed the Allende government while Washington's role was limited.[32] However, US involvement in the political and economic crisis that preceded the coup is well documented and its financial and technical support of the Chilean military is undisputed. The link between corporate interests and the US government has also been made.[33] To debate whether or not or how deeply it was involved at the actual moment of the coup is therefore academic. The preconditions that prompted the coup were so exacerbated by US political and economic sabotage that direct involvement became unnecessary. The United States did not, of course, create the opposition in Chile, but it actively aided and promoted Allende's adversaries. Furthermore, its involvement was explicitly directed towards achieving the end of the socialist experiment. The irony of the failure of social democracy in Chile is that it was adherence to the democratic process that contributed to Allende's fall and the imposition of the military dictatorship. In the name of maintaining the very democracy it was subverting, Washington manipulated class conflict in Chile to its own ends and Chile suffered 16 years of harsh military dictatorship as a consequence.

Manipulation of internal class conflict and the use of economic sabotage in a relatively open political context again proved to be useful strategies following the victory of the Sandinista National Liberation Front in Nicaragua in 1979. US pressure initially failed to topple the Sandinista government, however, which Nicaraguans legitimately re-elected in 1984, when the FSLN received 67 per cent of the vote on a 75 per cent turnout.[34] US hostility against the Sandinistas and revolutionary movements elsewhere in Central America escalated with the election of Ronald Reagan in 1980 and threatened to engulf the region as neighbouring countries became increasingly militarized by the US campaign, counter-insurgency actions increased with US military and financial assistance and Washington sabotaged every effort to achieve a negotiated settlement in the region. Events in Central America revealed more starkly than had the military dictatorships of South America the close relationship between Latin American militaries and the United States, facilitated through training, provision of equipment, financial support, alliances and bases. Its committed support to Central and South American militaries and military regimes made the United States directly complicit in the violence which those militaries used against their own people.

The Central American crisis of the 1980s demonstrated the use of ideological rhetoric to obscure the details of the confrontation. While Washington actively supported military and paramilitary action against the populations of Latin America, policy-makers intoned the sanctity of democracy and freedom and the evils of communism. In a masterly stroke, the Reagan administration solemnly insisted that the Sandinistas, governing an impoverished nation of less than three million people, threatened the security of the United States. Even as the United States illegally funded an army in an undeclared war on Nicaragua fought from Nicaraguan, Honduran and Costa Rican soil. In reality, the Sandinistas posed quite a different threat, of course. They represented a popular movement to pursue a development path radically different to the one inflicted on Nicaragua by the US-supported Somoza dynasty, including a redistribution of wealth without the limitations on civil rights which the Cuban government had imposed, and an assertion of national sovereignty openly defiant of Washington. The United States made it abundantly and violently clear that it would never accept Nicaragua's choice, and in 1990 the war-ravaged Nicaraguans capitulated and voted the Sandinistas from power.[35]

The US preoccupation with the Caribbean region, and the transfer of strategic responsibility for the Commonwealth Caribbean from London to Washington, was emphasized by Washington's response to Michael Manley's government in Jamaica between 1972 and 1980, and the New Jewel Movement which came to power in Grenada in 1979. The Manley case, like Bolivia and Peru before it, also provides an example of the choice reformers ultimately face: which interests will be supported as the reform process unfolds and class interests conflict. Manley instituted a partial land reform, implemented free secondary education, nationalized utility companies and resumed diplomatic relations with Cuba, all in the name of social democracy. In response, the United States pursued its historic tactic of economic subversion by undermining the bauxite and tourist industries on which Jamaica depended, cutting off aid and pressuring the IMF to lower Jamaica's credit rating. Manley wavered under the pressure, eventually capitulating to the IMF, thereby destroying his popular support. He later ended his dealings with the IMF, but too late to recover popularity and was defeated in the 1980 elections.[36]

The revolution in Grenada had more serious implications, for it represented an outright rejection of the Westminster model of government in the Commonwealth Caribbean. It occurred in a region where the United States expected complete control, and where it had already to contend with the survival of the Cuban revolution, a new revolution in Nicaragua, and incipient revolutions elsewhere in Central America. These anxieties explain why in 1983 the United States launched its largest military action since the Vietnam War against a tiny island inhabited by only 100 000 people. A serious internal split within the revolutionary government assisted the United States, which did not actually intervene until after Grenada's leader, Maurice Bishop, had been overthrown and killed. Washington then pledged to turn Grenada into a showcase of development in the Caribbean, a pledge on which it failed to deliver. Here there are parallels with Nicaragua post-1990, where promised economic boons did not materialize after the Sandinistas had been removed from power.[37]

The US intervention in Panama in 1989 provides a contemporary example of Washington's willingness to overthrow past allies who have outlived their usefulness or proved overly recalcitrant. The forcible removal from Panama of General Manuel Noriega by the US military made a mockery of Panama's independence. The fact of Noriega's corruption and his employment by the CIA did not alleviate the insult of the action for Panamanians. The consequence was a surge of anti-US feeling, making Noriega the latest in a long line of reactionary Latin American leaders who have appealed to nationalism in the face of US aggression to bolster their support. The Panama example additionally previewed the post-Cold War shift to new ideological beasts for the United States to slay, in this case drugs. The drug war also provided the rationale for an increased US military presence and support in Peru and Colombia.

In Haiti in 1994, Washington found itself caught between its own rhetoric and its preferred course of action. Following the military over-throw of President Jean Bertrand Aristide, the United States overtly sup-ported his return to power while covertly and indirectly undermining his authority. By the time a US-led multinational force reinstated Aristide, he had been so compromised that he abandoned his policies of economic nationalization and higher wages for workers in the export-processing zones and consented to implement the neo-liberal economic policies favoured by the United States. Meanwhile the composition of the army and police force remained largely unchanged. The United States thus succeeded in disbanding the multi-class coalition which had elected Aristide and preventing economic change which would have raised labour costs, at the same time as appearing to support a democratically elected president in opposition to a military regime.[38]

One of the significant features of the Haitian example was the impact of Haitian migration on US policy. The US coastguard turned back Haitians who attempted to emigrate illegally to the United States, while accepting Cubans. Washington argued that Haitians were economic, not political refugees, yet many who left were fleeing death-squad violence directed at supporters of Aristide. The United States attempted to deny that human-rights violations occurred in Haiti, in the face of incontro-vertible evidence, but the boatloads of stricken refugees fleeing the country made a mockery of the claim. Forced to acknowledge the violence, Washington then pledged to stop it but failed to take any significant action.[39]

The unequal economic relationship between Latin America and the United States, which José Martí warned against, has continued to the present day. The troubled relations between the United States and Mexico illustrate many of the problems which arise from this relation-ship. The 1980s debt crisis, which drove so many Latin Americans deeper into poverty and confirmed Latin America as a net exporter of capital in spite of heavy borrowing, was triggered by Mexico's inability to maintain debt repayments. Mexico under the presidency of Carlos Salinas (1988–94) was held up as a model of the success of neo-liberal policies, as it sold off state-owned assets, often to foreign capital, slashed subsidies to the poor and signed the North American Free Trade

Agreement (NAFTA) between the United States, Mexico and Canada, increasing both its number of dollar billionaires and the gap between rich and poor in the process.[40]

However, deeper insertion into the world economy left even a large and politically stable country like Mexico vulnerable to the fluctuations and weaknesses in that economy. It is no coincidence that poor and disaffected peasants in the Chiapas region chose the day that NAFTA came into effect to launch an armed rebellion in protest at their living conditions and encroachment on their land by ranchers. Meanwhile, a post-presidency Salinas left Mexico in disgrace, dogged by charges of corruption, while Mexico itself came near to financial collapse following loss of confidence by the foreign investors upon which the economy had come to rely so heavily. Only US loans averted collapse, with Mexican oil revenues offered as collateral. This trade symbolized the concession of the economic nationalism which Mexican oil represented and to which the neo-liberalist model objects, while the ongoing Chiapas rebellion and the government's choice of violent response over negotiated settlement starkly demonstrate the failure of neo-liberal policies to alleviate poverty or promote development.

Mexico also shares a long border with the United States, heavily guarded to stop Mexicans and other Latin American migrants fleeing economic destitution and political violence from crossing into the United States to search for work and a better life, the fulfilment of the American material dream which bombards them through advertisements, television and film. The US government goes to great trouble and expense to keep them out. Yet, as long as people watch their children die from hunger, or curable diseases, or suffer from the effects of poor nutrition, housing and sanitation, or live long enough only to become unskilled, badly paid labour, often working in conditions hazardous to life and health, the United States will not be able to stop the flow of migration from south to north. Nor will it be able to subvert the logic which argues that if export crops must be grown, then better to grow profitable coca leaves than work for low wages on foreign-owned plantations. Thus the economic and political stability which corporate capital craves cannot be maintained permanently, for it creates too many tensions and contradictions in its quest for profit and leaves behind an appalling trail of human waste.

The Export Processing Zones are perhaps the most concrete manifestation of the unequal economic relationship between the United States and Latin America. Host nations offer tax holidays, subsidized credit, and freedom from import duties on raw materials, unrestricted profit repatriation, construction of the zones and many other benefits in exchange for employment for locals. Cheap and docile labour is a condition of employment and attempts to unionize or improve working conditions are met with dismissal, force or closure of the factory.[41] The General Agreement on Tariffs and Trade (GATT) and the World Trade Organization (WTO), dominated by the United States and other western nations, have also proved to be effective methods of reinforcing corporate power at the expense of national autonomy. The WTO, following a complaint by the US multinational Chiquita and the Clinton administration, has ruled that small Caribbean banana producers should no longer enjoy preferential access to the European market under the Lomé Convention, which was designed to promote trade with developing countries. The complaint was made in spite of the fact that Chiquita already commands the majority of banana exports to Europe and Caribbean producers cannot compete. The Multilateral Agreement on Investment currently being finalized by the Organization for Economic Co-operation and Development (OECD) will give transnational corporations the right to sue national governments for profits lost through national laws which they believe discriminate against them. Thus corporate profit and the unrestricted movement of foreign capital will be enshrined as more important than a nation's right to protect its sovereignty, environment or people.

The methods the United States has used to protect its interests, however Washington has defined them, have varied over time, proving remarkably adaptable to different conditions and changing circumstances throughout Latin America. Although military force is the ultimate weapon that the United States wields, the proximity and strength of the opponent and the availability of other means to pursue its aims temper its use. The US government normally offers inducements and applies pressure to achieve its ends through a complex web of military, economic, political and cultural relationships. Washington has followed an historic pattern of responding aggressively to reforms which move away from capitalist development, and exploiting cleavages within the elite and the possibility of military suppression to contain popular mobilisation, maintain favourable investment conditions and trade agreements and protect its security interests, however defined. This pattern of behaviour conflates with the US government's ideological position, which may change in the detail but is based on an assumption of the inherent superiority of its own people and form of government, and its consequent right to dictate economic, political and moral positions to others.

The continued US obsession with Cuba, symbolized by the tightening of the blockade, illustrates the extent to which the United States continues to claim as its right the freedom to do what it chooses in Latin America and to punish those who prefer a different path.[42] In spite of US rhetoric, the blockade of Cuba is not about 'democracy' or 'freedom' or the US commitment to either. Washington has proved perfectly content to carry on cordial relationships with regimes guilty of civil and human rights abuses with which the Cuban government cannot begin to compete. For nearly forty years the United States has penalized Cubans, and by extension countries that trade with her, for asserting their national sovereignty in a way that is contrary to US interests and desires and which questions US justifications. Washington's response has been particularly ferocious because the prior dependent relationship was particularly extreme, and the break therefore especially offensive to US pride. The punishment continues because the Cubans refuse to return to the past relationship and the United States is unwilling to negotiate anything new. Meanwhile, Cuba stands as an example of the possibilities, limitations and dangers of attempting to pursue a development path in Latin America independently of the United States. The shanty-towns throughout Latin America remain testimony to the consequences of following in its wake.

Notes

I am indebted to Mary Turner and Christopher Abel for their comments and for discussions, which stimulated my ideas. Errors and omissions are my own.

1   José Martí, 'Congreso Internacional de Washington', in *Obras completas, tomo 6: Nuestra America* (La Habana, 1975), p. 46.
2   José Martí, 'La Conferencia Monetaria de las Repúblicas de America', in ibid., p. 160.
3   See Martí's letter to Manuel Mercado, written on 18 May 1895, the day before he was killed in battle, in *José Martí, Obras Completas, tomo 4: Cuba* (La Habana, 1975), p. 168.
4   Some good accounts of this period include Jules Benjamin, *The United States and Cuba: Hegemony and Dependent Development, 1880–1934* (Pittsburgh, 1977); Philip S. Foner, *The Spanish–Cuban–American War and the Birth of American Imperialism, 1895–1902*, 2 vols (New York, 1972); David Healy, *Drive to Hegemony: the United States in the Caribbean, 1898–1917* (Madison, Wisconsin, 1988) and *The United States in Cuba, 1898–1902: Generals, Politicians and the Search for Policy* (Madison, 1963); Louis Pérez Jr, *Cuba and the United States: Ties of Singular Intimacy* (Athens, 1990). See also, James L. Dietz, *Economic History of Puerto Rico: Institutional Change and Capitalist Development* (Prince-

ton, 1986). For a discussion of the attempt to 'Americanize' Cubans through the educational system, see Laurie Johnston, 'Por la escuela cubana en Cuba Libre: Themes in the History of Primary and Secondary Education in Cuba, 1899–1958', unpublished PhD diss., University of London, 1996, pp. 19–48; for the same in Puerto Rico, see Juan José Osuna, *A History of Education in Puerto Rico*, 2nd edn (Río Pedras, 1949).

5 Thomas F. O'Brien, *The Revolutionary Mission: American Enterprise in Latin America, 1900–1945* (New York, 1996), pp. 26–31.

6 Eduardo Galeano, *Open Veins of Latin America* (New York, 1973), p. 227.

7 Quoted in Walter LeFeber, *The New Empire: an Interpretation of American Expansion, 1860–1898*, (Ithaca, 1963), p. 106. It should be remembered that despite Blaine's disclaimer regarding annexation, the United States in the nineteenth century invaded, bought or annexed land from Alaska to Hawaii to Florida to Mexico (which lost half its territory) and all the native American land in between.

8 See, for example, Michael Hunt, *Ideology and U.S. Foreign Policy* (New Haven, 1987) and John J. Johnson, *Latin America in Caricature* (Austin, 1980). The contempt which US rhetoric has historically expressed for Latin America has prompted a mixed response among Latin Americans themselves. Many resisted US cultural and racial characterizations, defining themselves in opposition to the United States. In 1900, Uruguayan José Enrique Rodó published *Ariel*, an essay using the characters of Ariel and Caliban from Shakespeare's *The Tempest* as an allegory for Latin America and the United States. Ariel represented Latin America's reason and civilization against the barbarism and materialism of Caliban, or the United States. Yet, this type of cultural reaction notwithstanding, Latin Americans continued to move between envy and admiration for the United States. This tension is hardly surprising given the immense cultural influence of the United States, which permeates Latin America through US corporatism, Protestant missionaries, radio, television, film and literature and the extent of migration between the two regions.

9 Annual Report of the War Department for the Fiscal Year Ended June 30, 1900, Part II, Report of the Military Governor of Cuba on Civil Affairs, vol. 1, part 4 (Washington, 1901), pp. 205–6. For more on the school–city programme, see Johnston, pp. 30–31.

10 Quoted in Healy, *Drive to Hegemony*, p. 143.

11 The annexation of Hawaii in 1898 and the acquisition of the Philippines following the Spanish–Cuban–American war provided the United States with an entry into Asia and particularly China, thus sharpening the desire for a Central American canal.

12 Quoted in Frank Neiss, *A Hemisphere to Itself: a History of US–Latin American Relations* (London, 1990), p. 76.

13 The United States occupied all or part of: Cuba in 1898–1902, 1906–09, 1912, 1917–22; Haiti in 1914–34; Panama in 1908, 1912, 1918; Honduras in 1905, 1910, 1912, 1919, 1924; Nicaragua in 1912–25 and 1926–33; and the Dominican Republic in 1916–24.

14 The Platt Amendment, drafted by US legislators, consisted of eight clauses, which effectively undermined Cuban national sovereignty in favour of Washington, and allowed the United States the right to intervene on the

island at will. The United States insisted on the amendment's incorporation into the new Cuban Constitution as the price for its evacuation of the island. For the full text of the amendment, see Russell H. Fitzgibbon, *Cuba and the United States, 1900–1935* (Wisconsin, 1935), pp. 272–3.

15 In the Hay–Bunau–Varilla Treaty of 1903.

16 The most important exception to this pattern is the US relationship with Puerto Rico, which the United States still directly controls one hundred years after taking the island from Spain. Puerto Rico has been granted Commonwealth status, giving it some internal autonomy under US sovereign control, although it is not a state and therefore has limited representation in the US government. Islanders have US citizenship and migration to the United States has proved an important strategy for tackling poverty at a household level. Puerto Rico's somewhat uncertain status is neatly captured by a lawsuit between Wrangler, the jeans manufacturer, and a competitor, in which Wrangler challenged the right of its competitor to label its jeans 'made in the USA', because they are made in Puerto Rico. Wrangler's lawyers described Puerto Rico as a 'Third World country' inhabited by 'Indians and Creoles', a description which no doubt reflects the opinion of many in the United States. See 'Wrangler Faces Race Slur Protest' in *The Guardian* (London), 3 February 1998.

17 For an outline of the issues and debates, see Christopher Abel and Colin M. Lewis, *Latin America, Economic Imperialism and the State: the Political Economy of the External Connection from Independence to the Present* (London, 1985), Section IV: The Era of Disputed Hegemony.

18 For an account of US corporate relationships with Latin America during this period see O'Brien, *The Revolutionary Mission*.

19 US warships also sat off E1 Salvador during the *matanza* of 1932.

20 See Lorenzo Meyer, *Mexico and the United States in the Oil Controversy, 1916–1942* (Austin, 1977). Meyer notes that the compensation awarded exceeded the value of the oil companies' investments, thereby appearing to include the value of oil not yet extracted from the ground. See pp. 225–6.

21 The United States supported the creation of the OAS in part to offset any influence the newly formed United Nations might develop in the region. For an account of inter-American diplomatic relations, see Gordon Connell-Smith, *The United States and Latin America: an Historical Analysis of Inter-American Relations* (London, 1974).

22 For an account of this period, see James Dunkerley, *Rebellion in the Veins: Political Struggle in Bolivia, 1952–82* (London, 1984).

23 For further detail on this period, see Piero Gleijeses, *Shattered Hope: the Guatemalan Revolution and the United States, 1944–1954* (Princeton, 1991) and Stephen Schlesinger and Stephen Kinzer, *Bitter Fruit* (London, 1982).

24 'Overview: Economic Problems Confronting Cuba and the Underdeveloped World', in M. Kenner and J. Petras (eds), *Fidel Castro Speaks* (Harmondsworth, 1969), p. 31. It should be noted that the United States did not have a strong history of encouraging social and economic reform in Cuba.

25 Quoted in Jane Franklin, *The Cuban Revolution and the United States: a Chronological History* (Melbourne, 1992), p. 39.

26 'Turn toward Socialism: Cuba's Socialism Proclaimed', in Kenner and Petras, p. 131.

27 Martí to Mercado in *Obras Completas*, tomo 4, p. 168.

28 'The Second Declaration of Havana', in Kenner and Petras, p. 151.

29 Jagan had been forcibly removed from power by British troops following his election in 1953, in an operation encouraged and approved by the United States. For his first-hand account, see Cheddi Jagan, *The West on Trial* (London, 1966).

30 On the nationalist uprising, see Piero Gleijeses, *The Dominican Crisis: the 1965 Constitutionalist Revolt and American Intervention* (Baltimore, 1978).

31 For a study of this period of Peruvian history, see Cynthia McClintock and Abraham F. Lowenthal (eds), *The Peruvian Experiment Reconsidered* (Princeton, 1983).

32 It is interesting to note that a blueprint for the future appeared in documents of the International Telephone and Telegraph company which was opposed to Allende's election in 1970. ITT's analysis concluded that the Chilean military would not intervene to prevent Allende from taking office except within the framework of the constitution, that the head of the army would 'not budge an inch without Frei's okay' and that Frei [Allende's predecessor] would not move 'unless he is provided with a constitutional threat'. ITT advised that 'a constitutional solution . . . could result from massive internal disorders, strikes, urban and rural warfare. This would morally justify an armed forces intervention for an indefinite period.' See Bertrand Russell Peace Foundation, *Subversion in Chile: a Case Study in US Corporate Intrigue in the Third World* (Nottingham, 1972), pp. 30, 32.

33 Even those who place less emphasis on US involvement as a critical factor in the coup accept this. See, for example, Paul E. Sigmund, *The United States and Democracy in Chile* (Baltimore, 1993). Other views are presented in Lois Hecht Oppenheim, *Politics in Chile: Democracy, Authoritarianism and the Search for Development* (Boulder, 1993) and James Petras and Morris Morley, *The United States and Chile: Imperialism and the Overthrow of the Allende Government* (New York, 1975).

34 James Dunkerley, *Power in the Isthmus: a Political History of Modern Central America* (London, 1988), p. 279.

35 The literature on Central America during this period is voluminous. Some of the best works include Dunkerley, *Power in the Isthmus* and *The Pacification of Central America: Political Change in the Isthmus, 1987–1993* (London, 1994) and Walter LeFeber, *Inevitable Revolutions: the United States in Central America*, 2nd edn (New York, 1993). On the ideological and diplomatic war, see Noam Chomsky, *Turning the Tide: the US and Latin America* (Montreal, 1987) and David Ryan, *US–Sandinista Diplomatic Relations: Voice of Intolerance* (London, 1995).

36 For a brief but useful account of Manley's terms in office, see Fitzroy Ambursley, 'Jamaica: from Michael Manley to Edward Seaga', in Fitzroy Ambursley and Robin Cohen, *Crisis in the Caribbean* (New York, 1983), pp. 72–104.

37 Good brief introductions to the revolution in Grenada and its overthrow are Fitzroy Ambursley and James Dunkerley, *Grenada: Whose Freedom* (London, 1984) and James Ferguson, *Grenada: Revolution in Reverse* (London, n.d.). See also Tony Thorndike, *Grenada: Politics, Economics and Society* (London, 1985).

38   For an introduction to this period, see Deidre McFadyen, *et al.* (eds), *Haiti: Dangerous Crossroads* (Boston, 1995).

39   A captain in the US army who inspected a prison in Port-au-Prince himself, after failing to be assigned someone to do so, was court-martialed for his pains. See 'Court Martial for Trying to Stop Abuses in Haiti', *The Guardian* (London), 23 February 1995.

40   On debt, see Jackie Roddick, *The Dance of the Millions: Latin America and the Debt Crisis* (London, 1988). For a discussion of neoliberal policies in Latin America, see Duncan Green, *Silent Revolution: the Rise of Market Economics in Latin America* (London, 1995); Henry Veltmeyer, James Petras and Steve Vieux, *Neoliberalism and Class Conflict in Latin America* (Basingstoke, 1997); John Weeks, 'The Contemporary Latin American Economies: Neoliberal Reconstruction', in Sandor Halebsky and Richard L. Harris (eds), *Capital, Power and Inequality in Latin America* (Boulder, 1995), pp. 109–35.

41   For an excellent study of export-led industrialization in the Caribbean and its effects on the female workforce, see Helen I. Safa, *The Myth of the Male Breadwinner: Women and Industrialization in the Caribbean* (Boulder, 1995).

42   Washington tightened the blockade on Cuba in 1992, 1993 and 1996, hoping to capitalize on Cuba's economic crisis following the collapse of the Soviet Union to topple the regime. The American Association for World Health reported in 1997 that, as a consequence of the blockade, the average calorie-intake of Cubans had dropped by a third between 1989 and 1993, that sick children suffered agony through lack of medicine and that Cubans had died needlessly. The Association also reported that only the Cuban government's continued commitment to health spending had averted a humanitarian catastrophe. See 'Children Die in Agony as US Trade Ban Stifles Cuba', *The Guardian* (London), 7 March 1997.

3
'Adjusting to a New Period in World History': Franklin Roosevelt and European Colonialism

Paul Orders

In late November 1943, in a hotel near Cairo, Winston Churchill and Franklin Roosevelt discussed the future of Indochina. Churchill expressed concern that China might look to annex the French colony after the defeat of Japan. Roosevelt, an enthusiastic supporter of increased Chinese responsibilities in Southeast Asia, dismissed the Prime Minister's worries out of hand: 'Winston, this is something you are just not able to understand. You have 400 years of acquisitive instinct in your blood and you just don't understand how a country might not want to acquire land if they can get it. A new period has opened in the world's history, and you will have to adjust to it.'[1]

The comments reflect Roosevelt's strong conviction, expressed frequently until his death in April 1945, that global conflict sounded the death-knell of European colonialism. He was eager to 'adjust' to the 'new period . . . in the world's history'. From about mid-1942, he began to argue that Europe's colonial empires should be replaced by a network of independent nation-states and trusteeships, overseen by the United States and its great-power allies and linked to a new organization for world security.

Unsurprisingly, a large number of historians have sought to make sense of FDR's attitude towards colonialism.[2] Most have emphasized his antipathy towards Europe's 'formal' empires.[3] John Darwin notes how Roosevelt regarded colonialism 'with the same hostility and dislike as had Woodrow Wilson';[4] John Charmley highlights the President's belief that colonialism was an 'outdated system';[5] and Warren Kimball and Fred Pollock emphasise his 'general distaste for colonialism'.[6]

These and other historians, however, have disagreed strongly about the nature of FDR's anti-colonial project. Writing in the immediate aftermath of the war, commentators tended to locate Rooseveltian diplomacy in the idealist tradition of Woodrow Wilson. Numerous studies highlighted Roosevelt's noble objectives in the colonial sphere, above all his desire to improve the lives of colonial peoples and prevent future wars by purging the world of imperial rivalries.[7] Some historians recognised that this was only part of the story.[8] Most, however, agreed that liberal idealism was the key to understanding American anti-colonialism during the Second World War.

In the 1960s this orthodoxy was challenged by revisionist scholars following the footsteps of William Appleman Williams, whose arguments seemed extraordinarily relevant in the midst of the conflict in Vietnam.[9] Sympathetic to Williams' *Tragedy of American Diplomacy*, a new generation of historians explored the material factors that underpinned American foreign policy during the 1930s and 1940s and sought to understand how liberal ideology, often couched in the language of internationalism, served to mask Washington's aggressive pursuit of American commercial interests. Lloyd Gardner brilliantly outlined the commercial considerations that informed 'New Deal diplomacy', while Gabriel Kolko stridently contended that the Roosevelt administration pursued 'open door' policies that aimed to ensure that American business prospered from trade with colonial dependencies.[10]

In the 1970s international historians, taking advantage of newly opened official archive collections, developed more eclectic interpretations. Roger Louis, Christopher Thorne and Walter LaFeber illuminated the complexity of American anti-colonialism.[11] Roosevelt was shown to have been motivated by various contradictory impulses. Louis, for example, emphasised the President's belief that opposition to colonialism reflected the best interests of both the United Nations and the United States. The elimination of empires would reduce international tensions, help to increase world trade, and enable the United States to expand its commercial and strategic interests throughout the world.[12]

Crucially, Louis, Thorne, LaFeber *et al.* agreed that Roosevelt's radicalism on colonial issues waned as the war progressed. Other matters took precedence in American war diplomacy and the White House and State Department frequently adopted policies that were at odds with the President's broad sympathy with the aspirations of colonial peoples. FDR himself was anxious to maintain Anglo-American unity and sensitive to the dangers of creating power vacuums in strategically important areas of the world. In 1942 he did not push the British too hard to make concessions over India, despite Gandhi's resurgent liberation movement, for fear of undermining the recently established Anglo-American alliance.[13] Similarly, from mid-1944 he seemed prepared to allow the French to resume colonial responsibilities in Indochina, a colony that he had earlier earmarked for a United Nations trusteeship.[14] The implication of these arguments is that Roosevelt seemed increasingly prepared to tolerate, at least in the short term, the continuation of European colonialism in Africa, Asia and the Pacific.

More recently, however, Kimball and Pollock asserted that the President waged an 'unceasing public and private campaign aimed at eliminating European empires and setting the colonial world on the road toward independence'.[15] True, he occasionally adopted pro-colonial measures in order to facilitate the prosecution of the war and reinforce inter-allied relations during the transition from war to peace. But he continued to believe that colonial empires were remnants of a bygone age and would be dismantled in due course. More importantly, he continued to support policies to hasten decolonization. In sum, Roosevelt adopted 'the classic position of the moderate American reformer, seeking the middle ground between reaction and change'.[16]

The following essay will assess some of these arguments after tracing the development of FDR's thinking about colonial issues from the end of the First World War. It underlines the extent to which he supported the anti-colonial cause after Pearl Harbor. He was committed morally to improving the plight of small nations and colonial peoples. At the same time, he believed that anti-colonial policies would help to secure the United States' commercial and strategic interests overseas, particularly in regions that were likely to occupy an important role in American strategy after the war. But he was reluctant to push policies that were likely to damage US relations with key great-power allies. This does not mean that Roosevelt's anti-colonialism was characterised by words rather than deeds. The essay's main contention is that Roosevelt was convinced that the United States could moderate its anti-colonial policies during 1944 and 1945 without endangering decolonization in the long term.

By the end of the First World War Roosevelt, who had served as Assistant Secretary of the Navy since 1913, had established a reputation for himself as a militant nationalist, an advocate of a 'Big Navy' that could be used to defend the US overseas interests.[17] Peace required that he sing a different song. Woodrow Wilson's postwar foreign policy, outlined in the Fourteen Points of January 1918, was dominated by idealistic *causes célèbres* – peace, disarmament and the League of Nations. Roosevelt, with an eye on his own advancement within the Democratic Party, became a standard-bearer of Wilsonian internationalism, despite the US failure to join the League of Nations.[18]

For much of the following two decades he emphasized the importance of the US involvement in international affairs. War in Europe, he
reminded the American public, had revealed the country's exposure to
events abroad.[19] For Roosevelt international cooperation was the only
way to ensure that Americans enjoyed lasting peace and prosperity.

At the same time he thought that European colonialism represented
a major obstacle to cooperation between the Old and New Worlds.[20] The
US external economic and political influence, which had increased
steadily since the late nineteenth century, was checked by the existence
of Europe's colonial empires. Furthermore, imperial rivalries had served
to sour international relations in the run-up to 1914. Roosevelt hoped
that the League of Nations' mandate system, encompassing former
German colonies in Africa and the Pacific and set up at the Paris Peace
conference at the behest of Woodrow Wilson, would prove that the
colonial urges of Europe's leading powers could be tamed by making so-
called 'parent' states accountable to international opinion. In 1923 he
argued that colonialism was no longer a serious cause of international
tension. 'The whole trend of the times is against wars for colonial expansion. The thought of the world leans the other way. Populations themselves have a say. Subjects of dispute are being worked out more and
more by amicable means.'[21]

The grounds for such optimism disappeared in the 1930s. The onset
of depression and the rise of militarism poisoned the atmosphere surrounding colonial issues. The economic and political significance of
European colonialism increased after the British government sought,
from 1931, to overcome serious balance-of-payments problems by
restricting trade between imperial colonies and third countries outside
the British Empire. The expansionist ambitions of militarist regimes
in Rome and Tokyo increased the prominence of colonial affairs still
further. Italy's drive into Abyssinia, the first step in Mussolini's plan to
create a 'new Roman Empire', revealed the potential for a new scramble for territory involving Europe's great powers. Japan's invasion of
Manchuria highlighted the possibility of a similar problem in the Far
East. Such developments were viewed with foreboding in Washington.
In August 1936, at Chautauqua, New York, Roosevelt claimed that there
was no reason for the United States to fight in wars caused by 'ancient
hatreds, turbulent frontiers, [and] the "legacy of old, forgotten, far off
things"'.[22]

He had already demonstrated his ideas on how powerful nations
should conduct relations with dependent states that lay within their
orbits. In April 1933 he unveiled plans for the United States to act as a

'good neighbour' in its dealings with Latin America.[23] He and Cordell Hull, the Secretary of State, renounced gunboat and dollar diplomacy south of the Rio Grande. The contrast between the good-neighbour policy and European colonialism was stark. According to Walter Lippmann, Roosevelt's actions demonstrated that powerful countries did not need to impose formal colonial controls on dependencies. On this reading, the President's policy was 'the only true substitute for empire'.[24] Roosevelt sought to prove the point after the outbreak of war in Europe. In response to fears about Nazi infiltration of Latin America, he suggested that Antarctica and Western Hemisphere possessions of Nazi-occupied countries should come under the tutelage of a Pan-American trusteeship, which would offer them protection for the duration of the war and, if appropriate, prepare them for eventual independence.[25]

FDR also took steps to strengthen the US position in the Pacific, at the expense of British and French colonialism. American concerns about the threat of Japanese aggression and Pan American Airway's attempt to develop transoceanic air routes across the Central and South Pacific prompted Roosevelt to become a firm advocate of the need for the United States to obtain as many strategic possessions as possible in the Pacific. In late 1934 he signed an executive order that put several coral atolls in the Central Pacific under the control of the US Navy. Over subsequent years he became an enthusiastic supporter of American expansionism in the Pacific islands, many of which were claimed by Britain and New Zealand. In 1935 and 1936 three of the British-administered Line Islands were colonized by American soldiers as a prelude to a presidential annexation decree. In March 1938 strategically important Canton and Enderbury Islands in the British-claimed Phoenix group were also occupied.[26]

The moves followed the British and Australian governments' refusal to grant Pan American Airways landing rights in British Empire territories to enable the airline's completion of its proposed transpacific trunk route between San Francisco and Sydney. Stephen Early, Roosevelt's Press Secretary, claimed that American moves over Canton and Enderbury 'were motivated by the needs of commercial aviation'.[27] Roosevelt, however, downplayed the significance of aviation interests in the Central Pacific, arguing that Britain and the United States had a mutual interest in ensuring that Canton was never occupied by the Japanese.[28]

The British were furious at American behaviour, particularly over Canton, but their response was tame due to their wish to avoid confrontation with the Americans, Britain's prospective allies in a future struggle against Germany. In an exchange of notes on 6 April 1939 Britain and the United States agreed on joint ownership of Canton and Enderbury for a period of fifty years. The Roosevelt administration remained dissatisfied. On 16 August the State Department, with Roosevelt's support, submitted an *aide-mémoire* to the British Embassy in Washington claiming American title to 23 islands under British and New Zealand jurisdiction, including Christmas and Hull Islands, five islands in the Southern Line group, five in the Phoenix group, four in the Ellice group, and seven in the New Zealand-administered Union and Northern Cook groups.

For British officials the *démarche* revealed the aggressive, nationalist and expansionist impulses that often fuelled American attacks on European colonialism.[29] Throughout the dispute Roosevelt made very few references to the welfare of natives inhabiting large islands such as Canton and Christmas.[30] Yet he subsequently argued that the Anglo-American agreement over Canton was an early example of his trusteeship ideas in action.[31] In fact, the agreement indicated how international administrative arrangements encompassing island dependencies could be used to secure American strategic interests in the Pacific. Within months of signing the agreement the Americans had gained control of the islands' affairs and had started to build an airport on Canton, prompting British colonial officials in Fiji to quip that the condominium worked out in practice with Britain having the 'con' and the United States the 'dominium'.[32]

The Pacific islands dispute was soon overtaken by events in Europe and the Far East. The German invasion of Western Europe, in the spring and early summer of 1940, and the Japanese occupation of northern Indochina, in September, and southern Indochina, in July 1941, encouraged American and British policy-makers to look to collaborate in the sphere of colonial possessions. The new Churchill government was generally happy to meet American demands for bases in the Western Hemisphere. On 2 September 1940 Britain and the United States signed the 'destroyers for bases' agreement. The United States supplied Britain with old destroyers in return for long-term leases on a number of bases in British territories in the Western Hemisphere.[33] Roosevelt greeted the agreement, which proved that both countries were willing to enter into mutually beneficial security arrangements in the Atlantic, as 'the most important action in the reinforcement of our national defence . . . since the Louisiana Purchase'.[34] A comparable agreement was secured in relation to the Pacific when, in late 1941, British Commonwealth governments approved American plans to establish a chain of bases to support the movement of heavy bombers between Honolulu and the Philippines, via a number of territories including the disputed Christmas Island.[35]

Increased Anglo-American cooperation in the Atlantic and Pacific meant that there was no need for Roosevelt to press the British too hard over colonialism. In August 1941 he met Churchill at Placentia Bay, in Newfoundland. He allegedly took the opportunity to inform the Prime Minister that he was 'firmly of the belief that if we are to arrive at a stable peace it must involve the development of backward countries. . . . I can't believe that we can fight a war against fascist slavery, and at the same time not work to free people all over the world from a backward colonial policy.'[36] In a similar vein, according to Rexford Tugwell, the President warned the British that colonialism might have to be eliminated after the war and that the United States 'could not and would not underwrite colonialism or undertake to defend imperialism as against movements in various places – like India – for independence'.[37]

Yet Roosevelt appreciated Churchill's intransigence over colonial matters. He recognized that the British leader would react furiously to constant American criticisms of colonialism, particularly concerning British rule in India. In consequence, he was content to insert merely an ambiguous reference to colonial issues into the summit's public statement.[38] In the third clause of the Atlantic Charter Roosevelt and Churchill agreed to 'respect the right of all peoples to choose the form of government under which they will live; and they wish to see sovereign rights and self-government restored to those who have been forcibly deprived of them'. Eight days later the Prime Minister assured Leo Amery, Britain's Secretary of State for India, that the pledge could be invoked 'only . . . in such cases when transference of territory or sovereignty arose'.[39]

Churchill's interpretation was highly contentious. Amery himself feared that the Prime Minister, as co-author of the Atlantic Charter, had committed Britain to a policy of decolonization. His worries increased when, as a result of pressure from Roosevelt, the Indian Government became one of the Charter's signatories.[40] But Roosevelt proceeded with caution. Immediately after the Atlantic summit, Eleanor Roosevelt provided him with a critical report of British activities in the sub-continent. He seemed more concerned to maintain Anglo-American unity than to lambast the British over colonialism: 'I can have no thoughts about India.'[41] Even so, he was prepared to outline, in unequivocal terms, the United States' general objections to colonialism. At a White House dinner during the Prime Minister's visit to Washington in late 1941 and early 1942 he alleged that Churchill did not understand the nature of American thinking about empires. 'It's in the American tradition, this distrust, this dislike and even hatred of Britain – the Revolution, you know, and 1812; and India and the Boer War, and all that. There are many kinds of Americans of course, but as a people, as a country, we're opposed to imperialism – we can't stomach it.'[42]

Anti-colonial sentiment in the United States was inflamed by military and political developments in Asia. As Japanese forces surged southward and westward in the aftermath of Pearl Harbor, the US Senate Foreign Relations Committee demanded that India be granted increased autonomy.[43] The fall of Singapore, on 15 February, and Rangoon, on 7 March, sent shock waves throughout allied capitals.[44] With the Japanese seemingly poised to strike deep into Indian territory, Allied policy-makers grew increasingly concerned about the state of the country's defences. India was engulfed by political turmoil, with Gandhi's influential Congress Party refusing to support the allied war effort.

Chiang Kai-shek, who visited Delhi and Calcutta in February, warned FDR that the British had to make significant concessions to the Indians.[45] Roosevelt asked his 'Special Representative' in London, Averell Harriman, to sound out Churchill's views. The Prime Minister indicated that Whitehall was contemplating a declaration that India would after the war be granted Dominion status and the right to secede from the British Empire.[46] In response, on 10 March, FDR sent Churchill a lengthy cable outlining 'a new thought to be used in [relation to] India'. He invoked the American Revolution and the decision of 13 formerly British colonies to sign the Articles of Confederation – 'an obvious stop-gap government' – as an historical precedent that indicated the wisdom of establishing in India a 'temporary Dominion Government . . . charged with setting up a body to consider a more permanent government for the whole country'.[47]

The following day Whitehall sent Sir Stafford Cripps to India to discuss with Gandhi and other Nationalist leaders the possibility of a constituent assembly being convened after the defeat of Japan to frame an Indian constitution. Roosevelt, meanwhile, sent Louis Johnson, a former Assistant Secretary for War, to Delhi to assist these negotiations. Cripps failed to persuade Gandhi and his supporters of the merits of British proposals. In a message delivered to Churchill by Harry Hopkins, Roosevelt was blunt: 'The feeling here [in Washington] is almost universally held that the deadlock has been caused by the unwillingness of the British to concede to the Indians the right of self-government.' He urged that Cripps be allowed to persist in efforts to reach a compromise with the Congress Party, possibly along the lines he had suggested on 10 March. In addition, he warned Churchill 'that the prejudicial reaction on American public opinion [of a successful Japanese invasion of India] can hardly be overestimated'.[48] The Prime Minister was furious. He maintained that he would resign rather than compromise over India and that 'the President's mind was back in the American War of Independence ... he thought of the India problem in terms of thirteen colonies fighting George III'.[49]

Roosevelt pursued the issue no further. He had already indicated to Churchill that he was loath to interfere in the Indian problem: 'For the love of Heaven, don't bring me into this, though I do want to be of help. It is, strictly speaking, none of my business, except insofar as it is a part and parcel of the successful fight you and I are making.'[50] The President, whose overriding priority was the struggle against Germany, now concluded that further American pressure on the British over India would, in view of Churchill's intransigence, endanger inter-allied unity at a critical time in the war.

This reflected a geopolitical mindset which was geared towards Europe and the Pacific, where the allied war effort would be won or lost, rather than South Asia, where Americans had played an inconspicuous role in the past. On 9 March Roosevelt formally proposed, and Churchill agreed, to divide the world into three areas of strategic responsibility: an Anglo-American Atlantic and European sphere, a British 'middle area' extending from the Mediterranean to Singapore, and an American Pacific zone.[51] South Asia was to remain in the British sphere for the duration of the war. In effect, the region continued to exist on the margins of Roosevelt's consciousness. In this respect, he personified the attitude of most leading American policy-makers. The point is well made by historian Anita Inder Singh: 'Seen through the Atlantic–Pacific prism, India and the Indian Ocean simply did not appear important to the United States.'[52]

Roosevelt, however, retained a keen interest in the future of relations between colonizers and colonized. In June he outlined to Vyacheslav Molotov, the Soviet Foreign Minister, his preliminary views on the postwar peace settlement. He argued that the great-power allies – Britain, the Soviet Union, the United States and possibly China – would have to act as policemen in the postwar period to ensure international stability, and that the prospects for peace would improve considerably if colonies were brought under the auspices of an international trusteeship system to prepare them for 'self-government' or independence.[53] In early 1943 he visited the British colony of Gambia, *en route* to meet

Churchill in Casablanca. He came away with the impression that Gambians were 'treated worse than livestock. Their cattle live longer.'[54] On his return to Washington he developed the trusteeship idea, with reference to Indochina, in conversation with Anthony Eden.[55] To the disillusionment of the British, the United States' Declaration on National Liberation, of 9 March 1942, proposed to apply the principles outlined in the Atlantic Charter and create an international procedure whereby colonial powers agreed 'to prepare their dependent peoples for independence through education and self-government, and to publish timetables for the process'.[56]

Roosevelt, meanwhile, began to argue that the French Empire should be dismantled after the defeat of Japan. Intensely distrustful of Charles de Gaulle, whom he viewed as undemocratic, and contemptuous of the French record during the first years of the war, the President believed that the French had no moral claim to rule over dependent territories. During meetings of the Pacific War Council, an inter-allied consultative committee, he repeatedly drew attention to the iniquity of French colonialism. He lambasted the French performance in Indochina – 'after 100 years of French rule . . . the inhabitants were worse off than they had been before'.[57] He insisted that France's colonies should be brought within the purview of a United Nations trusteeship system. Indochina's period as a trusteeship, possibly under the auspices of China, would last between 25 and 30 years. The United Nations would have to control, and establish military bases in, strategically important French possessions. He summarized his plans to Churchill: 'Indochina should not be returned to [the French]; Dakar [in French West Africa] should be under American protection; Bizerta under British, and so on. There is no need to abolish French sovereignty in these places; the French flag can fly, "But if Great Britain and America are to police the world, they must have the right to select the police stations".'[58]

The future of British colonialism was also uncertain. In the Pacific various British island territories became part of an intricate network of American forward bases, supply centres, staging posts, and wireless and meteorological stations. The US Army and Navy were left to exercise considerable – in some cases absolute – control over island affairs. Their grip over British possessions tightened as the flow of American manpower and weapons into the Pacific increased. As over India, Roosevelt had to assuage British worries about the future of colonial dependencies. In March 1942 he publicly repudiated congressional suggestions that his administration should, in view of American military efforts against Japan, press territorial claims in the Pacific.[59]

Yet he and other American policy-makers were already looking to ensure that the United States' postwar strategic needs were met. Their discussions were defined by the experience of Pearl Harbor, which had destroyed the traditional US sense of geographical isolation, and a determination to ensure that the United States was equipped militarily to meet any future threat to its security. Roosevelt advocated an offensive, air-power-led, military posture.[60] This reflected the influence of post-hostilities planners, whose work was based on the assumption that the performance of aircraft would improve greatly within a short period of time and expose all countries to the threat of air attack. The Joint Chiefs of Staff were adamant: American forces should be in a position to fight the next war from a chain of air and sea bases in North America, the Atlantic and the Pacific.[61]

This doctrine of postwar 'defence in depth' encouraged an assertive attitude among American policy-makers towards the Pacific islands. Many believed that American planes would have to be able to reach Asia from secure island outposts.[62] Frank Knox, the Secretary of the Navy, informed Congress that air and sea bases would be vital to ensuring the disarmament of Japan. 'Our Lend-Lease programme will help materially to obtain the desired bases throughout the Pacific, and I am in favour of negotiation for these bases beginning without delay.'[63]

Roosevelt was more cautious. He told the Pacific War Council that the United Nations should be allowed to control Japan's League of Nations mandates in the Central Pacific – the Caroline, Mariana and Marshall Islands – but it was too soon to consider the question in detail.[64] He warned Knox not to initiate discussions with the British about these territories: 'I am anxious to clean up the problem of all the islands in the Pacific and the British would probably be delighted to confine the discussions to the Japanese Mandated Islands.'[65]

He subsequently informed the Pacific War Council that French Oceania might be transferred to international control since air services across the South Pacific would need access to airfields in the French islands. He 'did not want to commit [himself] to handing these back to France because of their enormously increased international importance'. The United Nations might take them over or even purchase them from France, which would need funds to finance its postwar reconstruction.[66] More generally, he argued that South Pacific islands – including those that belonged to the British Commonwealth – should be administered by a United Nations High Commissioner. To illustrate his argument, he pointed to the variable standard of public health in the region. American Samoa, he observed, was free of venereal disease; New

Zealand-administered Western Samoa was 'saturated'.[67] For Walter Nash, the New Zealand Minister in Washington, this pointed criticism of New Zealand's administration of its island mandate was a 'disturbing development'.[68] It provided firm evidence that FDR was unlikely to be satisfied with any attempt to re-establish the *status quo ante* in the Pacific after the war.

FDR and Hull were thinking in terms of a new international order in the Far East. In October 1943, in Moscow, Hull convinced the British and Soviet foreign ministers that China should be party to a declaration on general security listing Allied proposals for the postwar settlement. In November, at an Anglo-American conference in Cairo, Roosevelt gained Churchill's agreement to issue a statement that all Chinese territories lost to Japan, including Manchuria, Formosa and the Pescadores, would eventually be restored to China. British Commonwealth officials noted with concern how he and Hull seemed to view China as 'an essential and equal factor' with the United States in Asian and Pacific affairs. The Roosevelt administration backed the Chinese nationalist leader Chiang Kai-shek, and seemed to downplay possible Chinese designs on Indochina, Thailand, Burma and Tibet.[69]

Commonwealth concerns were well justified, for Roosevelt seemed to envisage a Sino-American axis dominating much of the Pacific and Asia. He informed Chiang, at Cairo, that he supported Hong Kong's return to China, looked forward to Chinese involvement as a trustee in the Pacific, and hoped that the United States and China would police Asia from bases in Indochina.[70] More subtly, he hoped that China, as one of the 'Big Four' powers, would be able to act as a counterweight to Russian and British ambitions in the Far East. Roosevelt used the Chinese leader's presence at a great-power conference in Teheran to deflect Churchill's opposition to American plans for Indochina: 'Now, look hear', he told Churchill in the presence of Chiang and Stalin, 'you are outvoted three to one.'[71] The exchange must have confirmed to Churchill his earlier fear that China would represent 'a faggot vote on the side of the United States in any attempt to liquidate the British overseas Empire'.[72] For the British FDR had no understanding of the corruption and backwardness that plagued Chiang Kai-shek's administration. American policy would serve simply to destabilise Far Eastern affairs. In consequence, Eden conveyed to FDR the Foreign Office's aversion to 'the idea of the Chinese running up and down the Pacific'.[73]

Yet American policy towards the region had yet to take a concrete form. American officials were divided over whether they should seek base rights on behalf of the United States or the United Nations. In most inter-departmental discussions the US Navy, which tended to argue that the United States should seek outright control of military facilities in former enemy territories, was pitted against the State Department, which was generally happy to work within the context of a world security organisation.[74] Roosevelt favoured international bases. He informed the Pacific War Council that he, Stalin and Chiang Kai-shek agreed that 'the policing of the Western Pacific and, therefore, the necessary air and naval bases should be taken over by those powers capable of exercising effective military control'.[75] He seemed to envisage a situation whereby each controlling power was accountable to an international authority. In effect, the United States would dominate bases in the Central Pacific under the auspices of an international security organization.[76]

American discussions about the postwar status of the Pacific islands also vacillated between nationalism and internationalism. In March 1944 Hull, echoing the gung-ho attitude of the US Navy, informed Congress that he advocated 'taking over any Pacific islands necessary to ensure peace and American security'.[77] Roosevelt and most State Department officials, however, maintained that the United States should seek to control the Japanese mandated islands as a trustee, acting on behalf of the proposed world security organization. Moreover, Roosevelt believed that any trusteeship system should extend to the South Pacific, where the disposal of mandated territories after the First World War had been 'hit or miss'. He indicated that a 'reassignment of these islands might be considered' in the near future.[78]

Crucially, debates in Washington about the pros and cons of trusteeship coincided with continuing expansion of American influence in the Pacific. During the second half of 1943 and the first half of 1944 local British Empire and French authorities frequently predicted that the US army and navy would be reluctant to vacate British and French territories after the cessation of hostilities. American-built bases in French Oceania, the New Hebrides and the Solomon Islands seemed to be permanent constructions that would continue in use for some time to come.[79] Canberra received reports of military administrators being trained in the United States to oversee the post-hostilities affairs of former occupied territories. A large area of the Far East would be 'subjected to direct American influence . . . British, Dutch, French and Australian interests would be closely affected'.[80] American surveys of French Oceania, led by the United States' leading explorer Admiral Byrd, expressed American interest in developing the islands as staging-posts for transpacific air services.[81] Further surveys tried to ascertain the Pacific islands' mineral wealth.[82]

The British Commonwealth was extremely concerned about American policies towards the Pacific. Dr H. V. Evatt, the Australian Minister for External Affairs, pondered gloomily upon American expansionism in the region and the possible impact of the Roosevelt administration's support for Chiang Kai-shek on 'White Australia'.[83] Peter Fraser, the New Zealand Prime Minister, criticized FDR's brusque handling of the French: New Zealand 'did not wish to upset the status quo in this region at all as she believes it would be much more conducive to security to leave it as it is'.[84] On 21 January 1944 they unveiled the Australian–New Zealand Agreement (or Canberra pact), in which they insisted on their countries' right to be consulted over the terms of the international peace settlement and outlined ambitious plans to establish a regional defence zone in the Southwest Pacific involving the Pacific Dominions, Holland, Portugal, Britain, the French Committee of National Liberation – but not the United States. The British government was broadly sympathetic to such thinking.[85] The French, for their part, were increasingly willing to cooperate with British Commonwealth authorities in the South Pacific.[86] In effect, Britain, France and the Pacific Dominions were united in opposition to the expansion of American power in the region.

Each government feared that the Roosevelt administration would make a concerted attempt to weaken Europe's empires after the war. But the President's views on colonialism during the last year of his life were ambiguous. On the one hand, he continued to argue that colonialism should be replaced by a system of trusteeships and newly formed nation-states, linked to a world security organization. Trusteeships would accelerate trends in world affairs towards self-government and represented the only means to achieve the United States' overseas security interests in a manner that was deemed acceptable by the American people. In July 1944 Roosevelt rejected a Joint Chiefs of Staff plan to annex strategically located Pacific islands.[87] Unlike in the late 1930s, he did not feel that the United States needed to adopt heavy-handed measures to reinforce American security in the Pacific.

On the other hand, FDR was flexible in his dealings with the British and French over colonial matters. In February 1944 he informed Charles Taussig, the White House's leading adviser on colonial issues, that the United States was 'having so much trouble with de Gaulle and the French Committee [of National Liberation] that he did not think the time was right to start any conversation on [the status of] Dakar'.[88] In October Washington finally accorded diplomatic recognition to the French Committee of National Liberation. This brought the Americans into line with the British government, which was increasingly close to the French in international affairs. Significantly, the British facilitated the entry of Free French representatives into Indochina and began to work closely with de Gaulle's troops in the British-led Southeast Asian Command.[89] In January 1945 the President sanctioned the use of French agents in Indochina.[90] In the spring, as the British increased pressure on the Japanese in Burma and hostilities broke out between the Free French and Japanese in Indochina, he agreed to French operations in Southeast Asia and began to explore the possibility of France acting as the colony's sole trustee in the postwar world.[91]

More generally, the President was prepared to reach a compromise with the British over the role of empires in the postwar world. He rejected Cordell Hull's argument, weeks before the Secretary of State left office, that the British and French governments should be asked formally to draw up timetables of independence or self-rule for their colonial territories.[92] Henceforth, discussions in Washington focused on trusteeships. Anglo-American attempts to hammer out a draft declaration on the subject had failed to make progress, with the British refusing to subject their colonial territories to 'international accountability'. Roosevelt, however, was conciliatory. At Yalta, in February, he, Churchill and Stalin agreed that postwar trusteeship provisions would apply only to mandates, territories detached from the enemy during the war, and dependent territories voluntarily nominated by parent states.[93]

Roosevelt's position was shaped by political and military circumstances. 'Our goal is, as you say, identical for the long range objectives', he wrote Harold Laski about the postwar peace settlement, 'but there are so many new problems arising that I still must remember that the war is yet to be won.'[94] In relation to Indochina, this meant that he was willing to adapt to military and political realities, including a growing crisis in China and the British government's determination to revive France as one of Europe's leading powers, in order to expedite the defeat of Japan in Southeast Asia. More generally, he seemed to believe that it would be futile and counterproductive for Washington to pressure the British and French over decolonization to an extent that would endanger the Grand Alliance during the transition from war to peace. In the weeks following the Yalta conference, he was increasingly perturbed about Soviet machinations in Central Europe and Stalin's profound distrust of American and British postwar policies. He had no wish to compound inter-allied difficulties by clashing with Churchill and de Gaulle over colonialism. More fundamentally, he recognized the economic, political and strategic desirability of a strong Britain and Anglo-American alliance. This squared with the thinking at the time of a number of other leading American policy-makers who thought that the United States should recognize the 'essential importance of having a strong Britain and British Commonwealth to work with'.[95] An increasing number of leading American policy-makers now seemed to accept that the dismantling of colonial empires would serve to destabilize large areas of Africa and the Far East.[96]

The situation, however, was not clear-cut. Many American policy-makers still wanted the United States to oppose European colonialism. In January members of the Australian Legation in Washington attended an Institute of Pacific Relations conference, in Hot Springs, Virginia, to find that most American delegates thought that the Dutch and French had been better colonists than the British;[97] around 80 per cent wanted London to grant Burma, India and Malaya independence immediately.[98] Roosevelt himself continued to believe that colonial liberation was a desirable, if long-term, goal. He was convinced that the Yalta trusteeship provisions, to be discussed at the founding conference of the United Nations Organization in San Francisco, would serve to expose the iniquity of colonialism and accelerate the decolonization process.[99] On 5 April, just over a week before his death, he reiterated his anticolonial ideas to the Filipino leader, Sergio Osmena. Independence for the Philippines, he argued, would confirm the passing of the colonial age.[100]

Roosevelt was opposed to colonialism in principle. But, as revisionist historians have pointed out, he often viewed colonial issues in terms of American national interests. In challenging the British in the Pacific in the late 1930s, he revealed his determination to improve the US overseas air links and access to vital strategic territories. After Pearl Harbor, his approach to colonial affairs was influenced by crucial geopolitical and strategic considerations. Impressed by the rapid development of air power, he was convinced that the United States needed to control a network of bases in the Pacific from which to launch military operations after the current war. He was more determined to weaken European colonialism there than in South Asia, a region which he believed would play a marginal role in American strategy in the future. From 1943 until his death, he sought to ensure that American security interests in the Pacific were not compromised by the British Commonwealth's and France's wish to influence the region's postwar affairs.

But Roosevelt was highly sensitive to the danger of allied disunity. He envisaged a postwar international order based on great-power collaboration, with dependent territories being overseen by a world security organization. International trusteeships would help to accelerate the decolonization process, secure American strategic objectives, and prove that the US interests coincided with those of the wider international community. He was not prepared, however, to push anti-colonial initiatives to an extent that threatened to damage irreparably the United States' relations with great-power allies. From 1942 his overriding objectives were the military defeat of Germany and Japan and the negotiation of a satisfactory international peace settlement. Both objectives required inter-allied unity. He refused to become embroiled in Anglo-Indian relations and, after voicing numerous criticisms of the French Empire, was willing to accept France's reestablishment as an imperial power. He decided against mandatory international overview of colonial empires in the postwar world and the adoption by colonial powers of timetables for the creation of independent nation-states in key dependencies.

Yet Kimball and Pollock were right to argue that Roosevelt never distanced himself from the goal of decolonization. He was convinced that the long-term trend in international affairs was towards the elimination of colonial empires. Cordell Hull subsequently acknowledged that the American government had never explicitly asked Britain, France and the Netherlands to grant 'immediate self-government' to their colonies. 'This, it was expected, "would come in time".'[101] Roosevelt probably felt that concessions to the British and French over colonialism in the short term would not serve to derail decolonization in the long term. In effect, international economic and political circumstances served to alleviate tensions between his idealistic and realistic instincts. To this extent, those historians who have sought to emphasize the President's growing conservatism in relation to colonial issues in 1944 and 1945 are wide of the mark. Rooseveltian idealism was not eclipsed by Rooseveltian realism. FDR was a standard-bearer of anti-colonialism even as he sought to secure the future of the United States' relations with Britain and France. He was already looking towards a new period in world history in which colonialism was an historical anachronism.

Notes

1 Cited in Warren Kimball, *The Juggler: Franklin Roosevelt as Wartime Statesman* (Princeton, NJ, 1991), p. 66.
2 See Phillip Darby, *Three Faces of Imperialism: British and American Approaches to Asia and Africa, 1870–1970* (New Haven and London, 1987), p. 174.

3 For the distinction between 'formal' and 'informal' empire, see David Reynolds, 'Roosevelt, Churchill, and the Wartime Anglo-American Alliance, 1939–45: Towards a New Synthesis' in Wm Roger Louis and Hedley Bull (eds), *The 'Special Relationship': Anglo-American Relations since 1945* (Oxford, 1986), p. 27.

4 John Darwin, *Britain and Decolonisation: the Retreat from Empire in the Post-War World* (London, 1988), p. 38.

5 John Charmley, *Churchill's Grand Alliance: the Anglo-American Special Relationship, 1940–57* (London, 1995), p. 52.

6 Warren Kimball, *The Juggler: Franklin Roosevelt as Wartime Statesman* (Princeton, NJ, 1991), p. 128.

7 See, for example, Charles A. Madison, *Leaders and Liberals in 20th Century America* (New York, 1961), pp. 313–14; Willard Range, *Franklin D. Roosevelt's World Order* (Athens, Georgia, 1959); Rexford G. Tugwell, *The Democratic Roosevelt: a Biography of Franklin D. Roosevelt* (Garden City, New York, 1957), pp. 591–2.

8 Richard Hofstadter wrote of 'the quick sympathy with oppressed colonials, the ideal of liberation and welfare, and yet the calculating interest in American [commercial] advantage' that defined FDR's thinking about colonialism. See Richard Hofstadter, *The American Political Tradition* (New York, 1954), p. 350.

9 William Appleman Williams, *The Tragedy of American Diplomacy* (New York, 1959).

10 Lloyd Gardner, *Economic Aspects of New Deal Diplomacy* (Boston, 1971 edition); Gabriel Kolko, *The Politics of War: the World and United States Foreign Policy, 1943–45* (New York, 1968).

11 Wm Roger Louis, *Imperialism at Bay, 1941–45: the United States and the Decolonization of the British Empire* (Oxford, 1977); Christopher Thorne, *Allies of a Kind: the United States, Britain and the War against Japan, 1941–45* (Oxford, 1978); Walter LaFeber, 'Roosevelt, Churchill and Indochina, 1942–45', *American Historical Review*, 80 (1975), pp. 1277–95.

12 Louis, *Imperialism at Bay*, passim.

13 For a general survey, see Gary Hess, *America Encounters India, 1941–47* (Baltimore, 1971).

14 LaFeber, 'Roosevelt, Churchill and Indochina'; Christopher Thorne, 'Indochina and Anglo-American Relations, 1942–45', *Pacific Historical Review*, 45 (1976), pp. 73–96.

15 Kimball, *The Juggler*, p. 127.

16 Ibid., pp. 131–2.

17 Fiona Venn, *Franklin D. Roosevelt*, pp. 11–12; Robert Dallek, *Franklin D. Roosevelt and American Foreign Policy, 1932–45* (Oxford, 1979), pp. 8–9.

18 Dallek, *Franklin D. Roosevelt*, pp. 11–12.

19 Ibid., p. 13.

20 Significantly, however, after the war he seemed to support proactive, even imperialist, American policies in relation to the Western Hemisphere. See Frank Freidel, *Franklin D. Roosevelt: the Ordeal* (Boston, 1954), pp. 135–7.

21 Dallek, *Franklin D. Roosevelt*, p. 16.

22 Edgar B. Nixon, *Franklin D. Roosevelt and Foreign Affairs, January 1933–January 1937, Volume III* (Cambridge, Mass., 1969), pp. 377–84.

23 Kimball, *The Juggler*, p. 109; William R. Keylor, *The Twentieth Century World: an International History* (New York, 1984), p. 220.

24 Kimball, *The Juggler*, p. 107.

25 Ibid., pp. 123 and 130.

26 For a useful official summary of the dispute see memorandum by Hohler, 'Conflicting Anglo-United States claims to sovereignty over certain islands in the Western Pacific', 11 June 1943, in Public Record Office, Kew [hereinafter PRO]: FO 461/2 (part 7). See also minute by Balfour, 5 May 1939, PRO: FO 371/22792 (A3385/21/45); and memorandum, 'Notes on the islands administered by New Zealand claimed by the United States', New Zealand National Archives, Wellington [hereinafter NZNA]: AAEG 950/112b. Historians have sketched the outlines of the story to the outbreak of war in Europe. See Ruth Megaw, 'The Scramble for the Pacific: Anglo-United States Rivalry in the 1930s', *Historical Studies*, 17 (1975), pp. 458–73; and W. D. McIntyre, *New Zealand Prepares for War: Defence Policy, 1919–39* (Christchurch, 1988), pp. 195–200. The first comprehensive survey of American–Commonwealth rivalry concerning the South Pacific islands during the Second World War appears in Paul Orders, 'Britain, Australia, New Zealand and the Expansion of American Power in the South-West Pacific, 1941–46', unpublished University of Cambridge PhD (1997).

27 Notes on the Islands Administered by New Zealand Claimed by the United States, n.d., NZNA: AAEG 950/112b.

28 Memorandum by McEwen, 'United States' Claims to Certain Pacific Islands', 26 March 1940, Australian Archives, Canberra [hereinafter AA]: A6006 1940/03/29.

29 See, for example, minute by Barton, 18 October 1939, PRO: FO 371/22795 (A7550/21/45).

30 Indeed, this disregard for indigenous populations also characterized FDR's plans, aired in late 1936, for a Pacific neutralization pact. See Darby, *Three Faces of Imperialism*, p. 105; Dorothy Borg, *The United States and the Far Eastern Crisis of 1933–1938* (Cambridge, Mass.), pp. 27–9.

31 Kimball, *The Juggler*, p. 257.

32 Memorandum by Casey, 'Notes after reading files on Pacific Islands Question at Government House, Suva, Fiji', AA: CRS A 3300/2 15.

33 Cablegram, Roosevelt to Churchill, 13 August 1940, in Warren Kimball (ed.), *Churchill and Roosevelt: the Complete Correspondence: Volume I: Alliance Emerging* (London, 1984), pp. 58–9.

34 Dallek, *Franklin D. Roosevelt*, p. 247.

35 F. L. W. Wood, *The New Zealand People at War: Political and External Affairs* (Wellington, 1958), pp. 202–3.

36 Theodore A. Wilson, *The First Summit: Roosevelt and Churchill at Placentia Bay, 1941* (Lawrence, Kansas, revised edition, 1991), p. 108; Louis, *Imperialism at Bay*, pp. 121–2.

37 Mario Rossi, *Roosevelt and the French* (Westport, CT, 1993), p. 143.

38 Kimball, *The Juggler*, p. 132.

39 Martin Gilbert, *Finest Hour: Winston Churchill, 1939–41* (1983), p. 1163.

40 Kimball, *The Juggler*, p. 133; Dallek, *Franklin D. Roosevelt*, p. 320.

41 Wilson, *The First Summit*, p. 109.

42 Dallek, *Franklin D. Roosevelt*, p. 324.

43 Ibid., p. 325.

44 'Our whole Eastern Empire has gone', mourned one British MP, 'Australia is as good as gone. Poor little England.' Nicolson diary entry, 30 March 1942 in Nigel Nicolson (ed.), *Harold Nicolson: Diaries and Letters, 1939–45* (London, 1967), p. 207. See also Winston S. Churchill, *The Second World War, Volume 4: The Hinge of Fate* (London, 1951), p. 81.

45 Dallek, *Franklin D. Roosevelt*, p. 325.

46 Cable, Churchill to Roosevelt, 4 March 1942 in Kimball, *Churchill–Roosevelt Correspondence*, Vol. I, pp. 374–5.

47 Cable, Roosevelt to Churchill, 10 March 1942, ibid., pp. 402–4.

48 Cable, Roosevelt to Churchill, 11 April 1942, ibid., pp. 446–7.

49 Dallek, *Franklin D. Roosevelt*, pp. 327–8.

50 Cable, Roosevelt to Churchill, 10 March 1942, Kimball, op. cit., p. 404.

51 Cable, Roosevelt to Churchill, 9 March 1942, *Churchill-Roosevelt Correspondence*, Volume I, pp. 398–9.

52 Anita Inder Singh, *The Limits of British Influence: South Asia and the Anglo-American Relationship, 1947–1956* (London, 1993), p. 5.

53 Louis, *Imperialism at Bay*, p. 155; Dallek, *Franklin D. Roosevelt*, p. 342; Robert Sherwood, *The White House Papers of Harry L. Hopkins, Volume II: January 1942–July 1945* (London, 1948), pp. 577–8.

54 David Dimbleby and David Reynolds, *An Ocean Apart: the Relationship between Britain and America in the Twentieth Century* (New York, 1989), p. 158.

55 LaFeber, 'Roosevelt, Churchill, and Indochina', p. 1279.

56 Kimball, *The Juggler*, p. 139; Louis, *Imperialism at Bay*, p. 231.

57 Rossi, *Roosevelt and the French*, p. 143.

58 Lloyd Gardner, *Approaching Vietnam: from World War II through Dienbienphu, 1941–1954* (New York, 1988), p. 40.

59 Memorandum by Gore-Booth, 'Discussion of the possible retention by the United States after the war of bases constructed and used by American Forces and of the possible acquisition by the United States of sovereignty over such bases', n.d., PRO: FO 461/2 (part 6).

60 Alan K. Henrikson, 'The Map as an "Idea": the Role of Cartographic Imagery during the Second World War', *The American Cartographer*, 2 (1975), pp. 21–2.

61 Michael Sherry, *Preparing for the Next War: American Plans for Post-War Defense, 1941–45* (New Haven, 1977), p. 4; W. D. McIntyre, *Background to the Anzus Pact: Policy-Making, Strategy and Diplomacy, 1945–55* (Basingstoke, 1995), pp. 66–7.

62 Letter, Johnson to Hornbeck, 12 January 1943, Library of Congress, Washington DC: Johnson papers, box 66; letter, Johnson to White, 8 April 1943, ibid., box 43.

63 Memorandum, 'American comment on post-war bases in the Pacific and the Australian-New Zealand Agreement', n.d., AA: CRS A 5954/1 654/14. See also *The New York Times*, 9 March 1943.

64 Cablegram, Australian Legation, Washington, to Australian Prime Minister's Department, 2 April 1943, AA: CRS A 5954 652/1.

65 Dallek, *Franklin D. Roosevelt*, p. 430.

66 Cablegram, Chargé d'Affaires, New Zealand Legation, Washington, to

Fraser, 31 March 1943, doc. 32, in Robin Kay (ed.), *Documents on New Zealand External Relations*, Volume 1 [hereinafter *DNZER, Vol. 1*] (Wellington, 1972), pp. 41–3. On another occasion Roosevelt asserted that 'French interests in the Pacific should be transferred to other people.' See cablegram, Nash to Fraser, 12 January 1944, doc.41, *DNZER, Vol. 1*, pp. 54–6. See also cablegram, Chargé d'Affaires, New Zealand Legation (Washington) to New Zealand Minister for External Affairs, 11 August 1943, doc. 33, ibid., pp. 43–5; Pacific War Council meeting, 12 January 1944, Franklin D. Roosevelt Library, Hyde Park, New York: Roosevelt papers, map room files, box 168, folder 2.

67 Cablegram, Chargé d'Affaires, New Zealand Legation, Washington, to Fraser, 31 March 1943, op. cit. Nash pointed the finger at the influx into Western Samoa of American troops. See draft memorandum by Nash, April 1943, NZNA: EA 2 1945/6a.

68 Ibid.

69 Minute, Clarke to Eden, 11 June 1942, PRO: FO 461/1; cablegram, Bruce to Curtin, 26 August 1942, AA: CRS A989/1 43/735/321; cablegram, Cox to New Zealand Prime Minister, 31 March 1943, doc. 32, *DNZER, Vol. 1*, pp. 41–3.

70 LaFeber, 'Roosevelt, Churchill and Indochina', pp. 1284–5.

71 Dallek, *Franklin D. Roosevelt*, pp. 428–9.

72 Ibid., p. 389; Gardner, *Approaching Vietnam*, pp. 22–3.

73 Dallek, *Franklin D. Roosevelt*, p. 390.

74 Letter, Leahy to Secretary of State, 11 March 1944, United States National Archives [hereafter USNA]: RG 218, folder 101, box 17; memorandum, Leahy to Royal, 7 February 1944, USNA: RG 218, folder 101, box 17; Louis, *Imperialism at Bay*, p. 367. Some military officials placed less emphasis on bases than others. See note of conversation with Bowman, 12 April 1944, British Library of Political and Economic Studies: Webster papers, 11/12.

75 Pacific War Council meeting, 12 January 1944, op. cit.

76 Extract from New Zealand Chargé d'Affaires, Washington, to New Zealand Minister for External Affairs, 11 August 1943, NZNA: EA 1110/3/7 (part 1).

77 Note on Pacific islands, March 1944, AA: CRS A 5954/1 654/14.

78 Pacific War Council meeting, 12 January 1944, op. cit.; memorandum embodying inter-departmental views on Pacific islands, n.d. [October–November 1943], op. cit.; memorandum for the President, 9 November 1943, USNA: RG 59, Notter file, 1312–5.

79 Draft cablegram, Australian Department of External Affairs to Australian High Commissioner in the UK, August 1943, AA: CRS A 989/1 43/735/321; memorandum by Forsyth, 'Pacific Islands – Current Position and Future Possibilities', 12 July 1943, AA: CRS A 6494 T1 SPTS/1/2; cablegram, Ballard to Secretary, Australian Department for External Affairs, 17 November 1943, ibid., letter, Shanahan to Sedgwick, 1 December 1943, House of Lords Records Office, London (hereinafter HLRO]: Beaverbrook papers, D/274.

80 Draft cablegram, Australian Department of External Affairs to Australian High Commissioner in the UK, August 1943, op. cit.; *Far Eastern Survey*, 17 November 1943.

81 Cablegram, Australian Legation, Washington, to Australian Prime Minister's Department, 29 September 1943, AA: CRS A 5954/1 652/1; letter, Shanahan

to Sedgwick, 1 December 1943, HLRO: Beaverbrook papers, D/274; cable-gram, Campbell to FO, 12 August 1943, HLRO: Beaverbrook papers, D/221; extract from New Zealand Chargé d'Affaires, Washington, to New Zealand Minister for Extrnal Affairs, 11 August 1943, NZNA: EA 1110/3/7 (part 1); memorandum, 'Recent United States Activities regarding Pacific Islands, March 1944, AA: A 6494 T1 SPTS/1/2.

82   Memorandum by Hunt, 21 November 1943, NZNA: EA 1 110/3/10.

83   Wayne Reynolds, 'H.V. Evatt: The Imperial Connection and the Quest for Australian Security, 1941–45', unpublished University of Newcastle (NSW) PhD (1985), pp. 219–23; Orders, 'Britain, Australia, New Zealand and the Expansion of America Power', pp. 172–94, 223–37.

84   Cablegram, Riddell to Canadian Secretary of State for External Affairs, 15 February 1944, National Archives of Canada, Ottawa: RG 25, vol. 3261, file 6074-40C (part 1).

85   A lengthy analysis of the agreement is contained in Orders, 'Britain, Australia, New Zealand and the Expansion of America Power', pp. 172–94, 223–37.

86   Ibid., pp. 310–11.

87   Louis, *Imperialism at Bay*, p. 373.

88   Dallek, *Franklin D. Roosevelt*, p. 460.

89   LaFeber, 'Roosevelt, Churchill, and Indochina', pp. 1291–3.

90   Ibid., p. 1291.

91   See Thorne, 'Indochina and Anglo-American Relations', p. 90.

92   Gary Hess, *The United States' Emergence as Southeast Asian Power, 1940–50* (New York, 1987), p. 368.

93   See John Sbrega, *Anglo-American Relations and Colonialism in East Asia, 1941–45* (New York, 1985), p. 149.

94   Thorne, 'Indochina and Anglo-American Relations', p. 90.

95   Cablegram, Halifax to Eden, 5 December 1944, PRO: FO 954/30/589–594. See also cablegram, Balfour to Eden, 16 June 1945, PRO: CAB 122/1035.

96   Thorne, *Allies of a Kind*, pp. 456–7, 464, 596–600; Hess, *The United States' Emergence as Southeast Asian Power*, p. 369; John Sbrega, *Anglo-American Relations and Colonialism in East Asia, 1941–45* (New York, 1983), pp. 133–5; Louis, *Imperialism at Bay*, p. 567; Robert Hathaway, *Ambiguous Partnership: Britain and America, 1944–47* (New York, 1981), p. 46; Melvyn Leffler, *A Preponderance of Power: National Security, the Truman Administration and the Cold War* (Stanford, Calif., 1992), p. 16. See also State Department policy paper, 'A brief estimate of situation of the United Kingdom, Australia, and New Zealand in the South Pacific on the conclusion of the war in the Far East', n.d., USNA: RG 59, lot 54D224, box 2.

97   Cablegram, Watt to Hood, 23 January 1945, AA: CRS A 1066/1 P45/153/2 (part 1).

98   Hess, *The United States' Emergence as a Southeast Asian Power*, p. 368.

99   Kimball, *The Juggler*, p. 151.

100 Ibid., p. 154.

101 Hofstadter, *American Political Tradition*, p. 349.

4
The United States and the International Trusteeship System

Victor Pungong

Introduction

The preceding essay by Paul Orders provides a brilliant review of the literature and arguments on Franklin Roosevelt's approach to decolonization. Orders highlights the contrast in opinion between those scholars who believe that Roosevelt remained consistent in his opposition to colonial rule till the very end, even though he was forced to moderate his anti-colonial policies in 1944 and 1945 in order to keep his European allies on board, and those who believe that the President became more conservative on the issue during the last two years of his life in deference to America's national security interests. Orders sides with the former, arguing that in both words and deeds the President remained steadfast in his support for decolonization and that 'Rooseveltian idealism was not eclipsed by Roosevetian realism.'

This essay uses the issue of international trusteeship – President Roosevelt's own prescription to cure the colonial disease – to show that there was enough divergence between the President's vision and position between 1942 and early 1944 and final policy outcome in 1944–45, to suggest an increasing conservatism on decolonization. What emerged after the war in the form of the United Nations Trusteeship system was a far cry from Roosevelt's original vision. Not only was the remit of the Trusteeship system limited in practice to the former mandated territories, the trusteeship agreements for these territories left the administering powers such a free hand as to seriously blur the distinction between Trust territories and ordinary colonies. Besides, during the postwar period, the United States, contrary to Roosevelt's expectations during the war years, showed little enthusiasm in using the trusteeship system to press the colonial powers for a speedy end to colonial rule.

These two outcomes were for the most part due to an increasingly conservative approach to the colonial issue that started during the last two years of President Roosevelt's life.

That Roosevelt opposed colonial rule in principle is not in question. What we are concerned with here is whether actual policy matched the President's idealism. The answer, at least as far as the issue of international trusteeship is concerned, is that it fell short of this. The need to keep America's European allies on board and to protect America's national security interests in the postwar world explain but do not diminish evidence of a growing conservatism on decolonization from 1944.

The landmark work on the United States and the evolution of the United Nations Trusteeship system remains William Roger Louis' brilliant study *Imperialism at Bay: the United States and the Decolonisation of the British Empire, 1941–1945.*[1] Louis' work points to a more conservative approach to the trusteeship issue during 1944–45. This essay approaches the subject from the point of view of ideals and final policy outcomes and further examines America's approach to decolonization within the framework of the United Nations trusteeship system in the immediate postwar period.

The concept of international trusteeship

The concept of international trusteeship is based on the principle that a territory under colonial rule is not the exclusive preserve of the power that controls it but constitutes a 'sacred trust' over which the international community has certain responsibilities.

This concept, which evolved in response to what were considered to be the excesses and unaccountability of colonial rule, is European rather than American in origin. Although some scholars have identified the origin of trusteeship in Spanish thought of the sixteenth century[2] as a guiding principle of colonial policy, trusteeship is closely associated with Edmund Burke's interpretation of a trust as derived from Roman law. Burke's ideas were based on the principle that every form of political power held on a people's behalf must ultimately be exercised in their benefit. Hence, his most famous pronouncement in 1783:

> All political power which is set over men, and privilege claimed or exercised in exclusion of them . . . ought to be in some way or the other exercised ultimately for their benefit. Every species of political dominion and every description of commercial privilege . . . are all in

the strictest sense a trust; and it is of the very essence of every trust to be rendered accountable and eventually to cease, when it substantially varies from the purpose for which alone it could have lawful existence.[3]

Burke, like most of his contemporaries, envisaged that a trustee power was only accountable at national level – in the case of Britain, to Parliament – and not to any international body.

However, when the colonial powers met in Berlin in 1885 to formalize their partition of Africa, they accepted international obligations with regard to the welfare and material well-being of colonial peoples and the suppression of the slave trade, although no international framework was put in place to monitor what became known as the Berlin Act.

At the turn of the century, some European intellectuals began to advocate some form of international supervision of colonial territories. For example, in 1902 Hobson argued that the determination as to whether colonial rule was directed towards the safety and progress of the civilization of the world and the improvement of the character of the peoples of the colonies, should not be left to the 'arbitrary will and judgement of the colonial powers, but must proceed from some organized representation of civilized humanity'.[4] Twenty years later, the renowned British colonial administrator Lord Lugard hinted at international obligations when he stated that the colonial powers had a mandate as 'trustees of civilization', for the commerce of the world, *vis-à-vis* another mandate for the welfare of the colonial peoples.[5]

If international trusteeship as a concept is European in origin, the impetus for transforming it into a workable system for the supervision of colonial territories undoubtedly came from the United States.

Trusteeship as an ideal of US foreign policy

The European colonial powers always regarded the US campaign for the international supervision of colonial territories as no more than a smoke-screen to facilitate access to the economic resources of the colonies and to spread American influence globally. The strong influence of economic interest on the US policy-making establishment has now been firmly established by writers like Gardner and Kolko.[6] Louis' study also supports this. He cites Benjamin Gerig, the State Department official who began his career in the Secretariat of the League of Nations and who supervized US trusteeship policy during the Second World War. In his first book, written in 1930, Gerig concluded with regard to the economic factor in America's Mandates policy, 'The Mandates System is undoubtedly the most effective instrument yet devised to make the Open Door effective. The Mandates principle is irreconcilable with that of national economic imperialism.'[7] Similarly, a memorandum on US participation in the administration of Trust territories sent to the Secretary of State on 20 December 1945, by the Division of Dependent Areas stated that 'American interest in the Dependent areas has traditionally been based on a broad humanitarian concern for the welfare of the inhabitants of these areas and a desire not to see these areas exploited for the benefit of a single power through restrictive trade practices.'[8] The strong influence of economic interest in America's trusteeship policy was reflected in the Mandate and later on the Trusteeship agreements, which guaranteed equal and unrestricted access for all members of the international community with respect to economic, commercial and industrial activities in the Mandated and Trust territories.

Influential though economic interests may have been, they did not constitute the principal foundation of America's advocacy of international trusteeship. America's policy on international trusteeship as well as on the colonial issue as a whole, stemmed from its own colonial origins and its attainment of independence after a successful revolution. A paper on US policy on dependent territories written by the Colonial Policy Review Sub-Committee of the State Department's Committee on Problems of Dependent Areas in 1950, aptly put it that 'confronted by a colonial issue, the average American will, as if by instinct, favor the peoples of a colonial area against their European rulers'.[9]

Backward, exploitative, undemocratic, and a major cause of war, was how the forefathers of international trusteeship, Presidents Wilson and Franklin Roosevelt, saw European colonialism and their thinking on the issue emanated from this, although it was also shaped by considerations of free trade and economic interest.

The Mandates system proposed by Wilson and incorporated in the Covenant of the League of Nations, while limited to territories detached from the former German and Turkish empires, enshrined the principle that colonial expansion was no longer acceptable and that the colonial powers should be accountable for their administration of colonial peoples. Roosevelt was even more vociferous in his hostility to and distaste for colonial rule. He once described conditions in the Gambia as belonging in the Stone Age and the people as treated worse than livestock by their British masters.[10] He believed colonialism was a thing of the past that ought to be brought to an end as quickly as possible. In the interim, the colonial powers had to be held accountable through an international trusteeship system for their administration of the colonies.

Between 1941 and early 1944, Roosevelt presented international trusteeship as his grand idea for resolving not only the colonial issue but many of the other major postwar problems as well. Shortly after signing the Atlantic Charter, the President began to develop his ideas for an international trusteeship system. His starting-point was that trusteeship should be based on unselfish service, with the four allied powers – the United States, Britain, the Soviet Union and China – providing tutelage to subject peoples until they could stand on their own feet.

During a 1942 meeting in Washington with the Russian Foreign Minister, M. V. Molotov, the President made it clear that his idea of trusteeship went far beyond the League of Nations Mandates system which left the administering powers almost total control of the mandates with only minimal supervision by the League.[11] What the President was proposing at this stage was for the internationalization pure and simple (under a committee of three-to-five allied powers) of all colonial possessions of strategic importance to the allies, such as the Japanese mandated islands and other colonial possessions in the vicinity of the Pacific basin, including those like Malaya, Singapore and Indochina, held previously by the British and French.

Also central to Roosevelt's thinking at this stage was the strong belief that the United States should not itself seek any territorial aggrandizement or control as a result of the war. Hence, during his meeting with Molotov, Roosevelt went out of his way to assure the Russians that the United States had no intention of annexing the Japanese Mandates and were quite willing to place them under international control. During 1943, the President's view of trusteeship crystallized. He became even firmer in his conviction that Indochina ought not to be returned to the French at the end of the war but placed under international trusteeship. The President made this clear to the Chinese leader, Chiang Kai-shek, during a meeting at the Cairo conference in November 1943. His son Elliott recorded his views:

> The French would have no right, after the war, simply to walk back into Indo-China and reclaim that rich land for no reason other than it had once been their colony. And he had insisted to Chiang that the most the French should expect was a trusteeship of their colonies responsible to a United Nations organisation, looking toward even-

tual independence, once the United Nations were satisfied that the colonies could manage their own affairs.[12]

By the time Roosevelt, Churchill, and Stalin met in Teheran later that month, Roosevelt had greatly expanded the territorial scope of his trusteeship ideas to include all areas in the vicinity of the axis powers considered by the allies as strategically important, including such places as New Caledonia and Dakar. He successfully sold his ideas to Stalin during the conference, but not to Churchill who suspected that they could include parts of the British Empire.[13]

By early 1944, the high point of Roosevelt's idealism, the President had again expanded the scope of his trusteeship plans to include virtually all colonial territories. In addition to international free ports and military bases, he talked about subjecting such places as the Gambia (a British colony) and Morocco (a French one) to regular international inspections.[14] In January 1944, he told the Pacific War Council that Korea should be placed under trusteeship for a 40-year period while the United States should be willing to act as 'police agent' in the Marianas, Carolines and Marshalls.

And these were not just empty ideals. During these years, the President fought hard to get his ideas accepted by his allies as part of the postwar settlement. He even risked alienating some of his principal allies in the process. His insistence that Indochina should be taken away from the French after the war and placed under trusteeship did not help relations with General de Gaulle. Although the President was more circumspect about including parts of the British Empire in his trusteeship schemes, the implications were obvious: if the French were deprived of Indochina and Dakar, why should the British be allowed to keep Malaya, Singapore, or even Hong Kong?

The President even formed alliances to push through his ideas. At Cairo, he discussed his trusteeship plans extensively with Chiang Kai-shek behind Churchill's back. He even offered the Generalissimo trusteeship control over Indochina as an inducement, as well as support for the establishment of Hong Kong as an international free port.[15] At Teheran and later on at Yalta, the President sought out Stalin in private and got his support for the Indochina project as well as for his plan for the creation of strategic trusteeship bases in the vicinity of the axis powers.[16] All this left Churchill rather isolated, if not humiliated, during these Conferences.

It may not have been practical to expand the trusteeship idea as widely as Roosevelt advocated. For example, it quickly became clear that there was strong opposition in Korea as well as in Iran against any notion of international trusteeship. Also, the President's ideas about big-power trusteeship over strategic or disputed areas depended on a level of big-power cooperation that proved to be elusive. However, in promoting the principle that the allied powers, including the United States, must not seek territorial aggrandizement as a result of the war and that all subject peoples should be held in some form of international tutelage until they could find their own feet, the President was reflecting sentiments that were shared by most Americans at a time when anti-imperialist fervour ran deep in American society. In 1942, Roosevelt's Under-Secretary of State, Sumner Welles, had proclaimed the end of imperialism in highly idealistic terms, 'Our victory must bring in its train the liberation of all peoples. Discrimination between peoples because of their race, creed, or colour must be abolished. The age of imperialism is ended.'[17] In the same year, the Republican presidential candidate declared that the war 'must mean an end to the empire of nations over other nations'.[18]

When matters came to a head, however, it was the necessity to win the war and to secure America's postwar national security interests that prevailed. In short, idealism gave way to realism.

Keeping up alliances

Even as Roosevelt pushed forward his trusteeship ideas between 1942 and 1944, State Department officials were busy preparing more realistic proposals that could be acceptable to the British.[19] For despite the President's principled and idealistic stance on the issue of trusteeship, the major preoccupation of his administration at the time was to win the war against the axis powers as soon as possible. For this, the United States needed to keep its allies – particularly Britain and Russia, and in a symbolic sense the French – on board. The British and the French quite naturally resisted any notion of placing any of their territories of captured colonies under any kind of international trusteeship. In fact, the British position was to oppose the creation of a trusteeship system in the first instance and if this proved unsuccessful, to ensure that any system created did not affect the British Empire. Churchill's famous pronouncement in November 1942, to the effect that the British meant to hold what was their own, was meant to underline this position. When Roosevelt sprang his strategic-bases scheme on Churchill at Teheran, the Prime Minister, suspecting that the scheme might include parts of the British Empire such as Gibraltar and Malta, stated bluntly that 'nothing would be taken from England without a war'.[20] De Gaulle for his part made it clear he intended to re-establish French control over Indochina as soon as he could muster the means.[21]

In the showdown at Yalta in 1945, it was the Americans who backed down. The briefing book which the American delegation took to the conference contained proposals that represented a significant climb-down from Roosevelt's earlier vision and position.

Churchill set the tone from the start. Mere mention of the word trusteeship by Secretary of State, Edward Stettinius, provoked Churchill into one of his most famous and stubborn defences of the British Empire:

> I absolutely disagree. I will not have one scrap of British territory flung into that area. After we have done our best to fight this war and have done no crime to anyone I will have no suggestion that the British empire is to be put into the dock and examined by every-one to see if it is up to their standard. No one will induce me as long as I am Prime Minister to let any representative of Great Britain go to a conference where they would be placed in the dock and asked to justify our right to live in a world we have tried to save.[22]

Roosevelt and Stettinius quickly reassured Churchill that the trusteeship formula they had in mind had nothing to do with the British Empire. Stettinius explained:

> The only thing contemplated as to territorial trusteeship is to provide in the Charter of the world organisation the right to create a trustee-ship if it desires to do so. Later on, we have in mind that the Japan-ese mandated islands be taken away from the Japanese. We have had nothing in mind with reference to the British empire.[23]

Thus the Americans themselves jettisoned a key cornerstone of Roose-veltian idealism on trusteeship – the universal application of the concept to all dependent territories – in order to accommodate the British. From the case-book, Stettinius outlined a trusteeship formula which limited the scope of the trusteeship system to existing mandates of the League of Nations, territory detached from the enemy as a result of the war, and other territory voluntarily placed under the adminis-tering powers.[24]

An opportunity to revisit the issue arose at the Conference on Inter-national Organization in San Francisco, when the Australian Foreign

Minister, Dr H. J. Evatt, fought passionately to get trusteeship applied to all colonial territories. He made reference to the universality of the Atlantic Charter and pointed out how close the universality of trusteeship was to the heart of the then late President Roosevelt.[25] The American delegation turned a deaf ear and the Yalta formula was adopted and incorporated into the United Nations Charter.

In the event, none of the adminstering powers voluntarily placed any of their dependent territories under the trusteeship with the result that the territorial scope of the United Nations trusteeship system was no wider than that of the League of Nations mandates system before it.

During 1944 right up to his death, President Roosevelt also retreated from his longstanding position that Indochina should be taken from the French and placed under international trusteeship. In October 1944, he granted de Gaulle's National Liberation Front full diplomatic recognition and in January 1945, allowed the use of French agents in Indochina.[26] In March 1945, he told his key adviser on colonial matters, Charles Taussig, that he was prepared to agree to France retaining Indochina and New Caledonia, provided she assumed the obligations of a trustee and adopted independence as the ultimate gaol.[27] It is doubtful whether even if Roosevelt had not died in 1945, the French would not have swiftly reestablished full colonial control over their former empire as they did. The wheel turned full circle later on in the fifties, when the United States actually started to provide military and other support to the French against nationalist forces in Indochina.

These 'compromises' should not in any way detract from the great achievement that the setting up of a trusteeship system (against strong British opposition) represented for President Roosevelt and American foreign policy, nor the enormous contribution that the President made to the process of decolonization. They do, however, point to a growing conservatism in American policy on the colonial question during the closing stages of the war and also indicate a wide gulf between high-minded idealism and reality which has always been and continues to be a hallmark of American foreign policy.

The objective of independence

Central to Rooseveltian idealism was the firm conviction that national independence was inherent in the natural order of nations, and that all dependent territories eventually had to achieve their independence. Indeed, the key objective of his trusteeship plans was to prepare dependent territories for independence. The Atlantic Charter was based on this premise and Roosevelt's insistence on its universal applicability was meant to underline his position.

Having made a significant concession to the British by limiting the territorial scope of the trusteeship system, the United States wanted for some kind of declaration stating the inherent right of dependent territories to independence, to accompany the provisions for a trusteeship system. In March 1943, the State Department came up with a draft declaration by which the colonial powers were to pledge the 'preservation of liberty, independence, human rights and justice' in dependent territories and to extend the principles of the Atlantic Charter to peoples of all nations.[28] It also stated specific responsibilities of the colonial powers in preparing dependent peoples for independence, including the provision of timetables for independence.[29]

The British strongly opposed the objective of independence in the draft. The Parliamentary Under-Secretary of the Foreign Office, Richard Law, remarked that the document enshrined 'the ideal of the dissolution of the British Empire and the substitution for it of a multiplicity of national sovereignties'.[30] On this issue, Roosevelt remained steadfast to the very end, although he rejected the State Department's proposal that the colonial powers be asked formally to draw up timetables for independence or self-government for their colonies.[31]

The President refused to settle for self-government as the ultimate goal for colonial peoples as proposed by the British. In March 1945 he reiterated to Taussig that the ultimate goal for dependent peoples had to be in independence and nothing else.[32]

Even on this commitment, described by some as constituting Roosevelt's last will and testament for dependent peoples[33] the United States was to retreat from it at the San Francisco Conference. At the Conference, opinion was sharply divided between the Russians, the Chinese and other anti-colonial states who wished to include the objective of independence and the British and French who argued for the goal of self-government instead. The United States was caught in the middle and had to decide whether it wished to side with anti-colonial powers or with its European allies. When it came to the crunch, the United States sided with its European allies. Despite strong appeals from some members of the American delegation, including Taussig, who pointed out that to repudiate independence would be a betrayal of the ideals of President Roosevelt and would align the United States with the colonial territories,[34] the United States delegation decided in favour of supporting the objective of self-government. One senior member of the US delegation, Harold Stassin, whose arguments proved decisive, pointed to the importance of the friendship with Britain and questioned whether it was desirable for the United States to promote independence throughout the world with all the instability that this was bound to come with.[35]

Although the Americans did manage to persuade the British to accept independence as a possible objective for trust territories, in addition to self-government, the absence of the objective of independence in what became known as the Declaration Regarding Non-Self-Governing Territories (Chapter XI of the UN Charter), represented a major retreat from Rooseveltian idealism.

It could be argued that self-government still left open the possibility of independence (as eventually did happen in practice) and that the American delegation achieved a major diplomatic victory by maintaining good relations with her European allies without closing the door on independence as an objective for all dependent territories. This does not, however, diminish the fact that this concession represented another major departure from Rooseveltian idealism that set the trend for the years ahead.

The United States and the United Nations Trusteeship System

The United States delegation to San Francisco did manage to persuade the colonial powers, including Britain, to accept a supervisory regime for the trust territories that was tighter than that provided for under the League of Nations Mandates system. The Trusteeship Council, the organ immediately responsible for the supervision of trust territories, was made accountable to the General Assembly.[36] This provision was significant in the context of the membership of both organs. The Trusteeship Council was organised in such a way that there was a balance of membership between those states that administered trust territories and those that did not. The administering powers therefore had a disproportionately strong voice in it. The anti-colonial bloc, comprising the Soviet bloc countries, most Asian and Latin American states (themselves former colonies), and newly independent former colonies, on the other hand, dominated the General Assembly. In time, the Assembly, eager to proceed with decolonization, asserted its authority over a Trusteeship Council, which was inclined to take a more cautious approach.[37]

Another innovative provision for the supervision of Trust territories, forced on the colonial powers by the Americans, was for the General Assembly and the Trusteeship Council, which had to receive and examine petitions from the inhabitants of trust territories.[38] This provision was later on put to good use by the peoples of the trust territories especially after the Fourth Committee decided to hear petitioners orally.

Also included (at American insistence) in the mechanism for the supervision of trust territories, was provision for the General Assembly, and under its authority the Trusteeship Council, to undertake periodic visits to the trust territories to carry out on-the-spot inspections. This measure was strongly opposed at San Francisco by the British, who refused to accept an unconditional right of inspection.[39] In the end, the Americans had to settle for periodic visits 'at times agreed upon by the administering authorities'.[40] Still, this measure represented a significant tightening of the supervisory framework provided under the League of Nations Mandate system.[41] It was later used by nationalist groups in the Trust territories to channel complaints and petitions to the Trusteeship Council and the General Assembly.

These provisions taken together, stringent though they were in comparison with those provided for under the Mandates system, pale in comparison to the enormous powers that the actual terms of trusteeship gave the administering authorities. One of the major weaknesses of the trusteeship system was that there was no legal obligation on states (including those administering mandates) to place their dependent territories under trusteeship.[42] Article 75 of the Charter stated that the Trusteeship system was for 'the administration and supervision of such territories as may be placed thereunder by subsequent individual agreements'. Although there was a moral obligation on the mandatory powers to place their mandated territories under trusteeship, there was no legal obligation for them to do so.[43] This loophole seriously undermined the negotiating position of the General Assembly with regard to the terms of trusteeship, as the administering authorities often threatened to withdraw the draft agreements (which in most cases they had singlehandedly drawn up) if they did not get the terms of trusteeship that they proposed.[44]

The administering powers were thus effectively able to secure for themselves in the trusteeship agreements the same powers as they had over their ordinary colonies, subject to the provisions for supervision and the obligations to keep the doors of the Trust territories open to the commerce of the world. The trusteeship agreements gave them full powers of legislation, administration and jurisdiction over the trust territories. Furthermore, they were allowed to administer these territories in accordance with their own laws and as integral parts of their own territories. They were even allowed to take their respective Trust territories into customs, administrative, or federal unions with adjacent territories, provided these were consistent with the objectives of the trusteeship system. Thus the British were able to administer the Cameroons as part of the colony of Nigeria, and the Togolands as part of the Gold Coast. Similarly, the French were able to incorporate their section of the Cameroons as well as the Togolands into the French Union.

As with the issue of national independence, the United States did score some points with regard to the mechanism for the supervision of trust territories. However, the package as a whole represented only a marginal improvement on the Mandates system and was a far cry from hopes of an anti-imperial revolution that Rooseveltian idealism had generated.

Even more significant in the context of this essay was the increasingly conservative position that the United States took on trusteeship matters both in the Trusteeship Council and in the General Assembly. The precursor to this was the US perception of the threat posed by the Soviet Union and communism and the onset of the Cold War. By the time the Trusteeship system came into full operation, the United States found itself in the unenviable position of having to choose between its sympathy with the cause of decolonization and supporting its European allies. This dilemma was amply reflected in a memorandum from the Assistant Secretary of State for International Organization Affairs, Francis Wilcox, to the Secretary of State on May 1956. Wilcox wrote, 'On this issue (decolonization), which preoccupies many UN members, affirmations of traditional U.S. attitudes tend to displease the colonial powers, while U.S. actions often alienate the anti-colonial nations.'[45] It is worthwhile noting from this citation the notion that the US merely *affirmed* its support for decolonization, while its *actions* alienated the anti-colonial nations.

As a matter of fact, more often than not, the United States either voted with its European allies or abstained on the major contentious issues that the Trusteeship Council and the General Assembly had to deal with. In fact, the near-paralysis of decision-making in the Trusteeship Council was partly the result of the US casting its vote most of the time with the administering powers. The US vote in the Trusteeship Council was crucial, since there was a balance of membership in the Council between administering states and non-administering states and since the US itself was classified as an administering state because of its trusteeship of the former Japanese islands. An alignment of the US with the non-administering states (most of which were fiercely anti-colonial), could have tipped the balance in the Council in favour of the latter. The US rarely did so on the most crucial issues. For example, one of the most important issues that the Trusteeship Council had to decide upon was whether to hear oral petitions from the inhabitants of the Trust territories. With opinion in the Council sharply divided between the administering and non-administering states, the United States came down on the side of the former. The US Representative, Francis Sayre, who held the presidency of the Council, explained: 'the hearing of oral petitions is a matter which is easily liable to abuse. If all comers felt they had a right to be given oral hearings, this Council would be swamped and we could not properly perform the work set before us.'[46]

Sayre may have been sincere in his assessment, but it was nonetheless evidence of a growing conservatism in America's approach to trusteeship and decolonization. His fears were not borne out when the General Assembly, impatient with the Trusteeship Council's indecisiveness, decided to take upon itself the function of hearing oral petitioners. This gave nationalist politicians in the trust territories an important new international platform on which to launch their campaign for the end of colonial rule.

On another contentious issue – whether the inhabitants of trust territories should be allowed to send representatives to participate without a vote in the Council's consideration of the annual reports – the United States similarly lined up with its fellow administering states against the non-administering states, arguing that such representation would divide responsibility for the administration of Trust territories.[47] However, nothing in the Charter or the Trusteeship agreement prohibited this kind of representation, which could have provided for a more balanced consideration of the annual reports.

Of all the contradictions in America's approach to trusteeship and decolonization, perhaps the greatest was the fact of America itself becoming an administering power. Although Roosevelt successfully resisted the military's plans to annex the Japanese mandated islands outright, the United States was not willing, for its own security reasons, to subject the islands to the same supervisory regime that applied to other Trust territories.[48] And so a special category of trusteeship – the strategic trust – was created for the islands, which gave the US special rights in the islands and provided for a less stringent supervisory mechanism. Washington was given complete control over the islands' airspace and was allowed to determine the extent to which it wished to apply its trusteeship obligations according to its security needs.[49] Furthermore, all functions of the United Nations relating to the strategic trust was exercised by the Security Council – a less anti-colonial body – rather than the General Assembly.[50] Not even the widely acknowledged strategic importance of these islands to American national security could disguise the irony of the power that had vehemently opposed colonial rule and territorial aggrandizement as a result of the war, sitting in the Trusteeship Council as an administering power alongside the European colonial powers.

Conclusion

That Roosevelt was opposed to colonial rule in principle and that he was a great champion of decolonization is not in doubt. However, the gap between his idealism on the issue of international trusteeship between 1942 and early 1944 and his final position in late 1944 and 1945 does suggest a more cautious, if not conservative approach on decolonization in the last two years of his life – a trend that continued into the postwar period.

The need to keep European war allies on board and to protect US security in the postwar period explains, but does not bridge, the gap between ideals and final policy outcomes on this issue.

The ease with which high-minded idealism very often gives way to the reality of national interest in the making of American foreign policy is best reflected in the following quotation from a policy paper on the colonial problem. It was prepared by the Colonial Policy Review Sub-Committee of the Committee on Problems of Dependent Areas in the State Department in April 1950: 'There would be little value in throwing our support to dependent peoples with a view to developing worthwhile democratic friends in half a century, if, by so doing, we might seriously jeopardise present American security and the survival of democracy itself.'[51] True, but where is the idealism in this?

Notes

1 Key works in the literature include Quincey Wright, *Mandates under the League of Nations* (Chicago, 1930); Duncan Hall, *Mandates, Dependencies and Trusteeship* (Washington, 1948); G. W. Keeton and G. Scharzenberger (eds), *The Trusteeship System of the United Nations* (London, 1956); E. J. Sady, *The United Nations and Dependent Peoples* (Washington, DC, 1956); G. Thullen,

Problems of Trusteeship: a Study of Political Behavior in the United Nations (Geneva, 1964); C. E. Toussaint, *The Trusteeship System of the United Nations* (London, 1956).

2   See J. H. Parry, *The Spanish Theory of Empire in the Sixteenth Century* (Cambridge, 1940).

3   *The Works of Edmund Burke*, vol. 4, p. 296, cited in A. Burns, *In Defense of Colonies* (London, 1957), p. 101.

4   J. A. Hobson, *Imperialism: a Study* (London, 1902), p. 232.

5   F. D. Lugard, *The Dual Mandate in Tropical Africa* (London, 1929), pp. 62–3.

6   Lloyd Gardner, *Economic Aspects of New Deal Diplomacy* (Boston, 1971); and Gabriel Kolko, *The Politics of the War: the World and United States Foreign Policy, 1943–1945* (New York, 1968).

7   Benjamin Gerig, *The Open Door and the Mandates System: a Study of Economic Equality before and since the Establishment of the Mandates System* (London, 1930), p. 199, cited in Wm R. Louis, *Imperialism at Bay: the Decolonization of the British Empire, 1941–1945* (Oxford, 1977), p. 91.

8   Memorandum on United States Participation in the Administration of Trust Territories, *Foreign Relations of the United States (FRUS): the United Nations, 1946*, pp. 544–5.

9   United States Policy towards Dependent Territories, ibid., 1952–54, p. 1078.

10   Elliott Roosevelt, *As He Saw It* (New York, 1946), p. 75.

11   Louis, *Imperialism at Bay*, pp. 156–7.

12   Elliot Roosevelt, *As He Saw It*, p. 165.

13   For a record of the Cairo and Teheran Conferences, *FRUS: the Conferences at Cairo and Teheran*, pp. 323–5.

14   Louis, *Imperialism at Bay*, pp. 354–7.

15   Ibid., pp. 279–82.

16   Ibid., pp. 456–7.

17   Cited in ibid., pp. 154–5.

18   Ibid., p. 199.

19   For an account of the State Department's trusteeship planning during the war, see ibid., pp. 159–86.

20   *FRUS: Cairo and Teheran*, p. 554.

21   Ibid., *The Conferences at Malta and Yalta*, p. 770.

22   Cited in Louis, *Imperialism at Bay*, p. 458.

23   Ibid., p. 459.

24   *FRUS, Yalta*, pp. 884–5.

25   Louis, *Imperialism at Bay*, p. 528.

26   Walter La Faber, 'Roosevelt, Churchill, and Indo-China, 1942–1945', *American Historical Review*, 80 (1975), pp. 1291–3.

27   *FRUS: United Nations, 1945*, pp. 121–4.

28   Louis, *Imperialism at Bay*, p. 231.

29   Ibid.

30   Ibid., p. 243.

31   Gary Hess, *The United States' Emergence as a South-East Asian Power, 1940–1950* (New York, 1987), p. 368.

32   *FRUS: United Nations, 1945*, p. 121.

33   Louis, *Imperialism at Bay*, p. 486.

34   *FRUS: United Nations, 1945*, pp. 793–4.

35 Ibid., pp. 792–3.
36 Leland Goodrich and Edvard Hambro, *The Charter of the United Nations: Commentary and Documents* (Boston, 1949), pp. 418–76.
37 For details of the conflict between the General Assembly and the Trusteeship Council, see G. Thullen, *Problems of the Trusteeship System: a Study of Political Behavior in the United Nations* (Geneva, 1964).
38 United Nations Charter, Article 87.
39 Louis, *Imperialism at Bay*, pp. 326–7.
40 United Nations Charter, Article 87 (C).
41 For a comparison, see Goodrich and Hambro, *United Nations Charter*, pp. 465–72.
42 Ibid., pp. 228–35.
43 Ibid.
44 Ibid., pp. 440–2.
45 *FRUS: United Nations, 1956*, pp. 23–4.
46 Trusteeship Council Official Records (TCOR), Second Session, Second Meeting, 1947, p. 32.
47 Ibid., Fourth Session, 1949, pp. 23–4.
48 For a detailed discussion of the question of the Japanese mandated islands in the United States' trusteeship planning see Louis, *Imperialism at Bay*, pp. 259–74 and pp. 366–78.
49 See Goodrich and Hambro, *Charter of the United Nations*, p. 454.
50 United Nations Charter, Article 83.
51 *FRUS: United Nations, 1952–1954*, p. 1104.

5

The Ironies of History: the United States and the Decolonization of India

Dennis Merrill

The rapid decline of colonial empires during and after the Second World War reshaped the international system and posed major challenges to the makers of American foreign policy. The United States had long championed the principle of self-determination and hoped to reap political and economic benefits by supporting independence movements in Asia, Africa and the Middle East. India, the most populous of colonial dependencies, whose Congress Party had acquired vanguard status in the decolonization movement, seemed a logical test-case for Washington's commitment to anti-colonialism.

Yet, as the Indian freedom movement, or *Swaraj*, gathered strength during the Second World War, America extended only muted sympathy for independence in India and elsewhere in the non-western world. Historians who have studied US policies toward the subcontinent, including Gary R. Hess, M. S. Venkataramani, and Kenton J. Clymer, have concluded the retreat flowed from American ambivalence on a number of issues.[1] First, the United States generally shared with its European allies the prevailing cultural and racial attitudes of the day, and doubted the capacity of darker-skinned peoples to practise self-government. Indeed, few US officials envisioned immediate decolonization for dependent areas. Most subscribed to President Franklin D. Roosevelt's hopes for a gradual transition to trusteeship under the United Nations, followed by a period of conservatively managed economic and political development.

Equally important, military exigencies during the Second World War did not permit a breach in the Anglo-American alliance. Caught up in a struggle with fascism in Europe and Japanese aggression in the Pacific, the Roosevelt administration placed liberal ideology and anti-colonial principles aside and made its policies toward India in light of what would strengthen the war effort. Concern over India's will to resist Japanese militarism momentarily motivated Roosevelt to urge Britain to consider Indian self-rule. But as the Japanese threat receded, and London adamantly resisted any change in the *status quo*, Washington chose not to follow up on the proposal.

Global strategic considerations continued to inhibit US support for decolonization during the early Cold War. Interestingly, the subcontinent was one area where the United States belatedly backed self-determination. That policy contrasted with strong opposition to nationalist movements in French Indochina, French and Italian North Africa, and other regions where nationalist movements took on a leftist hue, or where decolonization threatened to ignite political turmoil.[2] In the Cold War setting of the late 1940s Washington viewed India's upper-class Congress Party leaders as safely non-communist and observed that a weakened Britain sought voluntarily to transfer power. India's determination to remain non-aligned in the escalating Soviet–American confrontation, however, limited American support for the new nation.

This essay does not attempt a narrative of America's response to *Swaraj*. Rather, it employs several interpretative frameworks to explain the disjuncture between American principles and American actions. In recent years a number of historians have argued that American foreign relations can be best understood when placed within the broader historical context of world capitalism, or what the sociologist Immanuel Wallerstein has labelled the 'world system'.[3] From the perspective of global history, the different experiences of the United States and India, from the days of European voyage and discovery forward, explain the limited prospects for cooperation during the 1940s. Yet a study of systematic or structural forces alone cannot fully explain specific US policies adopted at particular moments in time. Ideological forces, the personalities of key decision-makers, and the ebb and flow of everyday politics also require close examination. Thus, cultural studies, and poststructural analysis, suggest how ideology and American perceptions of Indian society further influenced attitudes toward that country's freedom struggles.[4] Finally, an examination of wartime and postwar power politics, viewed through the prism of what the historian Melvyn Leffler has called the 'national security paradigm', illuminates more precisely how strategic considerations led US policy-makers to abandon anti-colonial goals.[5]

The destinies of India and the United States have been linked since Christopher Columbus set sail for Asia in 1492 and accidentally discovered America. For the next 450 years, India and that part of America which became the United States were influenced by parallel historical forces, such as colonialism, industrialization, and global war. At opposite ends of the world system, however, India and the United States underwent widely divergent experiences.

Although India and North America were once linked together as critical components of a far-flung British Empire, they underwent nearly opposite colonial experiences. British influence in India, traceable to the early 1600s, was initially weak and indirect, contained to a small portion of Bengal on India's north-east coast and administered through the British East India Company. But as the Mughal court in Delhi suffered increasing internal stresses during the 1700s, the East India Company was able to expand its influence, usually by concluding strategic alliances with autonomous Muslim and Hindu kingdoms. By the mid-1800s British power extended across much of the subcontinent, and after the unsuccessful Sepoy rebellion of 1857, the authority of the East India Company gave way to direct governance by Parliament.[6] As Whitehall assumed political control over India, British merchants, manufacturers, and financiers helped integrate the subcontinent into the British-led world economy. Throughout the nineteenth and early twentieth centuries, England's modern factory system relied upon 'peripheral' regions within the world system to provide cheap raw materials and markets for manufactured goods. India quickly emerged as England's single largest export market, and a reliable supplier of primary products such as raw cotton, jute, indigo, hides, oilseeds, tea, wheat, coal and mica. After 1924, colonial authorities permitted India to erect limited, protective tariffs for industries such as iron, steel and cement. But the depression of the 1930s and dislocations caused by the war in the 1940s prevented India from diversifying its economy and breaking the cycle of economic dependency.[7]

In the part of North America that became the United States, British colonial control was initially more direct, featuring the Crown's direct rule over English settlers. The native Americans, erroneously referred to as Indians, lacked the internal cohesion, military power, and economic resources of Mughal India and fell more rapidly to European expansion. Yet forces set into motion by the Seven Years War (1756–63) quickly undermined British authority. When London's ministries tightened navigation laws, increased taxes, and placed restraints upon self-government the colonists bristled with indignation. Ironically, subsidized importation of East India Company tea, grown in India, gave Americans a rallying point. The colonists possessed the resources, and just enough unity, to wage an anti-colonial revolution.

As the British conquered and consolidated their Indian Empire during the nineteenth century, American settlers pushed west across the North American continent and forged a nation. In contrast to British-controlled India, the United States system of government had a democratic orientation, which by the 1820s featured universal, white manhood suffrage. Freed from the confines of colonialism, the new nation also began to build a national economy.

As in India, a mid-century rebellion, the American Civil War, marked a turning point in the country's development. But in the United States victory went to an indigenous industrial power rather than a foreign one. The newly united nation abolished slavery and relegated the cash-crop, export economy of the South to secondary status. By the 1890s industry rather than agriculture had become the most dynamic sector in the American economy, and the United States accounted for one-third of the world's supply of iron and steel. Technological advances during the early twentieth century created additional opportunities in the manufacture of electrical equipment and chemicals.

Perhaps most in contrast to India, the United States at the turn of the century embarked on an imperialistic course of its own. American policymakers sometimes disavowed pretensions to empire and celebrated the doctrine of the 'open door', that all nations must remain free to trade and prosper. But the establishment of United States sovereignty in Puerto Rico, Guam, Hawaii, Samoa and the Philippines, and the creation of an American Canal Zone in Panama, and military interventions in the Dominican Republic, Cuba, Nicaragua, Haiti and Mexico prior to the First World War, confirmed the existence of an American empire.[8]

The divergent historical experiences of India and the United States helped set the stage for Washington's rebuff to *Swaraj*. Although both evolved as components of an interdependent, British-led world system, the United States by the early twentieth century had emerged as a modern, industrial hegemon, and shared little in common with colonial India. Yet the United States also possessed a proud anticolonial heritage that at times found expression in support for the self-determination of oppressed peoples. To comprehend why those sentiments did not find application in US policy toward India, it is necessary to examine the course of Indo-American relations up to the 1940s, particularly the US response to India's modern independence movement.

Given the geographic distance between the United States and India, and the firm grip that Britain maintained over the latter, it is not surprising that Indo-American relations remained minimal during the formative nineteenth and early twentieth centuries. Altogether the United States secured between 2 per cent to 4 per cent of its imports from India between 1900 and 1940, and shipped approximately 1 per cent to 2 per cent of its exports there. In 1940 US direct investment in India totalled only $48 775 000 – less than 1 per cent of total, private American investment abroad.[9] Nor were American diplomatic relations with India extensive. Down through the years consular posts were established at Calcutta, Bombay, and Madras, but the unpopular appointments often went unfilled.[10] American missionaries, both Protestant and Roman Catholic, forged links between the United States and India, but as late as 1900 numbered only 1500 or so.[11]

Due to their very limited contacts, Americans on the whole acquired only a superficial knowledge of the subcontinent. Missionaries and well-to-do travellers, who constituted the most frequent commentators on the region, usually advanced a view of India coloured by ethnocentrism and stereotypes. Short stories, poems, novels, and travelogues typically focused on the most 'mysterious' and 'exotic' aspects of Indian life and described the subcontinent as a land of maharajas, religious fakirs, sacred cows, and snake charmers. India was alternately romanticised as a place of special beauty, or condemned for its caste inequalities, child marriage, and depravity.[12]

Poststructural or postmodern scholars have explained how dominant cultures 'construct' identities of 'foreigners', which impose an exaggerated sense of 'otherness' on outsiders and rationalize the privileged status of the more powerful society. Using familiar points of reference, American observers often compared Indians to African-Americans, people of colour similarly assigned inferior rank in what the historian Michael Hunt has called the American hierarchy of race.[13] From this perspective, Indians and other non-western peoples were commonly portrayed as child-like, politically immature, and in need of supervision. The historian Andrew J. Rotter has explained how India and other colonial societies were also frequently portrayed in gendered terms – as weak, helpless, dependencies, akin to prevailing constructions of femininity in male culture. Such stereotypes implied the legitimacy of protection, indeed domination, by the West.[14]

Interestingly, Indians did not maintain a wholly favourable view of America either. Although many political leaders admired Washington and Jefferson as champions of anti-colonialism, few Indians ever had the opportunity to visit America. Thus many fell under the sway of the British-controlled press which usually depicted the United States as a land of ruffians, cowboys and gangsters. More thoughtful criticisms came from activists in the Indian freedom movement who observed US imperialism in Asia and Latin America. Jawaharlal Nehru, India's future prime minister, travelled to Brussels in 1927 to attend the International Congress of Oppressed Nationalities and after meeting with Latin American representatives was moved to denounce United States as well as European expansionism.[15] The 6000 Indian immigrants who arrived in the United States between 1898 and 1914 added to the negative imaging. Settled along the Pacific coast typically as contract labourers, these new Americans often encountered harsh racial and religious discrimination.[16]

Limited contacts and distorted cultural perceptions, coupled with the very different developmental experiences of the two nations, coloured America's response to *Swaraj*. The origins of the Indian freedom movement can be traced to 1885 when a group of largely British-educated, middle- and upper-class Indians organized the Indian National Congress. In its first years the Congress remained a narrowly based organisation that primarily sought educational and civil service reforms. It achieved a popular base, however, with the advent of Mohandas K. Gandhi. Returned home in 1915 from South Africa where he had challenged institutionalized racism, Gandhi abandoned his Western tastes and habits, clad himself in dhoti and shawl and took his message of non-violent civil disobedience to the Indian masses. His efforts transformed the freedom movement.[17]

The British responded to the growing agitation by implementing constitutional reforms that conceded limited Indian participation in the civil service and established weak legislative councils at the provincial level. Such measures regularly met the Congress Party's disapproval, and were usually followed by a period of protest. Britain's final offer came with the India Act of 1935 which, without setting a precise date, pledged to grant dominion status in the future. While the measure slightly increased the powers of provincial legislatures, it reserved the right of veto in the British Governor's office. Another important provision of the bill provided for the creation of separate electorates for Indian minorities – including Muslims. Although Congress leaders were sceptical of Britain's intention to grant dominion status, and viewed separate electorates as a ploy to divide and conquer, they responded positively. In 1937, the Congress Party for the first time contested provincial elections.[18]

The Indian freedom movement received mixed reviews in the court of American public opinion. US citizens on the whole obtained only limited news of events on the subcontinent, much of it disseminated by British journalists and government press releases. Thus, American newspaper editors often applauded Britain's gradualist reforms and viewed the Congress Party's persistent demand for independence as obstructionist. Gandhi's popularity waxed and waned: at times he was revered as a democrat and a great moral leader, yet he remained in many ways an enigma, and by the mid-1930s his belief in non-violence seemed obtuse and naive in the face of fascist aggression. Americans who identified themselves as liberals – including Democratic presidential candidate William Jennings Bryan, the journalist George Kirchwey, American Federation of Labor president Samuel Gompers, the civil rights activist W. E. B. DuBois, and Nebraska Senator George K. Norris – took a much more sympathetic view of the Indian Congress and often compared its campaign with America's drive for independence in 1776. But these outspoken advocates of self-determination sustained little impact on US policy.[19] Until the outbreak of the Second World War Washington virtually ignored India's independence movement, making no official pronouncements. Nor is there any record of extensive internal discussion of the matter.

The response was not atypical of America's attitude toward liberation movements. As heirs to a revolutionary heritage, many US citizens instinctively sympathized with the nationalist aspirations of others. Government endorsement of, or assistance to, rebellions, however, came about only when United States interests dictated such a course. Thus, during the first half of the nineteenth century – as the nation expanded across the continent – American policy-makers supported revolts in Florida, Texas, California, and Canada; but remained aloof from those in Latin America, Greece, and Hungary. As the United States emerged as an industrial power, its support for revolutionary causes diminished further. Modern uprisings that featured radical social and economic change, as did Mexico's revolution during the early 1900s and Russia's Bolshevik revolution in 1917, seemed especially threatening to America's growing overseas interests.[20]

Since the India subcontinent was not an area of political or economic significance to the United States, and Britain's plans for political devolution promised moderate, progressive change, US officials saw no reason to become involved.[21] Prevailing American assumptions on race reinforced these inclinations. President Theodore Roosevelt in January 1909 exuberantly praised British-imposed white rule in India: 'In India we encounter the most colossal example history affords of the successful administration of men of European blood of a thickly populated region in another continent', he pronounced. 'Indeed, if English control were now withdrawn from India, the whole peninsula would become a chaos of blood and violence.'[22]

By the early twentieth century, history and culture had dampened US enthusiasm for self-determination in India. At the same time, America's growing world power gave rise to a new constellation of global economic and security interests that further encouraged support for British rule in India. Whereas the United States and Great Britain had historically been geopolitical rivals, at odds over territorial borders in North America and maritime practices on the high seas, the late 1800s witnessed an Anglo-American rapprochement. With increasing consistency London gave tacit support to America's drive toward hegemony in Central America and the Caribbean. Reciprocally, the United States did not criticize British practices in South Asia. The convergence of strategic objectives between the two imperial powers solidified with US entry into the First World War in 1917 on the side of the Anglo-led Triple Entente.

It was during the Second World War, however, that global interests led for the first time to direct US involvement in Indian affairs. Although Britain's leaders appear to have been unwilling to reckon with certain harsh realities, the war signalled the decline of the British Empire and set into motion forces that ultimately led to Indian nationhood. The simultaneous rise of the United States to a position of global military and economic leadership provided an opportunity for Washington to assist, in a substantive and perhaps decisive manner, the Indian freedom movement. The Roosevelt administration's calculation of US national security concerns, however, ultimately caused the United States to remain aloof.

The outbreak of fighting in Europe in September 1939 and Viceroy Lord Linlithgow's unilateral decision to make India an active belligerent brought about the Indian National Congress's withdrawal from the provincial legislatures. The Congress made its position clear: grant India independence and the party would abandon Gandhi's non-violent teachings and enter the struggle against fascism. Prime Minister Winston Churchill, who once declared that England should 'crush Gandhi, and the Indian Congress, and all they stand for', refused to make even minor concessions.[23]

During the early stages of the war the Roosevelt administration continued to unhesitatingly link US interests to Britain's survival against Nazism. Placing a premium on relations with Britain, US officials dared not show support for Indian nationalism. Secretary of State Cordell Hull and Under-Secretary Sumner Welles vetoed recommendations from lower-echelon officials that aid to England be made contingent upon democratic reform in India. As Welles noted in one letter to Hull: 'it would be undesirable to do anything to upset the Indian applecart at this critical juncture'.[24]

In August 1941 Roosevelt met with Churchill at Placentia Bay, off the coast of New Foundland, and the two leaders issued the Atlantic Charter, a bold enunciation of the principle of self-determination as part of a broader statement of war aims. Yet there is no record of India, or any other colonial area, having been discussed at the meeting. In the following weeks, when Churchill reported to Parliament that the doctrine of self-determination embodied in the charter applied only to Nazi-occupied territories in Europe, and not to 'regions who owe their allegiance to the British crown', Roosevelt remained silent. Upon his return from Placentia Bay the President received a note from his wife, Eleanor, asking for his views on India. 'I cannot have probable feelings in India', Roosevelt replied.[25]

Roosevelt espoused 'feelings' on India only after the bombing of Pearl Harbor and America's entry into the war. He was motivated by considerations relating to India's importance as an allied base of operations for the Middle and Far East, rather than by an ideological disapproval of colonial practices. In early 1942, as the Japanese scored easy victories in Singapore, Malaysia and Burma, and marched westward towards India, the president observed that political unrest in India might work against United States interests. Roosevelt articulated his views to John G. Winant, the American Ambassador in Great Britain. 'As you may guess,' he informed Winant, 'I am somewhat concerned over the situation in India, especially in view of a slow retirement through Burma and into India itself. From all I can gather the British defense will not have sufficient enthusiastic support from the people of India themselves.'[26]

In early March 1942, the president decided to write to Churchill to urge the Prime Minister to make concessions to the Indian National Congress. He couched his message in cordial and friendly language. Avoiding any discussion of the broader issue of colonialism, Roosevelt stressed only the adverse military ramifications of political instability in India. He also patently promised not to interfere in the matter. 'For the love of heaven', he exclaimed, 'don't bring me into this, though I do want to be of help.' Nonetheless, he suggested that Britain establish a

'temporary dominion government' in India. While only vaguely outlining the structure of such a government, he referred to the American
Articles of Confederation that had served to unite the thirteen disparate
American colonies during their early years of independence, as a possible model. Only a highly federated form of government, Roosevelt
argued, could accommodate itself to the subcontinent's religious,
ethnic, and caste diversity.[27]

Except for the pledge of non-intervention, the letter to Churchill was
well crafted, and represented the administration's most substantial initiative on behalf of decolonization on the subcontinent. Given its con-
tents, Churchill probably did not know how to interpret the president's
stated reluctance to interfere. Did Roosevelt mean to stay out of the
India tangle? Or was he merely putting a good face on inevitably bad
news?

Churchill quickly concluded that he should move ahead and send to
India a Cabinet Mission, headed by Labour Minister Sir Stafford Cripps,
to negotiate with Congress leaders. Domestic criticism of his policies
had originally stirred Churchill to action, but Roosevelt's expression
of interest may have played a role as well. Outlining the goals of the
mission to Lord Linlithgow, Churchill acknowledged: 'It would be
impossible, owing to the unfortunate rumours and publicity and the
general American outlook to stand on a purely negative attitude, and
the Cripps Mission is indispensable to prove our honesty of purpose and
to gain time for the necessary consultations.'[28] The Prime Minister
announced on 11 March 1942 the dispatch of the mission, one day after
receiving Roosevelt's communication.

The Cripps Mission offered Roosevelt his greatest single opportunity
to help bring about a negotiated settlement in India, and to help move
the subcontinent on a peaceful path toward nationhood. Churchill
probably had no intention of moving beyond Britain's 1935 promise of
eventual dominion status, but Sir Stafford Cripps, a long-time advocate
of liberalizing British rule, overstepped his instructions and began negotiating with Congress leaders increased Indian participation in the
wartime government. Such arrangements fell short of the official
demand for immediate independence, but key Congress representatives,
including party president Jawaharlal Nehru, showed a willingness to
compromise.[29]

In the weeks just prior to the announcement of the Cripps Mission,
the Roosevelt administration had been planning to send a technical and
economic mission to India to survey the subcontinent's war-related

industries. The mission was to be headed by the West Virginia lawyer and former Assistant Secretary of War Colonel Louis Johnson, a person whose military experience would prove valuable on the strategic sub-continent. Johnson was also to replace Thomas Wilson was Commissioner at the United States diplomatic post in New Delhi. However, at about the same time that Churchill announced the Cripps Mission, Roosevelt and Under-Secretary of State Welles decided to replace Johnson as head of the economic mission with Dr Henry Grady, an economist and former Assistant Secretary of State.[30] Johnson's duties would be restricted to those associated with the diplomatic post. Colonel Johnson, an important Democratic Party financial supporter, protested over what seemed to him to be a demotion in rank and status. To pacify Johnson, Welles intervened and assigned him a new title, 'Special Representative of the President'.[31]

Although Johnson did not carry instruction from either the president or the State Department to participate in the Cripps negotiations, the headstrong Colonel soon became deeply involved. Johnson correctly perceived that while Cripps sincerely worked towards a settlement, Lord Linlithgow opposed any diminution of authority. He also knew that any deal reached between Cripps and the Congress would require final approval by Churchill. Johnson surmised that only President Roosevelt's personal intercession could assure the success of the Cripps Mission. But the administration, still fearful of upsetting the Indian applecart, proved reluctant to interfere any further. When Johnson cabled the State Department on 4 April 1942, requesting that Roosevelt raise the matter of the Cripps negotiations with Churchill, he received only a cursory reply. 'The President asked me to let you know', Under-Secretary Welles explained, 'that he does not consider it desirable or expedient for him at least at this juncture, to undertake any further personal participation in the discussion.'[32]

Probably because both the British and the Indians thought he had the confidence of the president, Johnson proved to be a skilful negotiator. Within one week he and Cripps had won tentative approval from both the Indian Congress and British officials for an agreement that guaranteed India's postwar dominion status and enlarged, to a small extent, Indian participation in wartime decision-making. The modest concessions testified to the eagerness of Congress to solve the impasse and cooperate in the war effort. But they also reflected the fact that Linlithgow had moved with great caution. Indeed, the Viceroy accepted the Cripps/Johnson Plan pending final instructions from Churchill. Real progress had nonetheless been made, and even Nehru estimated the chances of a compromise settlement to be about 75 per cent. An ecstatic Louis Johnson reported to the State Department: 'The magic name here is Roosevelt; the land, the people, would follow and love America.'[33]

Churchill received word of the Cripps/Johnson Plan from Lord Linlithgow on 9 April. The Viceroy reported that Colonel Johnson had left the impression that he operated at the behest of the American president. That same morning Harry Hopkins, Roosevelt's most trusted adviser, arrived in London to begin plans for a second war-front in Europe. Churchill summoned Hopkins to his office, but the war in Europe was not uppermost in his mind. Before Hopkins, Churchill read the Linlithgow cable aloud, and warned that it was most likely that the War Cabinet would reject the Cripps/Johnson Plan that afternoon.

It is conceivable that Churchill was bluffing. Hopkins's answer, however, left few doubts regarding American intentions. He recalled in his diary: 'I told the Prime Minister that Johnson's original mission had nothing whatever to do with the British proposals and that I was sure that he was not acting as the representative of the President in mediating the Indian business. I told Mr. Churchill of President's instructions to me that he would not be drawn into the Indian business except at the personal request of the Prime Minister.'[34] Churchill immediately cabled Linlithgow informing the Viceroy of Johnson's true status, and instructed him to reject the Cripps/Johnson Plan.[35]

The Cripps Mission offered the last real chance for a wartime Anglo-Indian settlement. After its failure Gandhi launched the famous 'Quit India' campaign in August 1942. Soon most Congress leaders were in prison, and the British government was more adamant than ever against compromise. From December 1942 to May 1943, William Phillips, who replaced Louis Johnson in New Delhi, implored Roosevelt to raise the issue again with Churchill, but the president demurred. There were no more letters to the Prime Minister on the subject, and India did not arise as a topic at any of the wartime conferences.[36]

Nor did the president make a public statement on India's behalf. In February 1944, Roosevelt made the one and only formal statement of his long presidency on India. Rather than a ringing statement of Wilsonian principle, it read simply as an explanation of US security doctrine. 'The American objectives in India or elsewhere in continental Asia', he declared, 'are to expel and defeat the Japanese in the closest cooperation with our British, Chinese, and other Allies in that theater.'[37]

Roosevelt's intervention at the time of the Cripps Mission might have proved fruitless. Yet by expressing displeasure with Britain's obstinacy, or by providing incentives for a diplomatic solution, the president might have contributed to India's freedom. The important point is that at the most strategic moment, Roosevelt backed away. Engaged in a conflict that threatened the vital security interests of the United States, Roosevelt, ever the realist, did what most world leaders would have done. He put the question of India's independence to one side and vigorously pursued his wartime objectives. The president's policies toward wartime India foreshadowed in many ways US approaches to decolonization for the next half-century.

Roosevelt's death in April 1945, and the end of the Second World War shortly after, did not bring major changes in US policy toward the subcontinent. Cold War with the Soviet Union replaced hot war with Germany and Japan as the major foreign-policy preoccupation. The two powers vied for influence in Europe, faced off in Iran, and exchanged insults and accusations at the United Nations. President Harry S. Truman, having practically no previous experience in foreign affairs, and confronted by a multitude of vexing problems, had little time for or interest in India. Therefore, the Truman administration merely continued Roosevelt's broad support for the British.[38]

Freedom nonetheless came to India when postwar British officials realized that their authority on the subcontinent was so badly eroded they had little choice but to cut their losses. It came, however, only after the independence movement had splintered along communal, Hindu–Muslim lines. Although the Congress Party had been, since its founding, a secular organization that disparaged religious and ethnic division, Mohammed Ali Jinnah during the 1940s had rallied increasing numbers of followers around the banner of the Muslim League. In May 1946, the newly established Labour Ministry sent a Cabinet Mission to India that established an all-Indian, interim government. Faced with an intractable Muslim League, Viceroy Prince Louis Mountbatten hastily decided to partition the subcontinent. In this bittersweet context, Pakistan and India emerged on 14 and 15 August 1947, respectively, as free and independent states.

The United States did not play any direct role in these developments, although it did pledge its support for British policy at each phase of the proceedings.[39] While the Truman administration preferred a unified India – all the better to ward off the communist threat – it accepted the creation of two states, each led by moderate, non-communist elites. Thus, the United States at best might be characterized at this point as having been a cautious supporter of Indian independence. Its record on the subcontinent, moreover, did contrast with its support for France and outright opposition to nationalist forces in Indochina, where Ho Chi Minh's Vietnamese nationalist movement was infused with Marxist-Leninism.

Yet America's reluctance to exert strong pressure on wartime Britain, and its preference to allow independence to unfold on its own, belied an underlying ambivalence toward Indian nationalism. As the Cold War replaced the Second World War as the defining crusade in US foreign policy, Washington's antipathy toward Third World nationalism deepened, and Indo-American relations suffered. Indeed, the troubled history of America's relations with independent India suggests that the ironies of world history, enduring cultural barriers, and the vagaries of power politics continued to keep the two nations apart.

Perhaps no clash in early US relations with India better illustrates the matter than Washington's antagonism toward Prime Minister Jawaharlal Nehru's foreign policy of Cold War non-alignment. Although Nehru repressed communist activity inside his country, he refused to adopt an anti-communist international posture. India's non-alignment sprang from pragmatic considerations: its location near Soviet and Chinese borders, its position of weakness, and its natural interest in Asian and colonial affairs rather than East–West relations. Indeed, relations with Pakistan, particularly confrontation over the dispossession of the border-sate of Kashmir, ranked as India's foremost concern. Most fundamentally, however, non-alignment grew out of India's drive for national self-determination. 'For too long we of Asia have been petitioners in Western courts and chancellories', Nehru declared in March 1947. 'That story must now belong to the past.'[40]

As decolonization swept across Africa, Asia and the Middle East after the Second World War, India again stood as a symbol of Third World nationalism. And once more, Washington found India a troublesome obstacle to its global agenda.[41] From Korea, to Berlin, to Vietnam, to nuclear arms, New Delhi stridently criticized Washington's Cold War policies, and sought dialogue with the Soviet Union and the People's Republic of China. It became a particularly vocal opponent of Washington's Cold War military alliances, including the Southeast Asian Security Organization (SEATO) and the Baghdad Pact, each of which included arch-rival Pakistan. India's stature as an Afro-Asian leader peaked in 1955 when Nehru joined with Sukarno of Indonesia and Gamel Abdel Nasser of Egypt to denounce US policies at the Bandung Conference of non-aligned states.

The Indo-American clash undoubtedly sprang from geopolitics and conflicting security interest. But reactions on both sides assumed a shrill and emotional tone, which suggested that cultural differences also played a role. Secretary of State Dean Acheson complained after meeting Nehru in 1949 that the Indian leader 'was one of the most difficult men with whom I have ever had to deal'.[42] Nehru's forcefulness provoked Secretary of State John Foster Dulles's memorable lament that 'neutralism' in the Cold War was 'a short sighted and immoral conception'.[43] And even President Kennedy, eager to demonstrate friendliness toward the Third World, complained that talking to the Indian leader was 'like trying to grab something in your hand, only to have it turn out to be just fog'.[44] Andrew Rotter has argued that as in the days of the British Raj, many American officials continued to perceive India as an inscrutable 'other', emotional, unpredictable, weak and feminine, and not fully up to the manly task of self-government.[45]

As was the case during India's freedom movement, Washington at times considered it within its interest to assist independent India. The most important example of collaboration came in the economic development arena, where US capital and technical assistance helped promote industrial growth, 'green revolution', and agricultural self-sufficiency. Once again, liberals – such as former first lady Eleanor Roosevelt, labour leaders Walter and Victor Reuther, and US Ambassador Chester Bowles (1951–53 and 1963–69) – were especially vocal supporters of India, hailing the new democracy as a model for US-backed development in the Third World. But large economic aid came only after the mid-1950s, and followed the extension of Soviet economic assistance to India and other key non-aligned states. Its impact, moreover, was partly offset by continued military aid to authoritarian Pakistan and the expense of an escalating Indo-Pakistani arms race.[46] Nor did collaboration in the economic field or ideological affinities quell Cold War political squabbles. Thus, the world's two largest democracies remained distant friends, unable to fully pursue their mutual interests.

America's response to decolonization on the Indian subcontinent was riddled with contradictions. Itself the bearer of a proud anti-colonial past, the United States nonetheless condoned British rule throughout the first half of the twentieth century. Even during the Second World War, when the Roosevelt administration appears to have had the opportunity to work for self-determination, Washington sought most to avoid a break with Great Britain. After independence, Indo-American relations continued to be plagued with inconsistencies as the two democracies bickered over how best to confront communism and bolster Third World nationalism, and failed to realize their prospects for partnership.

Behind the contradictions, and underpinning the contrasting responses to wartime and Cold War politics, lay the vastly different historical experiences of the two societies. By the 1940s and 1950s India and the United States, once linked by a common dependent status, had come to occupy opposite locations in the modern world system – separated by unbridgeable gaps in wealth, power, security interests and culture. While their destinies had often intersected, they had travelled very different paths to the twentieth century. Some Americans sympathized with India's aspirations and US officials at times found limited ways to advance India's cause. But in the last analysis, the ironies of history prevented Washington from fully making the Indian struggle for national independence a part of its own crusade for human freedom.

Notes

1   Kenton J. Clymer, *Quest for Freedom: the United States and India's Independence* (New York, 1995); Gary R. Hess, *America Encounters India, 1941–1947* (Baltimore, 1970); M. S. Venkataramani and B. K. Shrivastava, *Roosevelt, Churchill, and Gandhi* (Delhi, 1983).

2   For comparative purposes see: Lloyd C. Gardner, *Approaching Vietnam: from World War II through Dienbienphu* (New York, 1988); William Roger Louis, *Imperialism at Bay: the United States and the Decolonization of the British Empire, 1941–1945* (Oxford, 1977); Christopher Thorne, *Allies of a Kind: the United States, Britain, and the War against Japan, 1941–45* (New York, 1978). Also see Terry H. Anderson, *The United States, Great Britain, and the Cold War, 1944–47* (Columbia, Missouri, 1981); Scott L. Bills, *Empire and the Cold War: the Roots of US–Third World Antagonism, 1945–47* (New York, 1990); Robert M. Hathaway, *Ambiguous Partnership: Britain and America, 1944–47* (New York, 1981); Gary R. Hess, *The United States's Emergence as a Southeast Asian Power, 1940–50* (New York, 1987); Andrew J. Rotter, *The Path to Vietnam: Origins of the American Commitment to Southeast Asia* (Ithaca, 1987); Henry Butterfield Ryan, *The Vision of Anglo-America: the US-U.K. Alliance and the Emerging Cold War, 1943–46* (Cambridge, 1987).

3   On world systems theory see: Immanuel Wallerstein, *The Capitalist World Economy: Essays* (New York, 1979); Thomas J. McCormick, *America's Half-Century: United States Foreign Policy in the Cold War* (Baltimore, 1989).

4   For an introduction to how postmodern thought might be applied to the study of foreign relations history, see: David Campbell, *Writing Security: United States Foreign Policy and the Politics of Identity* (Minneapolis, 1992); Arturo Escobar, *Encountering Development: the Making and the Unmaking of the Third World* (Princeton, 1995); Clifford Geertz, *The Interpretation of Cultures* (New York, 1973); Edward Said, *Culture and Imperialism* (New York, 1993).

5   Melvyn Leffler, 'The National Security Paradigm', in *Explaining the History of American Foreign Relations* (eds.) Michael J. Hogan and Thomas G. Paterson (Cambridge, 1991).

6   Standard works on India's history include: W. Norman Brown, *The United States, India, Pakistan, and Bangladesh* (Cambridge, 1974), Third Edition; H. Dodwell, *Dupleix and Clive: the Beginning of Empire* (London, 1967); M. Bence Jones, *Clive of India* (London, 1974); A. Maddison, *Class Structure and Economic Growth: India and Pakistan since the Moghuls* (London, 1971); P. J. Marshall, *Problems of Empire: Britain and India, 1757–1813* (London, 1968); P. J. Marshall, *East Indian Fortunes: the British in Bengal in the Eighteenth Century* (Oxford, 1976); Persival Spear, *A History of India,* II (Middlesex, 1970); Daniel Thorner, *The Shaping of Modern India* (New Delhi, 1980); Stanley A. Wolpert, *A New History of India* (New York, 1982).

7   In addition to the works cited above, the following provide an introduction to the consolidation of the British empire in India: Amiya Kumar Bagchi, *The Political Economy of Underdevelopment* (Cambridge, 1982); Judith M. Brown, *Modern India: the Origins of an Asian Democracy* (Delhi, 1984); Sarvepalli Gopal, *British Policy in India, 1858–1905* (Cambridge, 1965); D. R. Gadgil, *The Industrial Evolution of India in Recent Times, 1860–1939* (Delhi, 1971); Dharma Kumar, *The Cambridge Economic History of India,* II, (Delhi, 1984); Sumit Sarkar, *Modern India, 1885–1947* (Delhi, 1983); B. R. Tomlinson, *The Political Economy of the Raj, 1914–1947: the Economics of Decolonization in India* (London, 1979).

8   On US empire see: David Healy, *Drive to Hegemony: the United States in the Caribbean, 1898–1917* (New York, 1988); Stanley Karnow, *In Our Image: America's Empire in the Philippines* (New York, 1989); Paul Kennedy, *The Rise and Fall of the Great Powers* (New York, 1987); Walter LaFeber, *The New Empire* (New York, 1963); Walter LaFeber, *The American Search for Opportunity, 1865–1913* (Cambridge, 1993); Lester D. Langley, *The United States and the Caribbean in the Twentieth Century* (Athens, Georgia, 1985); Louis A. Perez, *Cuba and the United States: Ties of Singular Intimacy* (Athens, Georgia, 1990); Thomas D, Shoonover, *The United States in Central America, 1860–1911* (New York, 1991); William Appleman Williams, *The Tragedy of American Diplomacy* (New York, 1988).

9   Hess, *Emergence,* p. 5; L. Natarajan, *American Shadow over India* (Delhi, 1956), pp. 3–5.

10 Hess, *Emergence,* pp. 5–6.

11 Ibid., p. 6.

12 Ibid., p. 3; W. Norman Brown, *The United States,* p. 394. The quintessential example of American ethnocentrism is Katherine Mayo, *Mother India* (New York, 1927), see especially Chapter 3, 'The Slave Mentality,' pp. 19–32.

13 On US attitudes toward race, see Michael Hunt, *Ideology and U.S. Foreign Policy* (New Haven, 1987).

14 On gendered images, see Andrew J. Rotter, 'Gender Relations as Foreign Relations: the United States and South Asia, 1947–64', *Journal of American History,* 81 (September 1994), pp. 518–42.

15 Jawaharlal Nehru, *An Autobiography* (Delhi, 1982), First Edition, 1936, pp. 161–5.

16 Natarajan, *American Shadow,* p. 17; Hess, *Emergence,* p. 7.

17 On the Indian independence movement and Gandhi, see: Michael Brecher, *Nehru: a Political Biography* (London, 1959); Judith Brown, *Gandhi and Civil Disobedience: the Mahatma in Politics, 1928–34* (Cambridge, 1977); Mohandas K. Gandhi, *An Autobiography: My Experiments with the Truth* (Boston, 1957), First Edition 1927; Sarvepalli Gopal, *Jawaharlal Nehru: a Biography* (Delhi, 1975); Nehru, *Autobiography*; Jawaharlal Nehru, *The Discovery of India* (London, 1946, reprinted New Delhi, 1981).

18 Ibid.

19 Hess, *Emergence*, pp. 8–10, 14–16; Natarajan, *American Shadow*, pp. 12–13.

20 On American attitudes toward revolution, see Hunt, *Ideology, and U.S. Foreign Policy*.

21 Venkataramani, and Shrivastama, *Roosevelt*, pp. 333–7.

22 Address at the celebration of the African Diamond Jubilee of the Methodist Episcopal Church, Washington, DC, 18 January 1909, in Theodore Roosevelt, *Works* (New York, 1926), XIV, pp. 260–1.

23 Venkataramani, and Shrivastama, *Roosevelt*, p. 3.

24 Memorandum by Adolf Berle, 5 May 1941, *Foreign Relations of the United States, 1941*, III (Washington, DC, 1959), pp. 176–7 (hereafter volumes cited from this series will be cited as *FRUS*); Adolf Berle to Sumner Welles, 5 August 1941, ibid., pp. 179–181; Memorandum by Chief of the Division of Near Eastern Affairs (Murray), November 7, 1941, ibid., p. 197; Sumner Welles to Secretary of State (Hull), 15 November 1941, ibid., 184–7.

25 Quoted in Hess, *Emergence*, p. 32.

26 Acting Secretary of State (Welles) to Ambassador in UK (Winant), 25 February 1942, *FRUS 1942*, I (Washington, DC, 1960), p. 604.

27 President Roosevelt to British Prime Minister (Churchill), 10 March 1942, ibid, pp. 615–16.

28 Hess, *Emergence*, p. 38.

29 Gopal, *Nehru*, I, pp. 276–87.

30 Henry F. Grady, Unpublished Autobiography, Henry F. Grady Papers, Harry S. Truman Library, Independence, Missouri.

31 Memorandum by Assistant Secretary of State (Shaw) of a conversation with Colonel Louis Johnson, 11 March 1942, *FRUS 1942*, I, p. 617; Hess, *Emergence*, p. 41; Venkataramani and Shrivastama, *Roosevelt*, p. 25.

32 Acting Secretary of State (Welles) to Officer in Charge, New Delhi (Merrell), for Johnson, 5 April 1942, *FRUS 1942*, I, pp. 627–8.

33 Johnson to Secretary of State, 9 April 1942, ibid., p. 610. On Nehru, see Gopal, *Nehru*, I, p. 283.

34 Quoted in Venkataramani and Shrivastama, *Roosevelt*, p. 30.

35 On the Cripps/Johnson negotiations, see also Clymer, *Quest*, pp. 55–72; Hess, *Emergence*, pp. 33–59; Venkataramani and Shrivastama, *Roosevelt*, pp. 1–54.

36 Clymer, *Quest*, pp. 74–156.

37 Venkataramani and Shrivastama, *Roosevelt*, pp. 268–70.

38 Clymer, *Quest*, 238–84; Hess, *Emergence*, pp. 157–82.

39 Ibid.

40 Speech inaugurating Asian Relations Conference, 3 March 1947, *Jawaharalal Nehru's Speeches*, I (New Delhi, 1958), pp. 302–3.

41 The standard work on US security policy toward South Asia is Robert J. McMahon, *The Cold War on the Periphery: the United States and South Asia*,

1947–1969 (New York, 1994). Also see H. W. Brands, *India and the United States: the Cold Peace* (Boston, 1990).

42 Dean Acheson, *Present at the Creation* (New York, 1969), p. 336.

43 M. S. Rajan, *India in World Affairs* (Bombay, 1964), p. 259.

44 Arthur Schlesinger Jr, *A Thousand Days: John F. Kennedy in the White House* (Boston, 1965), p. 526.

45 Rotter, 'Gender Relations as Foreign Relations'.

46 Dennis Merrill, *Bread and the Ballot: the United States and India's Economic Development, 1947–1963* (Chapel Hill, 1990). For a thoughtful, upbeat appraisal of Indo-American relations, see Gary R. Hess, 'Accommodation Amidst Discord: the United States, India, and the Third World', *Diplomatic History*, 16 (Winter, 1992), pp. 1–22.

6
How We 'Lost' Vietnam, 1940–54

Lloyd C. Gardner

In May 1972 the Senate Foreign Relations Committee held yet another set of hearings on the seemingly endless Vietnam War. The committee was still seeking to understand the 'origin and evolution of American involvement in Vietnam', the chair, Senator William J. Fulbright, explained.[1] The invited witnesses included academics with widely different viewpoints on the American war in Vietnam, who all agreed, however, that the problem began when President Roosevelt – or his immediate successor, President Truman – abandoned a supposed commitment to postwar independence for the French colony. They did not concur on why the reversal took place. The reason why policy-makers made that fateful decision, the Roosevelt expert Arthur M. Schlesinger maintained, was the precarious and chancy situation in Europe immediately after the war. 'The real reason', he told the committee, 'why we acquiesced in the British–French imperial determination . . . to put the French back . . . was because of our concern with the French situation in Europe. . . . In other words, our policy in Vietnam was based, in that period, essentially on European reasons rather than on Asian reasons.'[2]

Yet despite all that has been written on Vietnam since that time, we are even today still uncertain about how and why America became involved in its longest war. Some continue to argue the case for 'European reasons', and some put forward 'Asian reasons', while others take up the argument for 'American reasons'. In a sense, it is a matter of where the writer chooses to put his or her emphasis, for all three considerations were present as decision-makers reached their conclusions. To settle on one, however, and particularly the argument for 'European reasons', risks creating an impression of a passive United States, with few direct interests of its own, and worried only about the internal situation in France as the Cold War began. Another way of looking at the origins of the Vietnam War is to locate it in the struggles of the decolonization process, during which the United States pursued a consistent policy of attempting to 'weed out' the weakened colonial powers and replace their outdated visions of empire with a world order that would re-integrate the economies of Southeast Asia with the industrial nations to reestablish world prosperity – and, not incidentally, prevent nationalist fervour from being directed against the West. Hence Washington opted for a type of 'informal empire' in the Far East. The object of this empire was to facilitate cooperation among the emerging nations, and to make it stretch across from Korea to Southeast Asia. This was not, as historian Stephen Hugh Lee points out, empire by invitation; nor was it modelled after America's postwar policy in Europe, which, George Kennan had averred, should be to promote independence within the parameters of 'containment'. The quest in Asia was for interdependence – overseen and directed by the United States.[3]

Before the Second World War, French Indochina little concerned American policymakers. When the Japanese demanded military bases in the colony in mid-summer 1941, however, President Roosevelt offered to 'do everything in his power' to neutralize the area in the same way as Switzerland. He even assured the ambassador that if Tokyo abandoned its quest for military bases the guarantee he proposed would be good against any attempts of the Free French to dislodge Vichy authorities. But when the Japanese went ahead with their plans anyway, Washington put Tokyo on notice that it would not allow Indochina to become a staging base for further expansionist adventures. Deploring Japan's actions, Under-Secretary of State Sumner Welles nevertheless warned the Vichy government as well that traditional friendship and sympathy for 'the desire of the French people to maintain their territories' notwithstanding, 'American attitudes . . . will be governed by the manifest effectiveness with which those authorities endeavor to protect these territories from domination and control' by powers seeking to extend their rule by force and conquest.[4]

The French, in other words, had not proven themselves to be effective rulers of a strategic territory. This *Realpolitik* analysis linked up easily to traditional American anti-colonialism, both rhetorically and substantively. The two marched side-by-side throughout the war and reinforced one another in policy-makers' minds. It was difficult to separate out where one left off and the other began. From the beginning, this conjunction led American leaders to see the problem in Vietnam as one of getting the French out of the way, so as to deal with the central issue, whether Japan or communist-directed revolution. And that early judgement continued to inform Washington's thinking well into the period of deep involvement two decades after the war. To all those who charge that we are seeking to take France's place in Vietnam, said National Security Adviser McGeorge Bundy in 1965, he would give this answer: 'We simply are not there as colonialists.' Any fair-minded observer understood that fundamental point. 'Our innate lack of imperial zeal is visible to any observer in Vietnam and to the Vietnamese people.' The French never had such a reputation, and, therefore, became an easy target for communist and non-communist nationalists alike.[5]

Explaining Roosevelt's wartime policies, and the bewildering switch-backs from expediency to efforts to force a solution to the colonial 'problem', was a bit more difficult for his successors. Secretary of State John Foster Dulles, indeed, felt considerable resentment at Roosevelt's failure to carry out his avowed goal of replacing the French with an international trusteeship, thus leaving his successors to deal with the unhappy consequences. By allowing the colony to be reoccupied, Dulles complained privately, FDR and Truman put the United States in a false position. 'Originally,' he wrote in an unused response to critics of the 'compromise' at the 1954 Geneva Conference, 'President Roosevelt was against this on the ground that France did not have a good record as a colonial power and its return would not be accepted by the people.' He was right. The French could only maintain their position by the 'bloody massacres which started the colonial war', and that allowed the communists an opportunity to lead the nationalist movement.[6]

Roosevelt would have been pleased at Dulles's acknowledgment of his foresight, and his early determination that France was not a suitable agent to represent the West's interests in Southeast Asia, but he would have asked him to look again at the complexities of the wartime situation. It was generally agreed in wartime Washington, and widely acknowledged even in the metropolitan capitals of Europe, that nineteenth-century colonialism was a dying system. How the transition to something better could be achieved was another question. Roosevelt's impatience with Winston Churchill's view of colonial matters was famous. But he needed a partner; he needed, above all, not to drive the lesser colonial powers into an alliance with the fading, but still powerful British Raj. Roosevelt did claim that he had spoken to Churchill on at least 25 occasions about Indochina's future, singling that colony out as the most eligible place to impose a trusteeship 'solution'. Churchill, for his part, suspected, rightly, that the president did not expect to halt the decolonization policy at Indochina's borders with Burma – although

FDR would have, and did, put it differently, preferring to say that whatever else resulted from the war, colonialism had no future.

Roosevelt's 'plan' for facilitating the transition began with the idea of the Big Four, which he hoped to sell to Churchill, Russia's Josef Stalin, and Chinese leader, Chiang Kai-shek. He seldom linked the colonial issue publicly to postwar security matters quite so definitely as he did musing about what would come after the war to an intimate friend at the end of 1942. He hoped to go to Khartoum, Egypt, he told Margaret Suckley, and there meet with the other world leaders. He thought Stalin might understand his plan better than Churchill, and she paraphrased in her diary:

> In general it consists of an international police force run by the four countries – All nations to disarm completely, so that no nation will have the chance to start out to conquer any other – Self determination to be worked out for colonies over a period of years, in the way it was done for the Philippines.[7]

Roosevelt's friend gently suggested that perhaps the 'Empire owners' might not take to the idea so easily. What would Queen Wilhelmina think, for example, she asked? 'F.[ranklin] said he gave her a hint about it!.' His companion was still sceptical. 'Perhaps she didn't realize what he really meant.'[8] There was the rub. What did Roosevelt really mean? Though he frequently spoke about the colonial question to various foreign leaders, diplomats and cabinet members, and, improbably enough, about Indochina specifically even to the Turkish prime minister and the Egyptian 'heir apparent' one afternoon in his villa during the First Cairo Conference in late November 1943, when he finally got to Khartoum a year later, none came away with much of an idea how his schemes for easing the empires through the transition period would pan out.[9]

The case of the Dutch Empire offers a good example of the frustrations Roosevelt's behaviour caused advisers to feel. Like him, they agreed that the postwar security system would have to be all-encompassing, and that the prewar colonial system was not secure. A definite policy needed to be worked out before the final battles were fought in Europe. Even were there no nationalist pressure in the colonies, postwar conditions in France and Holland would hardly allow those countries, unaided, to reoccupy far-off territories previously under their sovereign control. With Japan eliminated, and China a very big question-mark, international control became the only answer. As soon as 'the lid is taken off' in Europe, mused the old New Dealer, now Assistant Secretary of State, Adolf Berle, there will be a 'European revolution', either along Stalinist lines or 'liberal and individualist lines'. Plans would have to be made so that it did not become the former by default, as the result of a general upheaval and chaos. A general security system 'on a global basis' needed to be in place as soon as the war ended. 'The territories of Indo-China, Thailand, the Indies, and so forth, have to be worked into some sort of a cooperative system.'[10]

But the president feared pushing things too fast. Perhaps it would be possible, if the colonial problem were handled as if the Big Three or Four all had a significant role to play, to avoid such a contest altogether. 'When we've won the war', he told his son Elliott, he intended to work with 'all my might and main' to prevent the imperial powers from manoeuvring the United States into supporting their ambitions.[11] Meanwhile, he would keep the Big Four idea in play, and see where that led. But that did not mean simply standing aside and allowing things to sort themselves out on their own. Because of their common ancestry, perhaps, Roosevelt believed he had a special relationship with 'Minnie', Queen Wilhelmina, enough so, apparently, that he thought he could drop hints and give little nudges that she should begin the process of granting self-government to the Netherlands East Indies. He no doubt believed that winning her over would be very useful with the tougher cases when it came to dealing with the French and the British – and, more vaguely, even the Russians. The queen was not particularly responsive to these 'friendly' suggestions, however, telling the president that while Java might, perhaps, become independent in something between 15 and 50 years, anything for the more backward areas was 'sheer speculation'.[12]

Roosevelt backed off even in this case from a direct confrontation, retreating behind a series of anecdotes. His aides, however, apparently believed that he had thereby signalled acquiescence in Dutch plans. More likely, he was continuing to size up the situation before taking further steps or issuing ringing manifestos. His main worry, all along, was that he would scare the lesser European powers into placing their faith in British leadership on this question. And so long as Churchill navigated according to Rudyard Kipling's compass, he would welcome their allegiance aboard the leaky HMS 'Rule Britannia'. Perhaps if they all baled together they could prevent the imminent danger of being capsized. At war's end, both Churchill and Roosevelt knew, American demands for change could hardly be ignored by a largely bankrupt world, in debt to the United States – and to the colonies as well. Certainly that was the case with the British in India. There were mechanisms already being put in place to ensure that the British Empire was not shut up, as Secretary of State Cordell Hull had once complained, like an 'oyster shell' against world trade.[13]

Churchill would never think of choosing Paris over Washington, of course, but he had no compunctions about using Holland and France as bailers and counterbalances to an overweening America. Roosevelt could afford to wait him out, on the other hand. He would never allow Britain to sink – out of plain self-interest – but there would be no bargaining as at Munich in a futile effort to save the empire. The Europeans would just have to learn to adjust to an empire-less existence. 'Don't think for a moment', Roosevelt admonished his son, Elliott, during a private moment at the Casablanca Conference, 'that Americans would be dying in the Pacific tonight, if it hadn't been for the shortsighted greed of the French and the British and the Dutch.'[14]

Banker Thomas Lamont, of J. P. Morgan & Company, veteran of many international negotiations going back to the 1920s put it this way in a speech in early 1941 – at the time the Lend-Lease debates over aid to Britain were just about to get under way. 'We will all look forward to a postwar world in which Great Britain will be our prosperous friend, not another depressed area. She must be kept a going concern.' And, he concluded solemnly, 'America must have a partner.'[15] None of Lamont's words lessened policy-makers' determination to prevent London from leading, or even thinking about leading, a bloc of colonial powers in defiance of American plans to restore an 'Open World' for goods and ideas, but Roosevelt saw no reason to push the British into a corner.

And, when it suited his purposes, he would play the gallant rescuer of European fortunes with blithe disregard for any inconsistencies. Thus his response when he heard from one of his diplomatic representatives and old friends that Queen Wilhelmina felt a sense of anxiety for 'her people in Holland . . . as a result of the fall of the Indies', and had been 'deeply touched' by Mr Churchill's vow at a meeting of the Pacific War Council that the restoration of the East Indies was a 'sacred trust'. The Dutch foreign minister had conveyed this information, along with a request that President Roosevelt offer similar assurances, even though 'he was well aware of the delicacy of the situation'. And so FDR did. 'You have been much in my thoughts', he wrote the queen, and he wanted her to know that he was well aware of the 'gallantry of the Netherlands' forces in the Netherlands Indies'. When Germany was defeated, it would not take long to drive the Japanese back into their own islands. 'The Netherlands Indies must be restored – and something within me tells me that they will be.'[16]

FDR was gratified when Wilhelmina broadcast promises of future reform for the Indies, as that seemed to demonstrate the wisdom of his policy of nudges and hints; but he also informed a British diplomat that the Dutch, 'the poor dears,' were very unlikely to get the East Indies back as they liked to imagine.[17] Observing these ploys, Free French leader Charles de Gaulle deplored Roosevelt's scheming forays into previously sacrosanct colonial questions, claiming that the president had somehow forced the Dutch to 'renounce their sovereignty over Java'.[18] That gave the president too much blame or credit. Roosevelt and de Gaulle never got along – not from the start. The president bridled at the Free French leader's demands to share in the planning of the North African invasion, and he was determined not to recognize de Gaulle's Free French regime as the government of France in exile. He had expressed the view that it would take 20 years or more for France to return to great-power status, and, as if to make the prophecy self-fulfilling, he had once listed France among those countries to be completely disarmed after the war.[19]

Roosevelt's much put-upon Secretary of State, Cordell Hull, excluded not only from many wartime conferences, but often also from the president's inner thoughts on postwar matters, was well versed, nevertheless, on Roosevelt's attitude towards French colonial possessions. 'He could not but remember', Hull recalled of Roosevelt's outbursts, 'the devious conduct of the Vichy government in granting Japan the right to station troops there, without any consultation with us but with an effort to make the world believe we approved.'[20] Because Roosevelt wished to maintain some sort of relationship with that same Vichy regime, however, he had had Under-Secretary Sumner Welles offer similar assurances in April 1942, that the United States recognized the 'sovereign jurisdiction of the people of France over the territory of France and over French possessions overseas'.[21]

In his letter to Wilhelmina, the president had stressed the extreme danger that Russia might be driven to her knees by summer, thereby allowing the Germans and Japanese to join hands. A statement on colonialism issued under such duress was a justified lie for the good of the cause. And, as if to drive the point home, only a month later, in a conversation with Russian Foreign Minister V. M. Molotov, Roosevelt broached the idea of international trusteeships, passing it off as Generalissimo Chiang Kai-shek's idea. 'There were', he wooed this new acquaintance whose nation he believed held the key to victory, 'all over the world, many islands and colonial possessions which ought, for our own safety, to be taken away from weak nations.' Besides Indochina, he listed Siam and the Malay States, as requiring interim trusteeships until they were ready for self-government.[22]

It no doubt pleased FDR when Molotov responded that the Soviet Union would give the matter serious attention, given that it was premised upon Allied cooperation to make sure Germany and Japan did not again threaten the peace. 'Starting from this principle, Mr. Molotov expressed his conviction that the President's proposals could be effectively worked out.'[23] So many things, Roosevelt believed, could be effectively worked out with a Russia willing to cooperate in this fashion. Encouraged that he was moving steadily towards his long-range goals, the president scarcely worried about the letters he had sent to the Dutch and French. With Churchill seated nearby at a session with the Sultan of Morocco during the Casablanca Conference several months later, the president suddenly launched into a discussion of his sympathy with all colonial aspirations for independence, suggesting that he would like to see postwar economic cooperation between the United States and the Sultan's country.[24]

Alone with his advisers, Roosevelt openly discussed with his military leaders the transfer of Dakar, Indochina and other French possessions to some postwar international authority. He congratulated diplomat Robert Murphy on his diplomatic dealings with the Vichy French rulers of North Africa before the landings. 'But you overdid things a bit in one of the letters you wrote . . . pledging the United States', he mildly reproached Murphy, 'pledging the United States Government to guarantee the return to France of every part of her empire. Your letter may make trouble for me after the war.'[25] But perhaps not, because Vichy would not survive, and he would handle de Gaulle. France was 'in the position of a little child unable to look out and fend for itself', Roosevelt said, and 'in such a case a court would appoint a trustee to do the necessary'. Including, it would seem, concludes historian Christopher Thorne, taking away some of the child's possessions.[26]

At the next two sessions of Allied high council meetings, Cairo and Tehran, Roosevelt approached Chiang Kai-shek first, and then Stalin, trying to line them up for his trusteeship plan. Inviting Chiang to be an active member of the Big Four, Roosevelt then proposed that China and the United States should consult together before any decisions were reached on matters concerning Asia. They should, for example, reach 'a mutual understanding' on the future status of Korea, Indochina and other colonial areas.[27] At his first meeting with Stalin, at Tehran on 28

November 1943, the two immediately plunged into a discussion of postwar France. To Stalin's opening statement that the French ruling classes were corrupt and 'should not be entitled to share in any of the benefits of the peace', Roosevelt rejoined that Churchill thought the country would recover quickly. But that was not his view. 'Many years of honest labor would be necessary before France would be reestablished. He said the first necessity for the French, not only the Government but the people as well, was to become honest citizens.' By its manifest weaknesses, they agreed, France had forfeited the right to reclaim Indochina.[28]

Stalin then declared that he 'did not propose to have the Allies shed blood to restore Indochina . . . to the old French colonial rule'. It was necessary to fight Japan in the political sphere as well as the military, 'particularly in view of the fact that the Japanese had granted at least nominal independence to certain colonial areas'. Roosevelt was delighted with Stalin's understanding of the basic issues. 'He was in 100% agreement,' the president said, 'and remarked that after 100 years of French rule in Indochina, the inhabitants were worse off than they had been before.' What did the Soviet leader think about a system of trusteeship to prepare the people for independence within a definite time period, perhaps 20 to 30 years? Stalin said he 'completely agreed with that view'.[29]

Chiang sent word to Roosevelt after the Cairo Conferences that he regarded the president not only as his friend, but as an older brother, to whom he would speak frankly. Roosevelt took this to mean that Chiang's government would follow his lead, a dangerous conclusion. 'I think that Stalin, Chiang & I can bring brother Churchill around', he boasted at tea on the White House porch to friends. Later, at dinner, he rambled on about the stakes in the colonial question:

> In regard to the Far East in general, which means the yellow race, which is far more numerous than the white, it will be to the advantage of the white race to be friends with them & work in cooperation with them, rather than make enemies of them & have them eventually use all the machines of western civilization to overrun & conquer the white race.[30]

Over the summer of 1944, however, the military and political situation in China worsened. His closest adviser, Harry Hopkins, confided that the president now had much less hope for China than he had had at Cairo. The president was still interested in a trusteeship solution,

Hopkins went on, but was now absorbed in European questions. As these factors loomed more important in the immediate future, senior State Department officials called for a change of emphasis in postwar planning for Indochina. American influence, wrote Joseph Grew and James Clement Dunn, could be better directed towards securing French promises to end their commercial monopolies, and to integrate Indochina into the world market. 'These areas [of Southeast Asia] are sources of products essential to both our wartime and peacetime economy. They are potentially important markets for American exports. . . . Their economy and political stability will be an important factor in the maintenance of peace in Asia.'[31]

Cairo and Tehran proved to be the high points for dreaming dreams about what could be accomplished through Big Four cooperation. Those around the president sensed that he now had to find another way to achieve his purposes. A Big Four-imposed trusteeship was no longer on the cards. The shift came before the end of the war, therefore, and while the internal French political situation became a cause for concern, its importance was in reinforcing prior decisions. Roosevelt, after all, had not expected France to recover for a long time. At the Yalta Conference, in February 1945, Roosevelt was able to devote little time to the Indochina question. His notion that he could manage Brother Churchill by manipulating Chiang and Stalin was replaced by an almost desperate effort to secure Russian cooperation in propping up the Nationalist regime by becoming China's (uninvited, perhaps) intercessor with Stalin. In a private conversation with Stalin near the end of the conference, Roosevelt admitted that 'for some time we had been trying to keep China alive'. Stalin shrugged off the implications of this statement, and posed as a disinterested observer, wondering why the Nationalists and Communists could not form a united front against Japan. On the matter of trusteeships, Roosevelt gave a rambling account of his troubles with Churchill, who feared that a trusteeship for Indochina would lead to pressure to create one for Burma. Stalin pointed out that the British were being shortsighted. They had already lost Burma once by relying on Indochina. And then he put a point that must have triggered some ideas in FDR's mind. 'It was not his opinion', he said, 'that Britain was a sure country to protect this area.' Perhaps it would be possible to work on something that would hold France up to a standard that would 'protect this area', and would disengage the colonial powers from one another.[32]

From the beginning of the war, Roosevelt had seen Indochina as an area needing protection. His statements about the Indochinese at Yalta indicated that he had never really given much thought to them as an independent factor – nor had his advisers, for that matter. He did, as we have seen, express concern over a Far East organized by some force alien to the 'white race', and turning its weapons against the West. Speaking with Stalin, he declared that the Indochinese 'were people of small stature, like the Javanese and Burmese, and were not warlike'. France had done nothing 'to improve the natives since she had the colony'. And now de Gaulle wanted ships to transport French forces to Indochina. Where was he going to get the troops? asked Stalin. 'The President replied that de Gaulle was going to find the troops when the President could find the ships, but the President added that up to the present he had been unable to find the ships.'[33]

In the weeks after Yalta, Indochina's fate came up in various ways. An aide recorded what turned out to be his final words on the question on 15 March 1945:

> I asked the President if he had changed his ideas on French Indochina. . . . He said no. . . . The President hesitated a moment and then said – well if we can get the proper pledge from France to assume for herself the obligations of a trustee, then I would agree to France retaining these colonies with the proviso that independence was the ultimate goal.[34]

President Truman did make some attempts to secure the 'proper pledge' from France, but he mostly just wanted the problem to go away. OSS (Office of Strategic Services) agents who had been in contact with Ho Chi Minh expressed disappointment that nobody paid much attention to their reports of Ho's keen interest in an American presence in Vietnam. The United States, he told one of these agents, Frank White, was in the best position to come to Vietnam's aid, but Washington could not be counted on because it 'would find more urgent things to do'.[35] Ho was right that Truman was preoccupied. He had to worry about civil war in China, and the danger that Russia might lodge itself in Manchuria and then claim a role in the postwar occupation of Japan. The atomic bomb, which was supposed to simplify at least some of his problems, actually made matters worse by speeding up the pace of events. No one could have foreseen just how fast the war would end, with temporary arrangements for disarming the Japanese merging into French reoccupation plans – while American military personnel simply stood by and watched. The British landed first, and behind them the French, who immediately set about 'restoring order' using typically colonial methods of beatings and intimidation to demonstrate who was boss. The Japanese had already succeeded, however, in undermining the *raison d'être* of Western imperialism, that Westerners had come as both exploiters *and* protectors. Frank White remembered the scene as the war ended. 'There were mobs in the streets [of Hanoi]. . . . All the elements of a combustive explosion were there.' He went on, 'Ho was there.' 'The French coming back; there were the Chinese. Everybody was . . . acting pretty independently. . . . Those of us who were filing reports from the field . . ., it was like dropping stones down a bottomless well.'[36]

Ho Chi Minh suggested to the American OSS agents that he welcomed American involvement in his country's quest for independence, and would more than welcome capitalist investment. He wrote Truman several letters encouraging him to see the Vietnamese Revolution as fulfilment of the promises of the Atlantic Charter and the San Francisco Charter of the United Nations. None of these were ever answered.

French officials, meanwhile, made their own offers. Even if France went socialist, an official of the Colonial Ministry told a State Department official, even if the Metropole nationalized mines, utilities, and heavy industries, all this would have no bearing on freedom of enterprise in Indochina. 'It is apparently the purpose', his American listener wryly noted, 'to make Indo-China a haven for private enterprise.'[37] But Washington's attention was riveted on reconstructing Europe. Ho went to Paris and struck a deal with the authorities there that provided limited independence for his 'Republic of Vietnam', the area around Hanoi now called Tonkin. It gave him a little breathing room, but the inevitable 'incident' took place in November 1946, when French warships bombarded the port city of Haiphong. Ho and his supporters retreated into the countryside to prepare their resistance to yet another conqueror, and the Franco-Vietnamese war began soon after.

In his talks with the OSS agents in Vietnam, Ho Chi Minh had downplayed both his own Marxist convictions and his connections with Moscow. Washington's indifference to his pleas for American aid and moral support pushed him towards the Soviet Union, and that, in circular fashion, set off alarm bells in the United States. In mid-1947, Secretary of State George C. Marshall bemoaned the stalemate in Indochina. The French were displaying 'a dangerously outmoded colonial outlook and methods', but how could the United States help its European ally find a non-military solution? 'Frankly we have no solution of [the] problem to suggest', Marshall confessed. 'It is basically [a] matter for [the] two parties to work out [for] themselves.'[38]

Benign neglect was hardly an answer to the deepening crisis. French inability to resolve the crisis either on the battlefield or at the conference table had wide ramifications that began with its role in European recovery and rearmament, but extended outward to East Asia. Instability in Southeast Asia would tempt the Chinese communists – filled with revolutionary zeal after their momentous victory – to intervene. Surveying danger areas of Southeast Asia in the wake of the Chinese communist triumph, Secretary of State Dean Acheson told a Canadian diplomat that the United States felt the French had recently taken the right steps in establishing a government under the Emperor Bao Dai. In actuality everyone knew that Bao Dai was really just another makeshift solution, but Acheson had to hope for the best. 'The American Government', he informed Ambassador Hume Wrong, 'in distinction from its earlier views would be ready to recognize and help Indo-China as soon as the French had acted.'[39]

Keeping the Chinese out was only half the answer. It was critical to keep Southeast Asia open to Japanese trade and investment. The Korean War speeded European cooperation for rearmament, but set off warning signals about the danger of Japan's isolation. The recovery of this 'workshop of Asia', Dulles told the Council on Foreign Relations as the Chinese intervened in Korea, depended upon finding a way for Japan to participate in the world economy, without, on the one hand, relying on reopening trade with communist China, or, on the other, disturbing the tenuous equilibrium in Europe. That left one place for Japan to go – Southeast Asia. 'The solution lies partly in the development of the Japanese capital goods industry and in enlarging markets for such products in the underdeveloped areas of Southeast Asia.' The French, for that matter, had not really seen fit, either, to carry out their hasty promises back in 1945 to hold open the door to Indochina for foreign investment and trade.[40]

Might not a solution to the overall problem lie in recognizing Ho as another Tito? A communist who stood alone and was amenable to Western overtures? 'Whether the French like it or not,' one State Department official protested the drift towards Paris, 'independence is coming to Indochina. Why, therefore, do we tie ourselves to the tail of their battered kite?'[41] Only as a last resort, Acheson declared, would he consider a Tito solution. It was a 'theoretical possibility' to build such a 'Nationalist Communist state . . . in any area beyond [the] reach [of the] Soviet Army,' but he thought that all communists in colonial areas called themselves nationalists, and would show their true allegiances only after gaining power and ruthlessly exterminating all opposition groups.[42]

Containment of communism, clothed in a military necessity, was then a political question. It had been sold to the public, however, as a military necessity, and while one Tito demonstrated that even communists could not tolerate Stalin's heavy-fisted rule, two Titos would suggest that the idea of a world communist conspiracy needed serious reexamination. The world situation was too delicate to permit clouding the issue that way. Moreover, whatever his original intentions, Ho's orientation was now all the more towards communist systems of economic organization. It would not do to see that 'system' as the wave of the future for former colonial areas. Not only would it change economic patterns in those areas, it could cause instability in Europe, struggling already with the dollar gap, as traditional markets and dollar earnings disappeared. Vietnam – the country of those small, peace-loving people – thus threatened to disturb the world with its revolution. A former economic planner in the State Department conjured up the image of 'the patient little man in the Kremlin [who] sits rubbing his hands and waiting for the free world to collapse in a sea of economic chaos'.[43]

Truman and Acheson bequeathed a truly vexed situation to their successors. Eisenhower's Secretary of State, John Foster Dulles, talked about liberating American foreign policy from the debilitating and morally unsatisfactory tenets of containment. The American response to the Soviet challenge had been too passive, he charged, and too concerned with protecting the interests of those whose time had passed. The European colonial powers were 'old, tired, worn out, and almost willing to buy peace in order to have a few years more of rest'. The Free World 'will only be saved if it gets out of us what is lacking in the rest of the world'.[44] No more than Acheson did Dulles think the Tito solution would work; instead, there must be a revival of America's anti-colonial tradition to discover an alternative to Ho Chi-minh's deception. In a pointed address to French National Political Science Institute in May, 1952, even before he knew he would be the next Secretary of State, Dulles lectured his audience on the modern 'White Man's Burden' in Indochina:

> You are there paying a heavy cost, in lives and money. I am glad that the United States is now helping substantially. *I should personally be glad to see us do more, for you have really been left too much alone to discharge a task which is vital to us all.*[45]

Dulles sought new initiatives for 'Liberation' policies not only in Southeast Asia, but also in the Middle East and Africa. It soon became clear, indeed, that liberation did in fact mean release from the constraints of following the stand-pat policies of America's allies in what was now being called the Third World. Southeast Asia was of particular concern, however, because an actual war was being waged there between the forces of revolution (communist-style) and the forces of reaction (nineteenth-century style), or so, at least, Dulles believed. The problem facing the Eisenhower administration was compounded, again so Dulles believed, by the newly dynamic Chinese revolution, which served as an example to countries struggling to emerge from decades of European domination. The Red Army in Eastern Europe had brought revolution on its bayonets; the Chinese held aloft the writings of Mao, promising believers the country would triumph over the city.

Dulles was deeply disappointed by the Korean truce in June 1953, though he understood it was politically necessary if the administration were to clear the slate for taking new initiatives. But the prospect of a permanently divided country, as the Korean 'settlement' appeared to endorse, was hardly the image that one could use to entice former colonial peoples to align themselves with the West. Dulles's boasts about the threat of the atomic bomb to break open the stalemate in the truce talks should be seen from this perspective – as a replacement for the now-discredited boasts of the original colonial masters that they could protect their 'native' allies against outside forces and restless underclasses. The French, meanwhile, staked everything on one last roll of the dice at Dien Bien Phu. Eisenhower briefly considered using the atomic bomb to relieve the besieged French garrison in the spring of 1954, but realized that his old army companions were right: military intervention in Vietnam would mean another ground war on the continent of Asia too soon after Korea, and, despite Dulles's best diplomatic efforts, there was little support in Congress or from the Allies.

Fearing that the upcoming Geneva Conference would inevitably lead to another round of European 'appeasement', Eisenhower issued a dramatic warning at a press conference:

> You have broader considerations that might follow what you would call the 'falling domino' principle. You have a row of dominoes set up, you knock over the first one, and what will happen to the last one is the certainty that it will go over very quickly. So you could have a beginning of a disintegration that would have the most profound influences.[46]

This was without doubt Eisenhower's most famous utterance on the tangle of issues surrounding the Vietnam crisis, and later presidents would all harken back to it as American involvement deepened into tragedy, elevating it to the status of proven theory to be ignored only at great peril to the 'national security'. In fact, it was no more than an abstraction, constructed without regard to Vietnamese history. From Roosevelt to Truman, and then to Eisenhower, the Vietnam riddle was how to get the French out of the way, without 'losing' the contest for the hearts and minds of the people – and the resources of the land. Just as the French had sought to make Vietnam part of their history, so, too, the Americans. In that profoundest way, beyond limitations of the definition of 'colonialism', Bundy was wrong: we were seeking to replace the French. After Geneva ended the French war in Vietnam, with an apparent agreement that all-Vietnamese elections would be held within two years to determine the political future of the country and its reunification, American policy-makers still believed that the central issue was how to get rid of the French. At a National Security Council meeting in October 1954, President Eisenhower made that clear. 'It is true that we have to cajole the French with regard to the European area,' he said, 'but we certainly didn't have to in Indochina.'[47] With those marching orders, Eisenhower and Dulles set out to find a suitable George Washington for Southeast Asia, and to thwart the un-American revolution. Their successors discarded one after another but never stopped trying.

Notes

1 US Senate, Committee on Foreign Relations, *Hearings: Causes, Origins and Lessons of the Vietnam War*, 92nd cong., 2nd sess. (Washington, 1973), p. v.
2 Testimony of Arthur M. Schlesinger, Jr, ibid., p. 116.
3 Steven Hugh Lee, *Outposts of Empire: Korea, Vietnam, and the Origins of the Cold War in Asia* (Montreal, 1995). This outstanding monograph provides a well-argued case for an activist American policy, and a consistent one.
4 Public statement by Under-Secretary of State Sumner Welles, 2 August 1941, quoted in *The Senator Gravel Edition: the Pentagon Papers* (4 vols, Boston, 1971), I, pp. 8–9.
5 Bundy to Donald Graham, editor of the Harvard *Crimson*, 20 April 1965, *The Papers of Lyndon B. Johnson*, Lyndon Baines Johnson Library, Austin, Texas, Files of McGeorge Bundy, Boxes 18–19.
6 Draft Memorandum, 9 July 1954, reprinted in William Appleman Williams,

et al. (eds), *America in Vietnam: a Documentary History* (New York, 1985), pp. 166–8.

7   Diary entry, 27 November 1942, in Geoffrey C. Ward (ed.), *Closest Companion: the Unknown Story of the Intimate Friendship between Franklin Roosevelt and Margaret Suckley* (Boston, 1995), p. 187. Warren F. Kimball, *Forged in War: Roosevelt, Churchill and the Second World War* (New York, 1997), concludes: 'Roosevelt was convinced that the pressure of nationalism in the European empires was the most serious threat to postwar peace' (p. 301).

8   Ward, *Closest Companion*, p. 187.

9   See Editorial Note, 'Roosevelt's Conversations with Various Callers,' 24 November 1943, in Department of State, *Foreign Relations of the United States: the Conferences at Cairo and Tehran* (Washington, DC: GPO, 1961), p. 345, and 'Memorandum of Conversation, 3 January 1944, ibid., p. 864. (Hereafter: *FRUS*.)

10 Diary entry, 27 October 1942, in Beatrice Bishop Berle and Travis Beal Jacobs (eds), *Navigating the Rapids, 1918–1971: from the Papers of Adolf A. Berle* (New York: Harcourt, Brace, 1973), pp. 421–2.

11 Elliott Roosevelt, *As He Saw It* (New York, 1946), p. 116. From the time it was published, Elliott Roosevelt's account of his father's deep dislike of European imperialism, and especially FDR's supposed suspicion of British machinations to hold on to every part of every empire lest their own be threatened, has been denounced as inaccurate in detail and exaggerated in conclusions. Subsequent documentary evidence from various archives and memoirs has, however, strengthened confidence in Elliott's reportage of his father's attitudes.

12 Kimball, *Forged in War*, p. 300. See also Albert E. Kersten, 'Wilhelmina and Franklin D. Roosevelt: a Wartime Relationship', in Cornelius A. van Minnen and John F. Sears (eds), *FDR and His Contemporaries: Foreign Perceptions of an American President* (New York, 1992), pp. 85–96.

13 See Lloyd C. Gardner, *Economic Aspects of New Deal Diplomacy* (Madison, 1964), pp. 275–80, for a brief discussion of the debates at the Atlantic Charter Conference in 1941, and the debates over Article VII of the Lend-Lease Agreement which committed London to wartime negotiations over postwar trade and the removal of empire preferences. For a recent account that deals with the British predicament, see John Charmley, *Churchill's Grand Alliance* (New York, 1995), pp. 89–101.

14 Roosevelt, *As He Saw It*, p. 115.

15 Ibid., p. 275.

16 Anthony D. Biddle to Roosevelt, 27 March 1942, and Roosevelt to Queen Wilhelmina, 6 April 1942, both in *The Papers of Franklin D. Roosevelt*, Franklin D. Roosevelt Library, Hyde Park, New York, PSF, The Netherlands, 1942. The Dutch Prime Minister, Dr Gerbrandy, who conveyed this delicate request, was at the same time expressing his hope to British officials that the centre of gravity in the Pacific War would not shift to Washington from London, out of concern for the future of the East Indies. See Christopher Thorne, *Allies of a Kind: the United States, Britain, and the War against Japan, 1941–1945* (New York, 1978), p. 219.

17 Thorne, *Allies of a Kind*, p. 218.

18 See Warren F. Kimball, 'A Victorian Tory: Churchill, the Americans, and Self-

Determination', in William Roger Louis (ed.), *More Adventures with Britannia* (New York, 1998).

19 Robert Dallek, *Franklin D. Roosevelt and American Foreign Policy, 1932–1945* (New York, 1979), pp. 377–8.

20 Cordell Hull, *Memoirs* (2 vols, London, 1948), II, p. 1595.

21 Thorne, *Allies of a Kind*, p. 217.

22 Notes of Roosevelt–Molotov Meeting, 1 June 1942, in Robert E. Sherwood, *Roosevelt and Hopkins: an Intimate History* (New York, 1950), p. 573. This remarkable book, published so soon after the war, would provide the most complete history of American policy for years to come, and still bears re-reading no longer for documents once unavailable elsewhere, but for a feel of the atmosphere.

23 Ibid., 573–4.

24 See Lloyd C. Gardner, *Approaching Vietnam: from World War II through Dien-bienphu* (New York, 1988), p. 35.

25 Robert Murphy, *Diplomat among Warriors* (New York, 1964), p. 192.

26 Thorne, *Allies of a Kind*, p. 218.

27 *FRUS, Cairo and Tehran*, pp. 323–5. Elliott Roosevelt, *As He Saw It*, has his father suggesting to Chiang, however, that the French might be allowed to serve as the trustee for Indochina responsible to a United Nations organiza-tion (p. 165). This interesting piece of evidence certainly predicts where FDR came out in the final months of his life, and suggests that his mind was never at rest on how to manage the transition.

28 *FRUS, Cairo and Tehran*, pp. 484–5.

29 Ibid.

30 Diary entry, 28 June 1944, Ward, *Closest Companion*, p. 314. Sumner Welles, who issued many of the official statements on colonial questions during the war, wrote in 1951 that by the end of 1943 Roosevelt had become convinced that the United States had to work with China in years to come to prevent a cleavage between the Eastern and Western worlds, for our 'own safety's sake.' Welles, 'Roosevelt and the Far East: II', *Harper's Magazine*, vol. 202 (March, 1951): 70–80.

31 Gardner, *Approaching Vietnam*, p. 45.

32 *FRUS, The Conferences at Malta and Yalta, 1945*, pp. 770–1.

33 Ibid.

34 Quoted in Gardner, *Approaching Vietnam*, p. 46. Warren Kimball argues that FDR's conditions for French reinvolvement in Indochina 'were a trap designed to get them to dissolve their entire empire, not just in Southeast Asia'. A sole trusteeship under the United Nations would force the French to accept international accountability. 'Sole trusteeship and international trusteeship would achieve the same result, independence.' *The Juggler: Franklin Roosevelt as Wartime Statesman* (Princeton, 1991), p. 153.

35 Senate Committee on Foreign Relations, *Hearings: Causes, Origins and Lessons of the Vietnam War*, pp. 156–7. See also Archimedes L. A. Patti, *Why Vietnam? Prelude to America's Albatross* (Berkeley, 1980) for another account by a former OSS officer stationed in Vietnam.

36 Ibid., 148, 182.

37 Gardner, *Approaching Vietnam*, p. 70.

38 Robert J. McMahon, 'Truman and the Roots of U.S. Involvement in

Indochina, 1945–1953', in David L. Anderson, *Shadows on the White House: Presidents & the Vietnam War, 1945–1975* (Manhattan, 1993), pp. 27–8.

39 Williams, *et al.*, *America in Vietnam*, pp. 97–8.
40 Gardner, *Approaching Vietnam*, pp. 111–12.
41 Williams, *et al.*, *America in Vietnam*, p. 91.
42 Ibid., pp. 95–6.
43 McMahon, 'Truman and the Roots of U.S. Involvement', p. 32. And see Andrew J. Rotter, *The Path to Vietnam: Origins of the American Commitment to Southeast Asia* (Ithaca, 1987), p. 141.
44 *Executive Sessions of the Senate Foreign Relations Committee (Historical Series)*, vol. 5, 83rd Cong., 1st sess. (Washington: GPO, 1977), p. 142.
45 Gardner, *Approaching Vietnam*, p. 135. Emphasis added.
46 Ibid., p. 196.
47 David Anderson, 'Dwight D. Eisenhower and Wholehearted Support of Ngo Dinh Diem', in Anderson (ed.), *Shadow on the White House*, p. 49.

7
The Limits of Ideology: US Foreign Policy and Arab Nationalism in the Early Cold War

Scott Lucas

In recent years, some historians have begun to interpret US foreign policy in the context of an American 'ideology'. Rather than focus exclusively or primarily on geopolitics, economics or diplomatic or military strategies, these authors have interpreted US activity through a framework of 'negative' beliefs such as anti-communism and racism and, more rarely, 'positive' values, such as freedom and democracy. These approaches have been invaluable in cutting through the facade of 'national security', the catchall phrase leading to many justifications of US conduct, and the movement to glorify figures such as Dwight Eisenhower. They have extended the critiques of scholars such as William Appleman Williams and engaged with theorists ranging from Friedrich Nietzsche to Noam Chomsky. Most significantly, the application of 'ideology' has provided the first comprehensive explanation of US policy towards Eastern Europe in the early Cold War, treating 'liberation' not as a rhetorical flourish of the 1952 presidential campaign but as a policy objective dating from 1948.[1]

Yet, just as it is important to recognise the role of 'ideology' in the making and implementation of US foreign policy, so it is essential not to apply it as a general overriding concept. Espousal of a system of American values as universal values was the backdrop rather than the script for US 'internationalism' in the Cold War. The clarion-call of freedom in the Truman Doctrine and NSC-68 was not necessarily followed by a quest for dominance – cultural, political or military – in each and every region. The relentless crusade against communism may have served as a touchstone for US foreign policy, but it did not lead to a homogeneous policy of support of or opposition to 'nationalism' or, for that matter, 'colonialism'. US policymakers may have distrusted revolution

140

and neutralism but they did not necessarily oppose leaders who promoted those ideas.

In July 1954 the veteran US Ambassador to Cairo, Jefferson Caffery, had an audience with Egyptian President Gamal Abdel Nasser. The meeting occurred at a vital point in Egypt's evolving relations with Western countries; 13 days later, the outline of the Anglo-Egyptian Treaty, which would end the presence of British troops in the country after more than 70 years, would be agreed. Caffery summarised for the State Department:

> It would . . . be a grave error not to take seriously the implication that the US, to deal effectively with this area, must to a certain extent adopt the attitude of an intelligent parent faced with a 'problem child'. . . .
>
> It is clear that Nasser believes (probably correctly) that he must go slow with his own people in the matter of alignment with the West. . . .
>
> While some parts of this interview are certainly cause for dismay, it would be unwise not to recognize that the schizophrenic overtones which occasionally emerge are not only symptomatic of the state of mind of a man with whom the West has little choice but to deal with are also indicative of the state of present-day Egyptian society. It is likely that this observation would hold true for a large part of the Middle East and even the oriental world in general. Since people in such a frame of mind must be handled with great patience and tact, it would appear unwise to attempt to force any rapid and overt pro-Western alignment of Egypt's leaders, since even should they favor such a course, existing public attitudes would probably preclude it. Our diplomatic objective of strengthening the Near East against outside aggression and internal subversion must be pursuant with circumspection and finesse.[2]

In evaluating the relationship between US policy in the Middle East and Arab nationalism in the early Cold War, Caffery's report is remarkable for several reasons. There is, of course, the paternal tone of Western superiors dealing with irresponsible wards, but this is far from a request for the US to stamp out or even control nationalism. To the contrary, Caffery's identification of the political realities within Egypt and the Middle East and the consequent limits on Washington's influence point to a far different strategy of partnership or, failing that, negotiation with Arab regimes. Nationalism was not to be opposed because it led to the establishment of a communist system; rather it was to be supported as a way to prevent such an occurrence.

Caffery's commentary indicates that, at a time when an ideological impulse propelled many areas of US foreign policy, much of Washington's approach to the Middle East rested upon a pragmatic assessment of diplomatic, military and economic costs and advantages. There were cases where nationalists were seen as the advance guard of a communist take-over, the evolution of the US quest to replace the government in Syria being the most notable example, but this was the exception rather than the rule; the general approach was accommodation with local movements. The basic line was driven by the sentiment expressed in a 1953 document: '[We should] seek to guide the revolutionary and nationalist pressures throughout the area into channels not antagonistic to the West.'³

This approach was especially pertinent in the Middle East because of a feature of policymaking, overlooked by many historians, highlighted by Caffery's despatch. In the early years of the Cold War, US policy in the Middle East was often defined not by a President and close advisers but by representatives in the field, by 'working-level' officials in the State Department, such as the Assistant Secretary of State responsible for the Middle East, and by other agencies. Foremost among those agencies was the Central Intelligence Agency, which had seized the opportunity to craft a new American approach towards Arab nationalism.

When an activist (and, arguably, ideological) Secretary of State, John Foster Dulles, emerged, this bureaucracy set parameters upon policy and operations. In the public depiction of his struggles with the communists, Dulles many have blustered about the evils of neutralism and the dangers of nationalism but Middle East policy before 1957 was marked by a practical, step-by-step approach. An anti-communist bloc could only be established after the US had cooperated with existing regimes, be it the British-backed systems in Jordan and Iraq or the 'nationalist' (and, it may be claimed, anti-British) leadership in Egypt, to establish Anglo-Egyptian, Arab–Israeli, and Anglo-Saudi settlements, as well as tentative steps towards a Middle Eastern defence organization. This pragmatism could lead to a policy in which the US, covertly cooperating with the British to 'isolate' Nasser in the region, could intervene to halt London's overt attempt with France and Israel to oust the Egyptian President. Only in the special case of Syria would the Eisenhower administration follow its anti-communist rhetoric to the point of attempting a coup against a nationalist regime.

Even the Eisenhower Doctrine of 1957, with its invocation to defend

Middle Eastern countries 'from any country controlled by international Communism',[4] was limited in its universal application. For almost a year, Washington might be unified in a crusade against Moscow's 'stooges' in Cairo as well as Damascus. By the end of 1957, however, US officials by choice or default again sought limited cooperation with Nasser. They were also forcing superiors like Foster Dulles to accept the necessity of working with aspects of Arab nationalism broader than the old-guard monarchies of Iraq, Jordan and Saudi Arabia.

The first complication with positing a thesis about a clash between US policy and Arab nationalism is that, in the immediate aftermath of the Second World War, the US was not the dominant Western power, politically or economically, in the region. The Middle East was not 'vital' to American security and, with the expansion of US commitments elsewhere, Washington was not eager to take on additional responsibility. US oil interests had established themselves in Saudi Arabia but the government's interest in the stake was limited to providing for the destruction of the oil-wells if Soviets invaded the country. The special case of US involvement in Palestine was shaped more by domestic politics (or, it may be contended, humanitarian motives) than by calculation of long-term strategic advantage.

On four occasions between 1947 and 1950, US and British officials held comprehensive talks on current issues and future policy in the Middle East, and each time the Americans made clear that they would not match London's presence in the region. While the US Government established that 'the security of the Eastern Mediterranean and of the Middle East is vital to the security of the United States',[5] the US commitment of economic and military power was to ensure maintenance of the Greece–Turkey–Iran tier of 'outer ring' defence rather than involvement in Egypt and the Levant. Pressed in 1949 by Britain, increasingly eager for US support and largesse, Washington went no further than an expression of general sentiment of cooperation, which noted the obstacles to any coordination of policy:

> The objectives of the two countries in the area were identical, although there might be a difference of method in seeking to attain them. . . . The difference in methods might arise from the fact that the influence and material interests of the UK and US were not the same in each country.[6]

The US did divert some aid from the outer ring to Israel and the Arab States but, as late as March 1951, official US policy emphasized, 'because of US commitments in other areas, it is in the US interest that the United Kingdom have primary military responsibility for Israel and the Arab States'.[7] The political and diplomatic position would continue to be underpinned by Britain's treaty relations with Jordan, Iraq and Egypt.

Even the first public sign of US commitment to the region, the Tri-partite Declaration of May 1950 with Britain and France, was significant as much for what it was not as for what it was. The pledge to obtain 'non-aggressive declarations from the Middle East countries' and to oppose any violation of *de facto* frontiers by 'aggressive action'[8] was pri-marily to check a potential arms race between Israel and the Arab coun-tries, and secondarily, to curb tensions between Arab countries, notably the Saudi rivalry with the Hashemite monarchies of Iraq and Jordan, and tacitly to confirm the *de facto* break-up of Palestine into territory held by Israel and Jordan. Apart from its general affirmation of regional order, it was not designed to prevent Soviet incursion into the Middle East or to challenge 'nationalist' forces in the region.

Indeed, the US was considering how to establish an accommodation with nationalism. In the 1949 talks with the British, George McGhee, Assistant Secretary of State for the Near East, stressed:

> The United States Government had found it advantageous to back nationalism against communism. But nationalism was not neces-sarily friendly to British and American interests. We should aim at putting the Middle East countries on their own feet and persuading them voluntarily to turn toward the West.[9]

The foundations for this involvement were established not by the higher echelons of the Executive but from working-level officials. The CIA's Kermit Roosevelt had written publicly in 1949, 'The poor grow poorer and the rich grow richer and everyone grows nervous.' Within a five-week period in summer 1950, the US Embassy in Cairo, led by the new ambassador, Jefferson Caffery, issued 12 reports on the deteri-orating situation.[10] In the State Department, McGhee seized the initia-tive by defining a US role as a catalyst to pull Britain and 'new' Middle Eastern regimes together. McGhee's campaign caused friction not with the Arab states but with the British, angered over the Assistant Secre-tary's intervention in Anglo-Egyptian conflict over a revised treaty as well as the British dispute with Iran over the nationalization of the Anglo-Iranian Oil Company.

Even more significant was the role of operatives in the CIA and the Office of Policy Coordination, the organization for covert action. Apparently with little input from the White House, State Department, or the military, these officials in 1949 used Syria, only recently independent from French control, as a test-case for intervention. The outcome was a military coup led by General Husni Za'im. The experiment failed when Za'im lasted less than five months before he was toppled, but the CIA saw great potential in supporting young military officers in other countries against antiquated political and economic systems.

Such initiatives took on added significance when, after the outbreak of the Korean War and the passage of the global strategy of NSC 68, the US was increasingly drawn into the Middle East. The State and Defense Departments now linked security in the Greek–Turkish–Iranian tier to stability in the region: 'It has been our view that, while Greece and Turkey have been considerably strengthened during the past two years, this increase in strength can be jeopardized by the patent weakness of the Arab States and, to a lesser extent, Iran and Israel.'[11] To combat 'political deterioration' and prop up Britain's military leadership, Washington would 'assist [the British] in strengthening their capabilities'.[12] This policy culminated in an agreement to join Britain in proposals for a Middle Eastern Command, which would sustain a Western presence in the Suez Canal Base, in exchange for British support for Turkish and Greek entry into NATO.[13]

Yet this cooperation with Britain was to be tied to a new relationship with emerging leadership in Arab countries, ensuring 'the coordination of American, British, and indigenous efforts of a concept of the defense of the Middle East as a whole'.[14] A conference of US ambassadors endorsed the approaches of McGhee and the CIA by recommending that 'US representatives in the Middle East, using all agencies at their disposal, give appropriate encouragement to liberal and moderate elements with a view to broadening the base of consent of the governed and produce desired reforms, suited to the culture of the particular country, which will contribute to well-being and stability in the long run'.[15]

Working-level officials recognized that, to achieve this goal, the US might have to develop links with opposition groups in countries where Britain was supporting the 'old guard'. Caffery led the call, warning, 'If the British maintain their stand . . . we must resign ourselves to the fact that the Canal Zone may, unless something unforeseen turns up, explode with a loud bang at no distant date, an explosion with a potential chain reaction of occupation, revolution, eventual Commie domination.'[16] The CIA pursued the new strategy through covert support of a new Egyptian leadership, eagerly arranging places on training courses and, in one case, specialist medical treatment in the US for young Egyptian military officers. By late 1951, the CIA's officials were conferring regularly with intermediaries for the 'Free Officers', including Nasser, as they discussed plans for the overthrow of King Farouk.[17] In Washington an interdepartmental committee chaired by Kermit Roosevelt considered how to 'encourage the emergence of competent leaders, relatively well-disposed toward the West, through programs designed for this purpose, including, where possible, a conscious, though perhaps covert, effort to cultivate and aid such potential leaders, even when they are not in power'.[18] Egypt was identified as the top priority.

The strategy was given further impetus when riots in Cairo in January 1952, burning foreign-owned property and killing several foreign nationals, raised the prospect of civil war and British reprisals. Caffery assessed, 'Time in Egypt is running out. This is not one that the Brit[ish] can win by stalling. Reoccupation, revolt, revolution may sound like over-emphasis but they are all visible on the cards in Egypt today.'[19] Kermit Roosevelt travelled to Cairo 'to straighten [the Egyptians] out'. His conclusion that King Farouk could not or would not deal with Egypt's problems and that no civilian government could function effectively reinforced the CIA's cooperation with the military dissidents.[20]

Thus the US not only had advance knowledge of the coup in July but also actively encouraged the action. Significantly Ali Sabri, a member of the new government's Revolutionary Command Council, visited US Assistant Air Attaché David Evans as the coup was occurring.[21] The Political Officer, William Lakeland, assured the State Department 'that he knew of the revolutionary elements and [denied] any relation between them and the communist organizations in Egypt'.[22] In contrast, the British were caught by surprise, Foreign Secretary Anthony Eden admitting, 'The coup happened so quickly that no one was aware as late as the morning before.'[23]

The US immediately tried to entrench itself as an ally of the new Egyptian government and a mediator between London and Cairo. Washington hailed the Revolutionary Command Council as the representative of political, social and economic progress and openly supported measures such as land reform. Most significantly, the Truman administration did not ally with Britain against Egypt in the continuing dispute over the Suez Canal Zone Base and the status of the Sudan. Both sides were pressed to come to the conference table, and Washington resisted British entreaties for sanctions against Cairo. For its part, the RCC [Revolutionary Command Council] hinted that it might be able to join the Middle Eastern Command.[24]

With this foundation in the field, continuity in relations had been established which would transcend the change from Democratic to Republican administration in 1953. The Eisenhower government, with all its anti-communist vigour, did not turn against 'nationalism'. Indeed, in its quest for advantage over Moscow in areas like the Middle East, its rhetoric was targeted more at British 'colonialism'.[25] Privately, Eisenhower maintained a steady if futile correspondence urging Prime Minister Winston Churchill to promote self-determination and eventual independence of British possessions, concluding:

> Should we try to dam [nationalism] up completely, it would, like a mighty river, burst through the barriers and could create havoc. But again, like a river, if we are intelligent enough to make constructive use of this force, then the result, far from being disastrous, could redound greatly to our advantage, particularly in our support against the Kremlin's power.[26]

Publicly, Foster Dulles announced on television that peoples in the Near East and South Asia were 'suspicious of the colonial powers. The US, too, is suspect because, it is reasoned, our NATO alliance with France and Britain requires us to try to preserve or restore the old colonial interests of our allies. . . . The day is past when [nationalist] aspirations can be ignored.'[27]

The view through this prism partly shaped the administration's conception of Arab nationalism. With no history of British occupation or influence for the US to 'correct', Washington would never cooperate with the Syrian government against the threat of colonialism. In contrast the Saudi regime, despite being an 'old guard' monarchy, was treated with sympathy by the Eisenhower administration not only because of its oil and its hosting of US airbases but also because of its long-running dispute with Britain over possession of the Buraimi Oasis.

A notable exception to this mindset was Iran, where the administration's fear of a communist take-over of power led it to join the British in the overthrow of the Mossadegh government in Iran, overturning previous US vetoes of covert action. Regarding Egypt, however, Eisenhower and his advisers were even more concerned than Truman's officials at avoiding any appearance of 'ganging up' with the British. In March 1953 the administration rejected a joint presentation with

British representatives of proposals to the Revolutionary Command Council. Two months later, after Secretary of State Foster Dulles' tour of the Middle East, it abandoned the Middle East Command. Foster Dulles told the National Security Council:

British position rapidly deteriorating, probably to the point of non-repair. Generally in the area . . . we find an intense distrust and dislike for the British. The days when the Middle East used to relax under the presence of British protection are gone. Such British troops as are left in the area are more a factor of instability rather than stability.[28]

In its attempt to get a revised Anglo-Egyptian Treaty, the State Department went so far as to draft a compromise agreement on the Suez Canal Base for the Egyptians to table as their own initiative.[29] The mediation culminated in farce when the legendary Robert 'One-Eye' McClintock, then the number-two official in the US Embassy in Cairo, was trailed by British intelligence services when he left a 'top secret' conference with British counterparts and went straight to Egyptian contacts. The State Department immediately removed McClintock from Egypt, although it resisted British demands to recall Caffery.[30] The Eisenhower administration also avoided an open break with London when, after furious lobbying by Prime Minister Winston Churchill and Foreign Secretary Anthony Eden, it did not complete offers of economic and military aid to Egypt.[31]

Behind this US balancing of British and Egyptian claims was the elaborate network of covert links with the Revolutionary Command Council. The initial contacts with US military attachés had been expanded as CIA operatives and Embassy officials like the Political Secretary, William Lakeland, conveniently a neighbour of Nasser, liaised with the Egyptian President through channels like the journalist Mohammed Heikal and General Hassan Touhami, another Council member.[32] A CIA official visiting Cairo in March 1954 wrote of the arrangements to Assistant Secretary of State Henry Byroade, 'We have an entree to [Nasser's] gang – Lakeland. It is useful while it lasts and we should preserve it, reinforce it if possible, but it is not the stuff out of which modern international relations are made. There is something 19th or even 18th century about this kind of a diplomatic contact.'[33] The contacts, however, were expanded as the CIA went to extraordinary lengths to further the relationship. Learning that Touhami had a special affinity for lions, the Agency, at great difficulty and expense, smuggled a cub into Egypt aboard a military transport.[34]

The US mediation culminated in success with the completion of the Anglo-Egyptian Treaty of 1954, in which Britain withdrew all military personnel from the Canal Zone Base but western powers were granted the right to re-enter in the event of war, but the covert relationship with the Egyptians was far from over. Instead, Washington tried to convert privileged contacts into a privileged political and military position. To convince Nasser to accept US military advisers as well as military aid, the CIA offered a $3 million bribe.[35]

Outside Egypt, the US deferred to Britain's political lead in countries like Iraq and Jordan, where London maintained its historic links with 'old' regimes, but Washington was now ready to take unilateral action for the sake of Middle Eastern defence. Aid to Turkey and Pakistan and the Turkish–Pakistani defence agreement were now linked to grants to Iraq, although Britain did insist upon a Memorandum of Understanding regulating the provision of US arms.[36] In Saudi Arabia the US protected its special relationship with the regime, and in Syria Washington continued its attempts to cultivate a favoured position with the 'independent' government of Adib Shishakli, the State Department assessing, 'While Shishakli is not pro-Western in a full sense, he has been fairly cooperative with the US, at least more so than his predecessor. There is no successor in sight who would be more inclined toward the US; in fact his disappearance could well herald a very anti-Western regime.'[37]

At the end of 1954, US policy in the Middle East entered a new phase. The revision of the Anglo-Egyptian Treaty had removed one obstacle to Western cooperation with Arab states in a regional defence system. Now the US had to remove the barrier of Arab–Israeli conflict. Far from sacrificing cooperation with states like Egypt on the altar of partiality towards Israel, Eisenhower and his officials emphasized:

> We were in the present jam [in the Middle East] because the past Administration had always dealt with the area from a political standpoint and had tried to meet the wishes of the Zionists in this country and that had created a basic antagonism with the Arabs. . . . It was of the utmost importance for the welfare of the US that we should get away from a political basis and try to develop a national nonpartisan policy.[38]

The administration put great stock in its refusal to send large-scale military aid to Israel and symbolic efforts such as the threat to suspend economic aid to Tel Aviv when Israel attempted to divert water, claimed by Syria, from the Jordan River.[39]

The search for 'a settlement of the irritating Israeli–Arab problem' had been launched in autumn 1953 with the despatch of a presidential emissary, Eric Johnston, to negotiate a division of the Jordan waters.[40] In December 1954 the US broadened the effort and agreed to collaborate with Britain in Project ALPHA, a top-secret effort at shuttle diplomacy. Plans, some mundane, some bizarre, for Israeli territorial concessions to link Egypt and Jordan, for resettlement of Palestinian refugees, and for a peace treaty would be mooted first to Cairo than to the Israeli government. The US would underpin an agreement with up to $200 million in economic aid.[41]

In retrospect, it seems fanciful that Nasser and Israeli Prime Minister David Ben-Gurion could have ever agreed terms but the Eisenhower administration would not admit defeat until the mission of a special envoy, Robert Anderson, to Cairo and Tel Aviv ended in misunderstanding and intransigence in March 1956. Until then the US, while balking at large-scale aid to Cairo, would go to great lengths to maintain relations with the Egyptian regime. For example, the US would not join the Baghdad Pact, agreed between Britain, Turkey and Iraq in April 1955, primarily because of the difficulty of accession in advance of an Arab–Israeli settlement but also because of Egyptian rivalry with Baghdad.

ALPHA's existence also shatters the notion that the Egyptian arms deal with the Soviet bloc, announced in September 1955, represented a break between the US and Egypt. To the contrary, the covert links established before the 1952 Revolution were never stronger, with CIA Director Allen Dulles instructing the Cairo station, 'Nasser remains our best hope and we believe State Department will within limits of overall policy cooperate to mitigate long-term effects of arms deal if Nasser in turn cooperates.'[42] Accordingly two CIA operatives, Kermit Roosevelt and Miles Copeland, helped Nasser draft the speech revealing the supply of arms from 'Czechoslovakia'. The State Department, as well as its British counterpart, briefly considered the removal of Nasser but restrained by the CIA, decided there was no better alternative. The Agency reassured, '[Nasser] is today no more anxious to come under Soviet domination than to join a Western alliance and is still convinced he can hold a middle path', and concluded, 'Western negotiations with Nasser would be long, difficult, and uncertain. If, however, the chosen alternative to this is an effort to isolate Egypt and destroy Nasser, this presents grave danger, as it would probably tempt Israel to attack Egypt.'[43]

Instead, Britain and the US proceeded with the offer of aid for construction of the High Aswan Dam, which was to be the centrepiece of

Egypt's economic development. Foster Dulles reasoned that 'the presence of so many engineers, technicians, and other people from the Free World in Egypt would constitute a strong influence in keeping Egypt on the side of the Free World'. More important, however, was his linkage of the offer to the success of ALPHA: 'Implicit in this proposed program of assistance would be the fact that the Egyptians were going to reach some genuine understanding with Israel.'[44]

Only when the fortunes of ALPHA waned over the following months did the US begin to move away from cooperation with Egypt. During a high-level summit with the British in Washington in January 1956, Foster Dulles complained, 'Nasser talked intelligently and made a fine impression. However, he made violent anti-Israeli statements on the one hand, while on the other saying privately that a settlement is possible', and exclaimed, 'Nasser might have become a tool of the Russians.' The Secretary of State's blunt assertions were due not to long-term reflection but to the news that the first talks between Robert Anderson, the President's envoy, and Nasser had not produced any results.[45]

Two months later, Anderson finally admitted defeat. His failure was due to the inability or unwillingness of Israel as well as Egypt to shift its position, particularly on the issue of territory. In a US election year, however, it was impossible to attribute blame for failure to Israel given the significance of the Jewish vote in both Presidential and Congressional contests. Instead the administration chose to press Nasser.[46] ALPHA was succeeded by Project OMEGA, a comprehensive initiative which included a cut-off of aid to Egypt and a corresponding increase in economic and military support to 'friendly' governments, propaganda to 'isolate' Nasser as a menace to his neighbours as well as to the West, and intervention in export markets to sabotage the price for Egyptian cotton.[47]

Not only Washington's policy on Egypt but also its entire approach to the Arab world had been altered by the inability to advance towards a peace settlement. In December 1955 the US had been angered by Britain's botched attempt to bring Jordan into the Baghdad Pact; in OMEGA the administration pledged support for the British position in Jordan and agreed to increase aid to Pact members and to join the organization's Military and Counter-Subversion Committees. Encouraging France and Canada to send jet-fighters to Tel Aviv discreetly circumvented the ban on export of 'major military items' to Israel.[48]

The effect reinforced the development of US policies towards Saudi Arabia, to be built up as the leader of a favourable Arab bloc, and Syria. In the case of the Saudis, the Americans not only resisted British calls for punitive action but also insisted upon London's compromise on the issue of the Buraimi oasis.[49] With Damascus, however, Washington saw no need for conciliation. In 1955, the combination of Syria as a 'test case' for US intervention, the fall of General Shishakli, and the fear of a communist take-over of power had led the State Department and CIA to renew covert attempts, including bribery and agents within Syrian political parties, to change the government.[50] Foster Dulles had complained at the Anglo-American summit that Syria was 'behaving much like a Soviet satellite'. However, his deputy had warned, 'Any of the suggestions thus far made by the Iraqis and Turks would put Nasser "off on a tangent" and would make it most difficult to deal with him on other problems, including an Israeli settlement.'[51] With the prospect of a settlement receding, an accelerated programme was incorporated in OMEGA, with the 'study [of] Syrian assets' for a possible coup.[52]

Yet OMEGA was far from a final confrontation with Nasser and Arab nationalism. The document emphasized, 'We would want for the time being to avoid any open break which would throw Nasser irrevocably into a Soviet satellite status and we would want to leave Nasser a bridge back to good relations with the West if he so desires.'[53] US officials repeatedly deflected calls from Britain for more drastic action, including the madcap proposals of British intelligence services for the overthrow of governments in Syria and Saudi Arabia as well as Egypt (with assistance from 'allies' like Turkey, Iraq and the 'snipcocks' in Israel) and the temperamental calls of Prime Minister Anthony Eden for Nasser's assassination.[54] Egypt's recognition of Communist China did not fundamentally change matters since even Foster Dulles acknowledged that Israel and other 'friendly countries' had established relations with Peking and said, 'We don't act on basis of any one single fact.'[55] Even the US decision to withdraw the offer of funding for the High Aswan Dam, the catalyst for Egypt's nationalization of the Suez Canal Company, owed as much to pressure from Congress as it did to the implementation of OMEGA.[56]

The US placed similar limits on its opposition to Nasser during the Suez Crisis. The immediate sentiment to 'move strongly in the Middle East' was soon replaced by the conclusion that 'the question of eventual military intervention does not seem to arise'.[57] In discussions with the British, US officials consistently returned to the strategy of a long-term combination of economic, diplomatic, and covert measures to weaken Nasser's position if the Egyptian leader would not cooperate with the West. For example, Foster Dulles told the British Chancellor of the Exchequer, Harold Macmillan, in late September, 'The US Govern-

ment was prepared to do everything it could to bring Nasser down, but
... the most effective way of doing so was to let the present situation
in the Canal continue and use other means of pressure which would
shortly be discussed between us.'[58]

Supporting the efforts for a peaceful resolution of the crisis, US officials maintained a covert liaison with Nasser and his advisers.[59] CIA
operatives informed the Egyptians of the extent of British plans for
Nasser's assassination and discussed a possible settlement with Ali Sabri
of the Revolutionary Command Council.[60] Robert Anderson undertook
a secret mission to Saudi Arabia, who acted as a surrogate negotiator for
the Egyptians; Eisenhower and Foster Dulles considered sending him
directly to Nasser.[61]

The US might have accepted the *fait accompli* of an Anglo-French occupation of the Suez Canal Zone and the toppling of Nasser if events had
occurred quickly. When they did not, the administration protected its
position by forcing a British cease-fire through diplomatic and economic
measures. Within days, the US Ambassador to Egypt, Raymond Hare, was
holding protracted talks with Nasser about the future of US–Egyptian
cooperation. Initially the Egyptian leader was urged to 'give thought to
developments in Hungary and note that what is happening there might
well be indicative of fate for those in Egypt who accept assistance from
[the] Soviet Union.' Once Nasser assured Hare, 'Egypt has had a long
struggle to get rid of foreign domination, and did not intend to repeat
that experience',[62] Eisenhower and Foster Dulles passed on their 'satisfaction that [Nasser] has spoken so fully and, we like to believe, so
frankly' about the future of the US–Egyptian relationship.[63]

In one sense the Eisenhower Doctrine, in which the President asked for
Congressional authority to cooperate with Middle Eastern countries 'in
the development of economic strength dedicated to the maintenance
of national independence' and to provide military aid including the
intervention of US forces 'against armed aggression from any nation
controlled by international Communism',[64] was a considered rejection
of rapprochement with Egypt. Despite the US intervention on behalf of
Egypt during the Suez War and the subsequent Nasser–Hare discussions,
the State Department assessed that

> Egyptian and Syrian military and economic dependence on the bloc
> [had been] increased. By support of the Arab nations and particularly

Egypt and Syria . . . the Soviet Union appeared as the defender of the sovereignty of small countries and of Arab nationalism against the threats of Western 'imperialism.'[65]

The Department recommended that the US foster an Iraq–Jordanian–Saudi bloc and 'utilize all appropriate opportunities to [CLASSIFIED] reduce Nasser's prestige and influence'.[66]

Eisenhower's inner circle rejected the possibility of accession to the Baghdad Pact, favoured by the military, because the US would be associated with the tainted British in the organization. A more intriguing proposal for US sponsorship of a new Afro-Asian grouping, presumably including Egypt, under the UN Charter to replace the Baghdad Pact was not viable because it was too significant a break with Britain and the Northern Tier system. That left the US with the option of a unilateral step to re-confirm and, given the perceived collapse of the British position in Egypt and the Levant, extend its interest in the Middle East.[67]

The immediate impact of the Doctrine went beyond regional strategy, however. Up to 1957 US policy, while inevitably part of a framework whose ultimate goal was containment of or victory over 'Soviet Communism', had been driven more by immediate objectives such as Northern Tier defence, resolution of the Arab–Israeli problem, and (arguably) economic and social reform. Much as the Truman Doctrine had done by expanding the issue of aid to Greece and Turkey into a global proclamation of US resistance to the communist advance, the Eisenhower Doctrine rhetorically shifted priorities by establishing that all policies had to be measured, first and foremost, by their contribution to the maintenance of an anti-communist system.

The ideological impact was most marked in the case of the Secretary of State. Dulles had always had a propensity to turn his public statements into clarion-calls against the menace of Moscow, notably through his 'neutralism is immoral' statement of June 1956; however, except in the case of Syria, he had not linked that anti-communism to a sustained attempt to topple a nationalist regime. After the issuance of the Doctrine, Dulles was far more likely to make an immediate reaction, which conflated the issues of communism and nationalism. For example, his initial response after the formation of the United Arab Republic of Egypt and Syria was 'that there was a strong possibility it was supported by the Russians and that if it materialized it would create a great danger that Jordan and Lebanon would be absorbed, putting Iraq and Saudi Arabia in peril'.[68] The Lebanese political crisis of 1958 led to a basic theory of linkage: 'Our failure to respond [to a "request" for US intervention] would destroy the confidence in us of all the countries on the Soviet periphery throughout the Middle and Far East.'[69]

Thus the rhetoric of the Doctrine polarized US policy into confrontation with 'bad' regimes and support of 'good' ones. Assessments that 'the increase of USSR, Syrian, or Egyptian influence in Jordan challenges United States interests in the Near East and should be prevented'[70] became fundamental assumptions. OMEGA was revised to sustain economic and diplomatic pressure on Egypt, and the possibility of a post-Suez rapprochement with Nasser was set aside while efforts to topple the Syrian government were renewed.[71] Far from succeeding, covert action would cause a crisis when the Syrians expelled American diplomats and moved closer to Moscow through economic and technical agreements. The US then pursued even more drastic steps, including Turkish and Iraqi intervention.[72]

Conversely, the Doctrine turned the President's fanciful notion of King Saud as the leader of the Arab world into a short-lived US policy. Eisenhower had written in March 1956, 'Our efforts should be directed toward separating the Saudi Arabians from the Egyptians',[73] but little was done until the following January when Saud was invited to Washington to be informed by Foster Dulles that, with British and French colonialism 'largely eliminated', 'the greatest danger at present was from international Communism, which started with a conspiracy of a small number of people who were able to take over all Russia and since then have seized control over approximately one-third of the peoples of the world'.[74] Even though Saud did not make a significant impression and was easily eclipsed by Nasser in episodes like the Syrian crisis, Eisenhower and Dulles persisted with the concept until he was effectively ousted from power in March 1958.

Yet, for all this activity, the Doctrine would not prove a turning-point in US policy in the Middle East. Even at the height of the US campaign in 1957, Washington recognized the limits on an ideological crusade. To potential Arab allies, the US stressed economic benefits rather than the struggle against communism.[75] During the April crisis in Jordan, US officials told British counterparts that the Doctrine might not be applicable since 'the trouble here was that the Jordan situation, despite its international overtones, was essentially an internal problem'.[76] Four months later, Foster Dulles warned for practical reasons that Eisenhower should 'avoid any statement or implication that you have as yet determined that Syria is now "controlled by International Communism" within the meaning of the Middle East Resolution'.[77]

The Doctrine would not mark a US–Israeli alliance against Arab countries, with Washington pressing Tel Aviv to give up territory seized during the Suez War and warning the Israelis against intervention in Jordan.[78] Nor did it lead to joint Anglo-American action. The US would take the token step of setting up Working Groups with the British as part of the Eisenhower–Macmillan reconciliation, but they had no significant impact.[79] Instead, the US pointedly acted unilaterally in 'crisis' situations, moving on its own to support King Hussein of Jordan in April 1957 and to send forces into Lebanon in July 1958 while refusing Anglo-American operations elsewhere.[80] Even the formation of a special Syrian Working Group in September 1957, given great emphasis in one recent study,[81] was a shadow of previous Anglo-American consultation. It was established only after months of unilateral US efforts had collapsed, and it never approached the level of cooperation in 1956.[82]

Most strikingly, there was no final break with Nasser despite Foster Dulles' periodic fits that 'Nasser must go.'[83] Significantly contacts with the Egyptian leader, both directly and indirectly through channels like Mohammed Heikal, Mustafa Amin, and Ali Sabri, were never suspended.[84] Nasser and Ambassador Hare met about once a month for conversations lasting several hours, with the President reiterating that 'he wanted to make [the Egyptian people] alive to nationalism and Arabism in order to combat communism'.[85]

Washington continually cautioned the British, driven by their hatred of the Egyptian leader, against confrontation and advised short-term conciliation on issues such as the future of the Suez Canal.[86] Some officials tried to check the attempt to topple the Syrian regime since the 'situation [was not] necessarily wholly irremediable over long run' and others reconsidered the position on Nasser.[87] A long conversation in September between the Egyptian leader and Hare and the subsequent collapse of the US efforts to stimulate an invasion of Syria[88] led Eisenhower to tell foreign leaders of his 'feeling [that] Nasser might be seeking to disentangle himself from Russians'.[89] When Foster Dulles mentioned 'the possibility – Egypt', his staff seized the opportunity to advise 'that we take appropriate opportunities to indicate our open-mindedness about improved relations with Egypt and our desire to continue relations at this stage'.[90]

The move to reconciliation led to a measure of US–Egyptian collaboration in crisis situations. In December 1957, for example, Nasser used an intermediary to ask the US to give him three months to check communist advances in Syria; the Assistant Secretary of State for the Near East, William Rountree, gave a cautious welcome.[91] After his initial outburst against the formation of the United Arab Republic, Foster Dulles was pulled into line by his officials, leaving the British to fume, 'The idea that it may be possible to get Nasser to play a game of "live and let live" has gained some currency.'[92]

By January 1958 the US was returning to acceptance of nationalist regimes that rebuffed alliance with Washington. NSC 5801 established the guideline, 'When pro-Western orientation is unattainable, accept neutralist policies of states in the area even though such states maintain diplomatic, trade and cultural relations with the Soviet bloc (including the receipt of military equipment) so long as these relations are reasonably balanced by relations with the West.' The NSC restated the wish to 'counterbalance Egypt's preponderant position of leadership in the Arab world by helping increase the political prestige and economic strength of other more moderate Arab states such as Iraq, the Sudan, Saudi Arabia, and Lebanon' but added that it would 'seek to determine whether Nasser's neutralist policy and his desire to remain free of great power domination provides the basis for understanding and cooperation'.[93]

So Foster Dulles' outburst that the United Arab Republic (UAR) of Egypt and Syria was Soviet-dominated was quickly checked by Allen Dulles' caution that 'the intelligence community does not believe that the USSR was behind the move toward union. . . . The evidence that we have indicates opposition to the union by Syrian Communists.'[94] Assessments that 'control of the Near East by radical nationalism of the Nasser brand would be inimical to United States interests' gave way, after talks on the nature of the UAR, to the judgement that Nasser would 'seek to stay neutral and to maintain at least tolerable relations with the West'.[95] A four-phase programme to improve US–UAR relations was authorized in April 1958.[96]

The transition in US policy was reinforced by the disappearance of alternatives, notably the eclipse of King Saud through bungled Saudi plots in Syria and the emergence of Prince Feisal as the dominant force in Saudi politics.[97] Thus in May 1958, the US asked Nasser to help broker a solution of the Lebanese crisis; the Egyptian President's plan became the blueprint for the eventual outcome.[98] Dulles chided his subordinates for 'working a little bit at cross-purposes' with him, as they again checked Dulles in his anti-Nasser outbursts.[99] The Secretary of State's various depictions of Nasser, before and after the Iraqi Revolution of July, as a Soviet puppet or a parallel of Hitler[100] were offset not only within the Department but also by other representatives on the National Security Council's Planning Board who argued 'in some cases it might be in our interest to promote policies which would coincide with

Nasser's immediate aims'.[101] The result was a NSC invocation in November, overruling Foster Dulles, that the US 'seek to normalize our relations with the United Arab Republic'.[102]

The ideological impulse of the Eisenhower Doctrine had not led to a break with Arab nationalism. Instead, it resurrected the prospect of cooperation with Egypt as a bulwark against communism, especially as fears grew of a communist-dominated Iraq in late 1958.[103] Foster Dulles not only withdrew his objections to discussions with Nasser but warned of 'an organized campaign from Israel in this country whose object was to check any rapprochement between Nasser and the U.S.' as Under-Secretary of State Christian Herter blocked British attempts 'to get Nasser to "lay off" Iraq'.[104] After protracted debate in April–May 1959, the NSC accepted the State Department recommendation of giving discreet support to Egypt in its anti-communist activities.[105] Economic aid was restored including support for a World Bank loan for development of the Suez Canal.[106]

I do not wish to vindicate the US approach to Arab nationalism. Official analyses often showed a woeful ignorance of the conception, both among leaders and among the 'masses'.[107] Public pronouncements, projecting an America dedicated to leading foreigners towards freedom, led to farce. When Eisenhower in a press conference in June 1956 suggested that the US would have to accept other countries' pursuit of non-alignment, the White House quickly clarified the notion of 'positive neutrality': 'The President does believe that there are special conditions which justify political neutrality but that no nation has the right to be indifferent to the fate of another or, as he put it, to be "neutral as between right and wrong or decency and indecency".'[108]

Significant opportunities to advance US cooperation with Arab nationalism were missed. The decision to abandon ALPHA and launch OMEGA against Nasser, dictated by the timing of the 1956 campaign rather than an Egyptian turn towards Moscow, was counter-productive. Even more misguided was the failure to capitalize after Suez on the wave of support for the US for its stand against the Anglo-Franco-Israeli invasion of Egypt.[109] Reducing 'Arab unity' to backing of an Iraqi–Jordanian–Saudi bloc against Egypt led to disastrous intervention in Syria and, on at least one occasion, the suggestion that Nasser should be 'liquidated'.[110]

My sympathy is with the trenchant critique offered to US officials by Syrian Foreign Minister Salah al-Din Bitar in June 1957:

Although the USG had stressed safeguarding the independence of Middle Eastern nations, it was evident that the USG does not comprehend the Arab desire for an 'independent' unity. The United States ... equates Arab nationalism with communism; it characterizes everything as either pro-Communist or pro-West, failing to recognize that there is a 'third way'.[111]

Yet, however misguided US policies in the Middle East might have been, it would be a meaningless caricature to characterize them as the inevitable and unchanging product of an equation of 'radical nationalism' with the Communist threat. If in 1957–58 Foster Dulles was rambling about 'Arab nationalism as a flood' which had to be contained by 'sand bags' around positions we must 'protect',[112] it was Eisenhower's 1953 warning of the futility of trying to dam up nationalism that would prevail. The National Security Council had to accept that 'Nasser had caught the imagination of the masses throughout the entire area' and that the US must 'be more skilful in identifying the interest of Arab nationalism with the free countries of the world and the western point of view'.[113] By August 1958, less than a month after the Iraqi revolution and the US intervention in the Lebanon, the NSC Planning Board was arguing that 'The ultimate Arab nationalist objective of some form of union which would really serve to strengthen the area is believed to be contrary to longer-term Soviet policy.' Thus the US should 'encourage Arab nationalism's resistance to the expansion of Soviet influence in the area, and to that end seek understanding with Nasser and other radical pan-Arab leaders in areas of mutual interest'.[114]

Without falling back on tired explanations like 'national security', we can recognize that in this case the ideological impulse was limited when policy was translated into practice. Beyond the differences of perspective between officials in Washington and officials in the field, even between officials in the State Department and officials in the CIA, there were immediate considerations such as opposition to obsolescent British-led political and economic arrangements or the sustained US effort for an Arab–Israeli settlement. Up to 1956, these led to some form of cooperation with Nasser. Conversely, the administration's decision to suspend ALPHA in March 1956 and, after Suez, the failure to renew the peace initiative – Foster Dulles argued, 'It did not make sense to think that he could solve problems which Moses and Joshua with Divine guidance could not solve'[115] – made it easier to challenge the Egyptian position.

Similarly the post-1956 policy of confrontation with 'radical nationalism' would eventually be modified not because of any change in US ideology but because of evolving regional conditions. The plans to topple the Syrian government in 1957 were undone not by Washington's enemies but by its allies, with Saudi Arabia and Iraq especially reluctant to play their roles.[116] The Iraqi Revolution of 1958, far from fuelling the campaign against Nasser, would link the US and Egypt in attempts to undermine the Kassem government.

In the end, US policy towards the Middle East was foolish, far too foolish to be redeemed by the national security school or the rose-coloured spectacle of 'Eisenhower revisionism'. However, there is no need to succumb to a homogeneous explanation of this foolishness. The tragedy lay not just in a blind anti-Communism, pursuit of an overriding economic or military interest, or a Machiavellian calculation of power politics; the real tragedy is that all were involved behind the hypocritical veneer of America's global mission. As Eisenhower wrote a friend in 1956, without any apparent trace of irony:

> In the effort to promote the rights of all, and observe the equality of sovereignty as between the great and the small, we unavoidably give to the little nations opportunities to embarrass us greatly. Faithfulness to the underlying concepts of freedom is frequently costly. Yet there can be no doubt that in the long run such faithfulness will produce real rewards.[117]

Notes

1 See, for example, Michael Hunt, *Ideology and U.S. Foreign Policy* (New Haven, 1987); Anders Stephanson, *Kennan and the Art of Foreign Policy* (Cambridge, Massachusetts, 1989); David Campbell, *Writing National Security: US Foreign Policy and the Politics of Identity* (Minneapolis, 1992); W. S. Lucas, 'Campaigns of Truth: the Psychological Strategy Board and American Ideology, 1951–1953', *The International History Review* (May 1996), pp. 279–302.

2 Cairo to State Department, Despatch 77, 12 July 1954, US National Archives (hereafter cited as USNA), Department of State Records, Central Decimal File, 774.00/7-1254.

3 NSC 155/1, 14 July 1953, Dwight Eisenhower Library (hereafter cited as DDE), Office of the Special Assistant for National Security Affairs, NSC Policy Papers, Box 5.

4 *Public Papers of the Presidents of the United States: Dwight D. Eisenhower, 1957*, pp. 6–16.

5 Annex to McGhee to Acheson, 27 December 1950, *Foreign Relations of the United States* (hereafter cited as *FRUS*) *1951*, V., p. 6.

6 Records of Anglo-American discussions, October 1949, Public Record Office, FO371/81907/E1023/3.

7 NSC 47/5, 14 March 1951, *FRUS 1951*, V, p. 94. See also Howard memorandum, 2 January 1951, USNA, Department of State Records, Central Decimal, 780.5/1-251.

8 Text of Tripartite Declaration on the Middle East, 25 May 1950, *FRUS 1950*, V, p. 135.

9 Quoted in Geoffrey Aronson, *From Sideshow to Center Stage: U.S. Policy Toward Egypt, 1946–1956* (Boulder, Colorado, 1986), p. 11.

10 M. A. Wahab Sayed-Ahmed, *Nasser and American Foreign Policy 1952–1956* (London, 1989), p. 33.

11 Cited in McGhee memorandum, 9 February 1951, USNA, Department of State Records, Central Decimal File, 780.5/2-951.

12 Acheson to Marshall, 27 January 1951, USNA, Department of State Records, Central Decimal File, 780.5/1-2751. See also Howard draft, undated, *FRUS 1951*, V, p. 24.

13 See USNA, Department of State Records, Central Decimal File, 780.5 Series.

14 Acheson to Marshall, 27 January 1951, USNA, Department of State Records, Central Decimal File, 780.5/1-2751.

15 Conclusions of Istanbul conference, 14–21 February 1951, *FRUS 1951*, V, p. 56.

16 Cairo to State Department, Cable 788, 30 November 1951, *FRUS 1951*, V, p. 428. See also London to State Department, Cable 2094, 30 October 1951, *FRUS 1951*, V, p. 414 and Cairo to State Department, Cable 754, 24 November 1951, *FRUS 1951*, V, p. 424.

17 Sayed-Ahmed, *Nasser and American Foreign Policy*, p. 41.

18 National Security Council staff study, 18 January 1952, USNA, Department of State Records, Records of the Policy Planning Staff, 1947–53, Box 14.

19 Cairo to State Department, Cable 1395, 21 February 1952, USNA, Department of State Records, Central Decimal File, 774.00/2-2152. Secretary of State Dean Acheson, in his one of his rare interventions on the Egyptian situation, commented acidly, 'The [British] "splutter of musketry" apparently does not stop things as we had been told from time to time that it would.' [Acheson–Franks meeting, 27 January 1952, HST, Acheson Papers, Memoranda of Conversation, Box 67].

20 Aronson, *From Sideshow to Center Stage*, pp. 39–43.

21 Cairo to State Department, Cable 178, 25 July 1952, USNA, Department of State Records, Central Decimal File, 774.00/7-2552. More than a week after the coup, the Revolutionary Command Council finally met British and French officials but only in the presence of Evans, the US representative [Cairo to State Department, Cable 238, 1 August 1952, USNA, Department of State Records, Central Decimal File, 774.00/8-152].

22 Sayed-Ahmed, *Nasser and American Foreign Policy*, p. 45.

23 Eden minute, 5 August 1952, PRO, FO371/96932/JE1052/398G. British intelligence was so poor that its Embassy's first assessment of the coup was that it was led by 'a young Air Force officer . . . generally considered to have

... sympathies' with the Wafd party. In fact, the Free Officers saw the Wafd as a corrupt force responsible for much of Egypt's ills. [Cairo to Foreign Office, Cable 1060, 23 July 1952, PRO, FO371/96877/JE1018/204.] Subsequently the British, either from wildly inaccurate information or from a desire to set the US against the new regime, would declare that the fundamentalist Muslim Brotherhood was an integral part of the revolutionary government. [London to State Department, Cable 493, 25 July 1952, USNA, Department of State Records, Central Decimal File, 774.00/7-2552.]

24   Alexandria to State Department, Cable 47, 29 July 1952, USNA, Department of State Records, Central Decimal File, 780.5/7-2952.

25   See, for example, CIA memorandum, 'Political and Psychological Exploitation of Bermuda', undated, DDE, Jackson Papers, Box 2, Bermuda Conference Briefing Book.

26   Eisenhower to Churchill, 22 July 1954, DDE, Ann Whitman Series, DDE Diaries, Box 4, DDE Personal Diary, January–November 1954. Churchill replied bluntly, 'I am a bit sceptical about universal suffrage for the Hottentots even if refined by proportional representation. The British and American democracies were slowly and painfully forged and even they are not perfect yet.' [Churchill to Eisenhower, 8 August 1954, DDE, Ann Whitman Series, DDE Diaries, Box 8, DDE Diary, August 1954.]

27   Washington to Foreign Office, Cable 1174, 2 June 1953, PRO, FO371/104257/23.

28   Foster Dulles memorandum, 1 June 1953, USNA, Department of State Records, Records of the Policy Planning Staff, 1947–53.

29   State Department to Cairo, Cable 17, 4 July 1953, *FRUS 1952–1954*, IX, p. 2108.

30   State Department to Cairo, Cable 1401, 14 January 1953, USNA, Department of State Records, Central Decimal File, 641.74/1-1453; Strang minute, 29 January 1953, PRO, FO371/10273/JE10345/1; Cairo to Foreign Office, Cable 1149, 23 October 1953, and subsequent minutes PRO, FO371/102818/JE1192/560G.

31   See PRO, PREM11/395/File and PRO, PREM11/699/File.

32   Cairo to State Department, Cable 315, 9 August 1952, and subsequent minutes, USNA, Department of State Records, Central Decimal File, 774.00/8-952.

33   Hart to Byroade, 31 March 1954, USNA, Department of State Records, Central Decimal File, 774.00/3-3154. The official was taken aback that much of his interview was 'taken up by banter among Nasser, Haikal, and Lakeland. Some of this was at the expense of the [US Information Service] bulletin "Sadaqa" and was ridiculed by Haikal as was technical assistance. At one point I choked back a desire to turn to Nasser and say, "Since you apparently agree with these statements, shall we withdraw technical assistance?"'

34   Author's interview with Miles Copeland.

35   Allen Dulles to John Foster Dulles, 27 October 1954, DDE, John Foster Dulles Series, Telephone Calls, Box 3, September–October 1954. Nasser took the money but used it to build an ostentatious tower, supposedly nicknamed 'Roosevelt's Erection' after Kermit Roosevelt.

36   See USNA, Department of State Records, Central Decimal File, 780.5 Series.

37   State Department memorandum, 'Syria', 5 May 1953, *FRUS 1952–1954*, IX, p. 1204.

38   Foster Dulles memorandum of conversation, 18 October 1955, DDE, John Foster Dulles Series, Subject, Alphabetical, Box 10, Israeli Relations 1951–1957. See also the extract from the Jackson Committee report of June 1953 in Sayed-Ahmed, *Nasser and American Foreign Policy*, p. 99.

39   Eisenhower minute, 8 October 1953, DDE, Ann Whitman Series, DDE Diaries, Box 5, Telephone Calls, October 1953.

40   Eisenhower diary notes, 8 October 1953, DDE, Ann Whitman Series, DDE Diaries, Box 4, DDE Diary, October 1953.

41   Hanes to Russell, 15 February 1955, DDE, John Foster Dulles Series, Special Assistants Chronological, Box 7, February 1955.

42   State Department to New York, Cable TEDUL 4, 27 September 1955, USNA, Department of State Records, Central Decimal File, 774.56/9-2755.

43   Unsigned CIA analysis, undated, DDE, John Foster Dulles Series, White House Memoranda, Box 18, Conversations with Allen Dulles. See also 267th NSC meeting, 21 November 1955, DDE, Ann Whitman Series, National Security Council, Box 7.

44   268th NSC meeting, 1 December 1995, DDE, Ann Whitman Series, National Security Council, Box 7.

45   W. S. Lucas, *Divided We Stand: Britain, the US, and the Suez Crisis* (London, 1991), pp. 87–9; Eden–Eisenhower meeting, 30 January 1956, DDE, James Hagerty Series, Diary Entries, Box 5, Sir Anthony Eden.

46   See Eisenhower diary entry, 8 March 1956, DDE, Ann Whitman Series, DDE Diaries, Box 13, March 1956 Diary.

47   Foster Dulles memorandum, 28 March 1956, DDE, Ann Whitman Series, DDE Diaries, Box 13, March 1956 Diary.

48   Foster Dulles memorandum, 28 March 1956, DDE, Ann Whitman Series, DDE Diaries, Box 13, March 1956 Diary; Paris to State Department, Cable DULTE 5, 3 May 1956, DDE, Ann Whitman Series, Dulles–Herter, Box 5, May 1956.

49   See Eisenhower diary entry, 8 March 1956, *US Declassified Document Reference System*, 1978, 123E.

50   See, for example, Lucas, *Divided We Stand*, pp. 68 and 114.

51   Eden–Foster Dulles meeting, 30 January 1956, DDE, Ann Whitman Series, International, Box 20, Eden Visit.

52   Foster Dulles notes, 27 March 1956, DDE, John Foster Dulles Series, Subject, Alphabetical, Box 10, Israeli Relations 1951–57.

53   Foster Dulles memorandum, 28 March 1956, DDE, Ann Whitman Series, DDE Diaries, Box 13, March 1956 Diary.

54   CIA London Station to Director of Central Intelligence, Cable LOND 7064, 1 April 1956, copy in author's possession.

55   Foster Dulles to Snyder, 23 May 1956, DDE, John Foster Dulles Series, Telephone Calls, White House, Box 10, January–August 1956.

56   See Foster Dulles to Allen Dulles, 19 July 1956, DDE, John Foster Dulles Series, Telephone Calls, Box 5.

57   Goodpaster memoranda, 27–28 July 1956, DDE, Ann Whitman Series, DDE Diaries, Box 16, July 1956 Diary, Staff Memoranda; London to State Depart-

ment, Cable 517, 29 July 1956, DDE, Ann Whitman Series, Dulles–Hereter, Box 5, July 1956.

58 Foster Dulles–Macmillan meeting, 25 September 1956, DDE, John Foster Dulles Papers, General Memoranda of Conversations, Box 1. See Lucas, *Divided We Stand*, pp. 211–13 for the assertion that Macmillan deliberately deceived Eden and Cabinet colleagues on the extent of US support for British military action.

59 For contacts between Nasser and 'private' US representatives who were friends of Eisenhower, see Eisenhower–Hoover discussion, 28 July 1956, DDE, Ann Whitman Series, DDE Diaries, Box 16, July 1956 Miscellaneous.

60 See *The Times* (London), 19 June 1975, 1; Cairo to State Department, Cable 382, 15 August 1956, USNA, Department of State Records, Central Decimal File, 974.7301/8-1556.

61 Foster Dulles to Eisenhower, 31 August 1956, DDE, Ann Whitman Series, Dulles–Herter, Box 5, August 1956; Eisenhower to Foster Dulles, 7 September 1956, DDE, John Foster Dulles Series, Telephone Calls, White House, Box 10, September–December 1956.

62 Quoted in Sayed-Ahmed, *Nasser and American Foreign Policy*, p. 143.

63 State Department to Cairo, Cable 1520, 10 November 1956, DDE, White House Office, Office of the Staff Secretary, Subject, State Department, Box 82, Suez Canal Crisis; State Department to Cairo, Cable 2046, 20 December 1956, DDE, Ann Whitman Series, Dulles–Herter, Box 5, December 1956.

64 *Public Papers of the Presidents of the United States: Dwight D. Eisenhower, 1957,* 6–16.

65 OCB Progress Report on NSC 5428, 22 December 1956, *FRUS 1955–1957,* XII, p. 422. See also Special National Intelligence Estimate, 'Outlook for the Syrian Situation', 16 November 1956, *FRUS 1955–1957,* XIII, p. 601.

66 Attachment to Hoover to Eisenhower, 21 November 1956, *FRUS 1955–1957,* XII, pp. 343–51.

67 Eisenhower–Foster Dulles discussion, 8 December 1956, DDE, Ann Whitman Series, DDE Diaries, Box 20, December 1956; Ashton, *Eisenhower, Macmillan and the Problem of Nasser* (London, 1996), pp. 104–5.

68 Quoted in Herter to Eisenhower, 30 January 1958, *FRUS 1958–1960,* XII, p. 36.

69 Quoted in Nigel Ashton, *Eisenhower, Macmillan and the Problem of Nasser,* p. 162.

70 Rountree to Hoover, 26 November 1956, *FRUS 1955–1957,* XIII, p. 68.

71 Wilkins to Rountree, 9 May 1957, *FRUS 1955–1957,* XVII, pp. 608–10; State Department to Ankara, Cable 287, 31 July 1957, *FRUS 1955–1957,* XVII, p. 696.

72 See the documents in *FRUS 1955–1957,* XIII, pp. 645–719.

73 Eisenhower diary entry, 8 March 1956, *US Declassified Document Reference System,* 1978 123E.

74 Eisenhower–Saud meeting, 30 January 1957, *FRUS 1955–1957,* XIII, p. 418. Saud's visit was immediately followed by a stop in Washington by Iraqi Crown Prince Abdul Ilah. See *FRUS 1955–1957,* XII, pp. 1024–37.

75 Eisenhower–Saud meeting, 30 January 1957, *FRUS 1955–1957,* XIII, p. 422; Jidda to State Department, Cable 619, 11 April 1957, *FRUS 1955–1957,* XIII, pp. 492–3.

76 Herter–Caccia meeting, 14 April 1957, *FRUS 1955–1957*, XIII, p. 93.
77 Foster Dulles to Eisenhower, 20 August 1957, *FRUS 1955–1957*, XIII, p. 641. Foster Dulles was especially concerned about Israeli intervention in Syria.
78 Foster Dulles–Caccia meeting, 24 April 1957, *FRUS 1955–1957*, xiii, p. 106.
79 See Foster Dulles–Lloyd meeting, 25 October 1957, *FRUS 1955–1957*, XIII, pp. 509–15; Baghdad to State Department, Cable 337, 11 October 1955, *FRUS 1955–1957*, XIII, pp. 548–53 and subsequent documents. Compare this interpretation in Ashton, *Eisenhower, Macmillan and the Problem of Nasser*, pp. 122–3.
80 See for example Erika Alin, *The United States and the 1958 Lebanon Crisis* (New York, 1994).
81 Ashton, *Eisenhower, Macmillan and the Problem of Nasser*, pp. 122–39.
82 Note the references in Goodpaster memorandum, 7 September 1957, *FRUS 1955–1957*, XIII, pp. 685–9.
83 Jackson log, 24 January 1957, DDE, C. D. Jackson Papers, Box 69.
84 See, for example, Cairo to State Department, Cable 2222, 10 January 1957, *FRUS 1955–1957*, XVII, pp. 16–21; Cairo to State Department, Cable 2625, 15 February 1957, *FRUS 1955–1957*, XVII, pp. 173–7.
85 Cairo to State Department, Cable 2222, 10 January 1957, *FRUS 1955–1957*, XVII, p. 17.
86 See Eisenhower–Macmillan meetings, 20–21 March 1957, *FRUS 1955–1957*, XVII, pp. 450–1, 453; Eisenhower diary entry, 21 March 1957, *FRUS 1955–1957*, XVII, pp. 461–2.
87 DELETED to Foster Dulles, 24 August 1957, *FRUS 1955–1957*, XIII, pp. 652–3.
88 Cairo to State Department, Cable 608, 1 September 1957, *FRUS 1955–1957*, XIII, pp. 664–9; Rountree to Strong, 29 October 1957, *FRUS 1955–1957*, XIII, pp. 735–6; Rountree-El-Bitar meeting, 7 November 1957, *FRUS 1955–1957*, XIII, pp. 740–4.
89 Eisenhower–Menderes meeting, 18 December 1957, *FRUS 1955–1957*, XIII, p. 168.
90 See Rountree to Foster Dulles, 4 November 1957, *FRUS 1955–1957*, XVII, pp. 785–7. See also Eisenhower to Foster Dulles, 13 November 1957, *FRUS 1955–1957*, XVII, p. 795.
91 Cairo to State Department, Cable 1426, 11 December 1957, *FRUS 1955–1957*, XIII, pp. 744–7.
92 Quoted in Ashton, *Eisenhower, Macmillan and the Problem of Nasser*, p. 147.
93 NSC 5801/1, 24 January 1958, *FRUS 1958–1960*, XII, p. 29.
94 354th NSC meeting, 6 February 1958, *FRUS 1958–1960*, XII, p. 39.
95 Cairo to State Department, Cable 2120, 18 February 1958, *FRUS 1958–1960*, XIII, pp. 427–9; Cairo to State Department, Cable 2444, 20 March 1958, *FRUS 1958–1960*, XIII, pp. 435–6; Rountree to Foster Dulles, 16 April 1958, *FRUS 1958–1960*, XII, p. 54; National Intelligence Estimate, 'Trends in the Middle East', *FRUS 1958–1960*, XII, p. 63.
96 Cited in Rountree to Herter, 7 February 1959, *FRUS 1958–1960*, XIII, pp. 512–15.
97 Rountree to Foster Dulles, 14 March 1958, *FRUS 1958–1960*, XIII, p. 719; Special National Intelligence Estimate, 'Implications of Recent Govern-

mental Changes in Saudi Arabia', 8 April 1958, *FRUS 1958–1960*, XIII, pp. 726–8.

98 Cairo to State Department, Cable 3029, 20 May 1958, *FRUS 1958–1960*, XI, pp. 67–70, 101–3; Cairo to State Department, Cable 3241, 7 June 1958, *FRUS 1958–1960*, XI, pp. 101–3.

99 See Ashton, *Eisenhower, Macmillan and the Problem of Nasser*, pp. 158–61.

100 See, for example, Cabinet meeting, 18 July 1958, *FRUS 1958–1960*, XII, pp. 79; 374th NSC meeting, 31 July 1958, *FRUS 1958–1960*, XII, p. 129.

101 Furnas memorandum, 4 August 1958, *FRUS 1958–1960*, XII, p. 136.

102 383rd NSC meeting, 16 October 1958, *FRUS 1958–1960*, XII, p. 176; 384th NSC meeting, 30 October 1958, *FRUS 1958–1960*, XII, p. 182.

103 Rountree to Foster Dulles, 10 October 1958, *FRUS 1958–1960*, XII, p. 168; 391st NSC meeting, 18 December 1958, *FRUS 1958–1960*, XII, p. 364. This is not to say that the Eisenhower administration was filled with joy at the combination with Egypt against the new Iraq. The President characterized it as 'a case of whether we decided to support a baby-faced Dillinger or an Al Capone'. [393rd NSC meeting, 15 January 1959, *FRUS 1958–1960*, XII, p. 377.]

104 395th NSC meeting, 29 January 1959, *FRUS 1958–1960*, XII, pp. 371–8; Herter-Lloyd meeting, 4 April 1959, *FRUS 1958–1960*, XII, p. 411.

105 404th NSC meeting, 30 April 1959, *FRUS 1958–1960*, XII, pp. 443–5; 407th NSC meeting, 21 May 1959, *FRUS 1958–1960*, XII, p. 458. The significant holdout against the accommodation with Nasser was Vice-President Richard Nixon.

106 State Department to Cairo, Cable 2729, 17 March 1959, *FRUS 1958–1960*, XIII, pp. 518–19; Jones to Herter, 24 September 1959, *FRUS 1958–1960*, XIII, pp. 552–5.

107 See, for example, the prediction of continued stability in Iraq in National Intelligence Estimate, 'The Outlook for Iraq', 4 June 1957, *FRUS 1955–1957*, XII, pp. 1048–56.

108 White House press statement, 7 June 1956, DDE, John Foster Dulles Series, Telephone Calls, White House, Box 10, January–August 1956.

109 See, for example, Lodge to Eisenhower, 21 December 1956, DDE, Ann Whitman Series, administration, Box 24, Henry Cabot Lodge.

110 Gordon Gray oral history, 25 June 1975, DDE, Oral History Collection, OH-34.

111 Quoted in enclosure to Damascus to State Department, Despatch 18, 15 July 1957, *FRUS 1955–1957*, XIII, p. 624. Similar sentiments also came from 'friends' of the US such as King Saud and Lebanese diplomat Ghaleb Turc. [Foster Dulles-Saud meeting, 31 January 1957, *FRUS 1955–1957*, XIII, p. 439; Cairo to State Department, 1 December 1958, *FRUS 1958–1960*, XIII, pp. 502–3.]

112 White House conference, 23 July 1958, *FRUS 1958–1960*, XII, p. 98.

113 358th NSC meeting, 13 March 1958, *FRUS 1958–1960*, XII, p. 46; Eisenhower-Lloyd meeting, 17 July 1958, *FRUS 1958–1960*, XII, p. 76.

114 Rountree to Foster Dulles, 10 October 1958, *FRUS 1958–1960*, XII, p. 168.

115 Foster Dulles-Bowie discussion, 12 January 1957, *FRUS 1955–1957*, XVII, p. 29.

116 See, for example, White House conference, 28 August 1957, *FRUS 1955–1957*, XIII, p. 659; Foster Dulles memorandum, 2 September 1957, *FRUS 1955–1957*, XIII, pp. 669–70; White House conference, 7 September 1957, *FRUS 1955–1957*, XIII, p. 685.

117 Eisenhower to Hazlett, 3 August 1956, DDE, Ann Whitman Series, DDE Diaries, Box 17.

8

The United States and the Decolonization of Black Africa, 1945–63

John Kent

The Second World War produced an upsurge of anti-colonialism on a global scale. In the US, imperial trading blocs were seen as causes of conflict and war, while colonialism, with its denial of self-determination, was at odds with American values and the struggle for freedom in the face of Fascist tyranny. Sumner Welles, Secretary of State Cordell Hull's rival and deputy, was particularly keen to end colonialism when in charge of postwar planning in the State Department. He hoped to replace colonial administrations with international bodies responsible for the development of dependent peoples. Such institutions would have to prepare the way for independence particularly in Africa, as Welles believed that 'Negroes are in the lowest rank of human beings.'[1]

When such radical anti-colonial ideas disappeared with the scandal that produced Welles's departure from the State Department in 1943, the low opinion of Black Africans was to remain an influence on American policy towards colonialism. There was little or no detailed knowledge of the African continent within government circles in 1945, and American attitudes were based more on general perceptions of colonialism and African people. In wartime Washington the African empires of the European powers were seen by both Hull and Welles as impediments to the expanded US wartime economy's reversion to peacetime production without the recurrence of recession. Colonialism was thus incompatible with an international economic order in tune with American political values and American economic interests.

However, the anti-colonialism of Roosevelt's wartime administration continued to weaken and was to have little or no impact on American policy towards decolonization in Africa or elsewhere. Initially this was because of the strategic concerns of the US military, who opposed international controls over former colonial territories in the Pacific, where they required unfettered use of military bases. By the end of the 1940s the fears of a lack of markets had proved exaggerated and Cold War concerns had assumed overriding significance in dictating US attitudes to Africa and decolonization. In many respects African decolonization and US policy from this point on can be seen as adaptations to the requirements of the Cold War.

In order to understand the dilemmas produced by the Cold War, it is important to distinguish military requirements for hot war from the military and political requirements of the Cold War. The two were quite separate, with the political struggle against left-wing movements, particularly those controlled or influenced by Moscow, always assuming precedence over the military threat of the Soviet Union. NATO's alleged military importance or the strategic importance of Africa were never seen as overriding the battle for the hearts and minds of nations and peoples who were deemed likely to fall prey to the political tenets of communism. It was of course the case that America's NATO partner had an enormous political significance, especially during the 1940s, when the Cold War was an essentially European concern. Yet by the time John F. Kennedy became president, the relative importance of Africa as a Cold War battleground had dramatically increased and the future stability of the continent was more and more in doubt.

Essential to American perceptions of the anti-colonial struggle in Africa was the fear that communism would take over nationalist movements, particularly if legitimate demands for freedom were resisted. Yet, if they were not resisted, then the European powers might be alienated. Moreover, if Africans were granted premature independence, weak states would be susceptible to communism. These were the dilemmas faced by the US for much of the period.

Colonial problems were of concern to a number of government departments and offices, and as early as 1948 attempts were made to define a common approach to colonialism. It was 1950, following the reorganization of the State Department to provide for regional bureaus, before a formal policy statement was prepared on Africa. By then the US foreign service had arranged a conference of diplomatic and consular staff in Africa, which was held in Lourenço-Marques between 27 February and 2 March 1950. It was preceded by the discussions of a panel of experts from within the United States and members of African interest groups.

With the position in Europe stabilized through Marshall Aid, what emerged from these discussions was an American version of the dual mandate. Africa was now seen not just as an area where the US required access to economic resources (particularly strategic raw materials), but as an area where economic stability had to be provided for. In economic terms a mutually profitable relationship between the European powers and their dependent territories was to be encouraged. In political terms it was deemed necessary to foster self-government without jeopardising close relations with the European powers.[2] Thus the kind of premature independence that could produce chaos and instability and open the door to communism would be avoided.

The desire to move towards the end of colonial rule within a framework of cooperation with the European colonial powers involved an awkward balancing-act that increasingly had to deal with anti-colonial feeling at the United Nations. Not alienating the Europeans remained a Cold War requirement and pressure for the rapid end of colonial rule was limited by perceptions of Africans as backward or primitive peoples. American representatives in colonial Africa tended to doubt whether Africans were capable of self-government or even civilized behaviour. 'Peoples in Black Africa are basically primitive rather than backward due to racial characteristics and environmental influence.' Without European guidance in day-to-day affairs Africans would be lost and,

> without the discipline and control of Western nations, ancient antagonisms would burst their present bounds and numerous races or tribes would attack traditional enemies in primitive savagery. The native people of Africa tend always to mistrust the leadership of their own kind because in themselves they have not yet as a people achieved sufficient evolutionary stature to understand the existence of motivation other than the compulsion of self-interest of a very low order or fear.

In a continent deemed to be full of primitive ignorance, superstition and extensive illiteracy there would be a need for a long period of tutelage.

> To endow these African groups prematurely with independence and sovereignty would only result in creating political entities which would almost immediately become pawns of the Kremlin. Constructive effort without European stimulation would cease and the advances already achieved in bringing these areas a few steps forward from the conditions of the bush and the jungles would in a few years under native control, and as a result of native sloth, dishonesty,

incompetence and uncooperativeness revert to the status of conditions now observable in these portions of Liberia which are under direct native supervision.[3]

From the other side of the continent came views which not only portrayed the African as primitive but which hailed the virtues as well as the necessity of continued British involvement in the economic and political development of Africa. It was claimed that no part of Africa had ever developed into a civilization; the continent had been invaded by Western civilization and 'there was no point in wringing one's hands about it'. If it was suggested that the white man should leave, 'moral integrity would require us to pack up and leave the US which we occupy by much the same rights'. Africans could within a generation have participation in the central government but the greatest disservice the white man could do would be to leave Africa. 'The world, it is submitted, is better off for the Romans having civilised the Gauls, the Franks and the blue painted Britons.' It was also claimed that Africa had advanced in the previous sixty years from the Bronze Age to the early Middle Ages and therefore there was no point in comparing blacks in the Central African Federation to those in the US. 'The American negro is to Africans in Central Africa as the present day white American is to the common man in the days of Charlemagne.'[4]

American officials' distorted views of Africa were matched by distorted views of the United States when the racial question was addressed in the context of British efforts to create a multi-racial society in Central Africa. Black and white people there were deemed to be 'looking to the United States for examples as to how we achieved harmonious relations with our own Negro race'. Yet it was also argued as early as 1952 that the adoption of the correct racial policy was vital; it could affect the fate of future generations not only in Central Africa but throughout the whole of Black Africa, and the survival of Western influence might hinge upon it.[5] The implementation of multi-racialism as part of the decolonization process was subsequently to prove impossible despite American and British support for it and it was the Americans who were first to accept this.

In the meantime American policy-makers struggled to find a means of reconciling the demands of Africans for self-determination with support for the colonial powers. The policy statement in 1950 defined the security interests of the United States in most dependent areas as being best served by a policy of support for the European allies coupled as necessary with suggestions for the acceleration of economic, social and political development;[6] this remained the basic State Department line throughout the decolonization process despite the desire of the Office of Dependent Area Affairs to be more supportive of anti-colonial policies which were easier to sell to the United Nations.

Full support for African people could lead to colonial powers withdrawing from NATO.[7] On the other hand, the colonial issue was seen as such an international bone of contention that it might not only detract from the East–West conflict but displace it at the centre of the United Nations stage.[8] The question then and subsequently was not whether European, Cold War or military security issues should take precedence over African issues but whether the Cold War could best be fought by cooperating more with Africans than Europeans. The Working Group on colonial problems in the State Department failed to provide an answer and it was wound up in September 1952.

The Republican administration which came to power in January 1953 then reactivated studies of the colonial issue in an effort to overcome what the new Secretary of State, John Foster Dulles, felt was an unnecessarily ambiguous US policy. Responsibility was given to the Office of Dependent Area Affairs and in the summer of 1953 the US representative on the UN Trusteeship Council, Mason Sears, produced two memoranda. Equivocation was to be avoided by embarking on a campaign against the root evil of communism, which was to be portrayed as the new and more potent form of colonialism.[9] Western colonialism should not be regarded as any obstacle to freedom because of the commitment to decolonization. This had the advantage of encouraging European unity around the enhanced fear of communism and giving the US more grounds to press the European powers to hasten rather than hamper the process of orderly evolution to self-determination. In a speech in October, Henry Byroade, the assistant secretary for Near Eastern, South Asian and African Affairs, reiterated Sears' ideas but also stated that self-determination could mean closer association, as in the French Union, and drew attention to the dangers of premature independence.[10] Dulles followed this up with a speech in which Western colonialism was placed in the context of a global struggle between despotism and liberty as a springboard for the future. Orderly evolution from colonial status to independence could be achieved, he claimed, as in Indochina (*sic*), the Sudan and the Philippines.[11]

None of this ensured that the speed of the transition to self-government or self-determination would be acceptable to both Africans and Europeans. One suggestion was that

As a means of diminishing the threat to Western interests posed by nationalist demands . . . the United Stated should make the most practical use of economic, technical and where applicable military assistance so as to influence the process of political change to effect the best compromise of Western interests and to offer the maximum promise of stable non-Communist regimes.[12]

Yet if the European powers increased the speed of change but did not move fast enough to satisfy the Africans, the United States would still find it difficult to preserve the necessary stability in Black Africa.

By 1954 the Bureau of Near Eastern, South Asian and African Affairs was pointing to African dissatisfaction with the rate at which their aspirations were being met. Yet Dulles remained cautious, repeating in February 1955 his 1953 public statement on the US desire for an orderly transition from colonial rule to self-government 'with zeal balanced by patience'. Over the remainder of the decade the voices of caution had to confront the desire to accept the growing chorus of African demands for more rapid political change. With the perceived rigidity of the colonial powers and increased African demands for political and economic power, the US could not undermine its European allies but at the same time could not afford to alienate the Africans. The dilemma remained.[13]

In East and particularly Central Africa, the Americans were concerned that the British were not moving more rapidly to African majority rule. But generally after 1955 what emerged was not increasing pressure on the colonial powers but a growing desire to work with them to satisfy African aspirations and build on what the Americans saw as the benefits of colonialism. Thus Dulles allegedly told Macmillan at the Geneva conference in the summer of 1955 that he had suddenly realized all the US views about colonialism had been wrong and that the period of British hegemony had been the happiest period Africa had ever had.[14]

This did not remove the US colonial dilemma, which was made more acute in 1954–55 by the intensification of the Cold War after Stalin's death.[15] With the new Russian leaders eager to extend Soviet power and influence outside the areas contiguous with the Soviet Union, the Cold War competition for the hearts and minds of Asian and African people began in earnest. Soviet aid to India and the Middle East in 1954 and 1955 was followed by increased involvement in Africa made manifest in the Soviet delegation to Liberia, the establishment of diplomatic relations with Libya, the offer to exchange ambassadors with the Sudan and the willingness to provide Libya and Liberia with exports of industrial products in exchange for agricultural surpluses on easy terms.[16] The British and the Americans were in agreement that the Cold War in Africa was of enormous significance. One US official commented at the pre-United Nations Anglo-American talks on colonial questions in 1956, that colonialism was the principal battleground between East and West and Selwyn Lloyd informed Dulles in early 1957 that the battle for the next ten years would lie in Africa.[17]

One way of speeding up progress to self-government or self-determination was through timetables, as favoured by Mason Sears. In 1955 Sears had come to the conclusion that the US was frequently too solicitous of British, French and Belgian views and that is was important to 'make friends with the Africans even if we alienate or irritate our European allies'. Fixing final dates for independence was, however, seen as too radical by the State Department, who believed that the US could befriend Africans without alienating Europeans.[18]

Timetables would have been based on readiness for self-government and independence. Yet in the second half of the 1950s it eventually became clear that the timing of independence would not be influenced by economic or social criteria; outside West Africa this fact, after lengthy internal debates, was accepted sooner by the Americans, the French and the Belgians than by the British. It is true that stability was still seen as related to social and economic development and that differences over the pace of change continued to influence US African policy. Thus the US consul-general in Leopoldville questioned the wisdom of claiming Africans were not ready for independence and urged that the US should stop wooing the colonial powers, as this was only assisting the growth of communism.[19] On the other hand, in Dakar it was argued that colonialism should not be condemned in the abstract without considering the facts of everyday life. In much of Africa it was claimed that the people were not capable of managing their own affairs and the consul recalled that in the US it used to be said 'Beneath the starry Flag civilise them with a Krag.'[20] Support for this line came from the US consul-general in Nairobi who lamented the fact that an impression had been created that the US stood categorically against colonialism and for self-government.[21]

The belief that Africans were backward and still incapable of governing themselves fitted well with Dulles' apparent new-found appreciation of the benefits of colonialism. In Dar es Salaam the American consul-general thought Nyerere was naive to believe that Tanganyika would be ready for self-government between 1967 and 1969. Many Africans were seen as having developed little beyond the stage of child-like animosities and personal jealousies. Thus the creation of independent states was likely to produce a vacuum into which Asian and Russian influence would flow.[22] In the State Department a further consideration was that if the European powers were pushed too far they might be prepared to jeopardize important arrangements which the US believed to be necessary. In essence much of what the US wanted to accomplish in Africa, which was geared to the demands of stability for Cold War reasons, could, in political and economic terms, only be done through the colonial powers.[23]

Increasingly, as the transfer of power gathered speed, US policy-makers were looking to develop aid policies which would supplement those of their European allies. Americans desired to preserve the economic links between Europe and Africa because they were seen as beneficial to both continents. American cooperation with the colonial authorities was seen as necessary and desirable given that the US could not afford the kind of large-scale aid programmes that would guarantee the western orientation of African states prior to and immediately after independence. Colonialism was in that sense a progressive force, as reported one congresswoman in 1956 after a tour of Black Africa.[24]

Growing Cold War concerns about stability were helping to bring US ideas on decolonization into line with the British and, after the *loi cadre* of 1956, the French, under the auspices of cooperation to achieve the common goals of viable and stable self-governing states. In June 1956 the State Department proposed the establishment of an official committee of British, French, American and possibly Belgian representatives to recommend ways of combating what was seen as the Soviet campaign of subversion in Africa.[25] It should be noted that the Americans, like the Colonial Office, did not see an actual communist threat from within the continent at this time. Unlike the Foreign Office and the French, what concerned the Americans was the potential threat from Soviet-inspired communism, which they always saw as likely to increase. Thus they were sceptical of French claims, made at the official level and by de Gaulle, that their actions in Guinea were necessitated by the fact that Sekou Touré was a communist.[26]

This tendency to seek greater cooperation with the colonial powers between 1955 and 1957 and to promote joint efforts at nation-building produced regular meetings on African policy between the US and its NATO partners. These mainly involved the British, with whom regular talks on colonial issues began in 1950. In October 1958 Dulles and Selwyn Lloyd agreed that it would be useful to discuss prospects for Africa on an Anglo-American basis and a working group was set up in 1959.[27]

The first National Security Council paper on African policy in August 1957 referred to the growing importance of Africa's influence on world affairs and the US desire for orderly progress to self-government in co-operation with the European powers; the Euro-African links should be retained and the US should support 'constructive nationalism' and work with the metropolitan powers on specific development projects.[28] In 1957 some in the State Department saw nationalism reaching its peak in Africa in 1962 and 1963 rather than in the 20 to 30 years previously assumed, yet there was an awareness of the dangers of rapid progress towards independence.[29] Dulles, often unfairly branded as a crude anti-colonial cold warrior, told Selwyn Lloyd that US policy was not to exert pressure that would result in premature independence.[30] In some ways, as European colonialism entered its final phases in Black Africa at the end of the 1950s, it experienced growing popularity in the United States, with the exception of Portuguese rule. In 1958 another Congressional visit to Africa produced a report which notes that the nineteenth-century version of colonialism had disappeared and been replaced by enlightened administrations sensitive to native problems and aspirations.[31]

This was not simply because of the perceived need to work with the colonial powers in preparing backward Africans for communist-free independence. As more countries demanded self-government, the Americans realized that, to satisfy African aspirations, political change would have to precede social and economic development, with potentially disastrous consequences. Africans wanted the 'ragged shirt of independence rather than the warm blanket of colonial protection'. With Africans deemed to be 'practically leaping from the stone age into the twentieth century' there were doubts if the western European framework of political systems and economic and social advances would work in Africa.[32] Colonialism in these circumstances had all the hallmarks of a stable, long-lost age.

By 1958 the British were convinced that the Americans understood the dangers of independent regimes in Africa not experienced enough to fend off 'insidious friendliness or subversive attacks from Cairo and Moscow'.[33] American concern centred on French Black Africa following de Gaulle's return to power. A US national intelligence estimate concluded that

> present conditions and trends in French Tropical Africa are leading to a situation several years hence which could be inimical to western interests. The region will probably witness the creation of a collec-

tion of weak and unstable African states, at odds with each other and with their neighbours, and highly vulnerable to both internal and external communist influences.[34]

There was certainly no suggestion that in these difficult circumstances the US should try and swim against the political tide, as Eisenhower feared some Europeans might, by attempting to slow down progress to independence. Eisenhower wanted 'to be on the side of the natives for once.'[35]

The revised NSC paper on US policy towards Africa south of the Sahara continued to approach the problem in terms of encouraging an accommodation between African nationalists and the colonial powers.[36] The US was not going to rock any European boats. In a speech in November 1958 Dulles expressed support for the principle of independence but also reiterated the need to base this on adequate political, economic and social structures, even though the US was privately discounting this and feared that newly independent African nations would be marked out as special prey by the communists.[37]

This was even more so after Guinea's vote in September 1958 for independence rather than membership of the French Community. The Americans saw this and the riots in the Congo as more significant for British Africa than those in London did and feared that the inability of white settlers in British Africa to adjust would cause problems. Sears predicted in January 1959 that a crisis was developing in British Africa, which seemed to be confirmed by the Nyasaland riots in March and the Hola camp massacre in June.[38] At the UN Henry Cabot Lodge noted that his contacts were 'vividly impressing me with the rapidly evolving revolution in Africa'.[39]

The period between spring 1959 and autumn 1960, when the British colonial secretary announced a review of the Northern Rhodesian constitution, was one in which the Americans most feared that the British in Central and East Africa were not responding adequately and speedily enough to events. Again this was accompanied by the fear that conceding to African demands would replace one Cold War difficulty with another. In January 1959 the British colonial secretary envisaged self-government in Tanganyika in 1970 with Kenya following around 1975.[40] Even after the riots in Nyasaland, this kind of timetable was confirmed by a memorandum, 'Africa the Next Ten Years'.[41] The Americans, on the other hand, believed that Kenya might obtain independence within five years.[42]

As 1960 began, the National Security Council discussed the implications of early independence for British East and Central Africa in pessimistic terms. Allen Dulles, the director of the Central Intelligence Agency, believed that the chances of African countries achieving orderly economic development and political progress to self-government were nil. Eisenhower agreed that countries would be independent long before they were politically or economically ready for it. With the director of the Bureau of the Budget claiming that many Africans still belonged in the trees, this presented a serious problem to which Nixon, who felt some African peoples had only been out of the trees for fifty years, offered a solution. Strongmen, as in Latin America, were Nixon's answer, as he believed it was naive to hope for African democracy. And as he explained, the US must avoid assuming that the Cold War in Africa was a struggle between communism and western-style democracy even though this could not be said publicly.[43]

In terms of US policy this meant that before independence the US must avoid serious 'misunderstandings' with the colonial powers while encouraging them to increase economic assistance to promote stability. The most important area was the Central African Federation, where it was believed the British had done too little too late.[44] In November 1959 the British were telling the Americans that partnership in the Federation would succeed and no constitutional changes were foreseen in Nyasaland or Northern Rhodesia before the constitutional review at the end of 1960. American officials responded that the pace of change was too slow and that while they did not want the UK to abandon its responsibilities too soon, the gap between European concessions and African aspirations was widening.[45] The US should remain publicly uncommitted on the thorny question of whether the Federation should continue in its present form but maintain public support for the concept of multi-racialism. However, given the doubts about the latter's viability there should be a shift in US programmes in order to extend influence with the Africans who will 'inevitably and increasingly hold the key to the future' of the Federation. The Americans had accepted the inevitability of moves towards African majority rule in Central Africa before the British, and wanted them implemented as part of a strategy of retaining the initiative. On the other hand, if they were not, the US should not do anything to undermine British prestige in the Federation.[46]

In 1960 the Americans were to resist entreaties from Kenneth Kaunda to pressure the British for constitutional change in Northern Rhodesia.[47] They remained cautious partly because the British were moving towards African majority rule in 1960 and partly because they were aware of the potential for racial conflict in which white settlers were extremely critical of US anti-colonialism. Stability based on agreement between Africans and Europeans remained the priority. The Americans were enormously encouraged by developments in 1960 with the Lancaster House Conference on Kenya in January effectively selling the pass in the Federation by conceding the principle of an elective African majority. The release of Hastings Banda in April 1960, with the promise of an early Nyasaland constitutional review, further encouraged the Americans. The consul-general in Salisbury believed that the time was ripe to assist the British with the economic and social development of Nyasaland now that, unlike in November 1959, they had accepted the need for vigorous action.[48] The Americans were disappointed that, given the potential for instability, the British were not doing more with economic assistance in Central Africa.[49]

Other developments were to continue to cause concern in Salisbury and Washington. The consul-general was disturbed by the attitudes of the more moderate whites in the Federation. He was particularly concerned by a speech of Lord Malvern's, the Federation's first leader, which claimed that Africans would clamour for secession until it was made quite clear that it was not on offer. Malvern described the African as a 'decent fellow if he is given a chance and if people will only get down to talking to him and explaining the other side of the picture', but the trouble is that 'he is being carried away by people who have been to Britain and America and have come back with left-wing ideas in their heads'. The consul commented that after reviewing 'such a procession of tired clichés' one is left to 'wonder disconsolately concerning the antediluvian thinking prevalent among even the middle of the roaders in this country'.[50]

Throughout the ending of colonial rule in the period prior to 1961, US support for the European powers was based on the latter's acceptance of the principle of self-determination and on progress to self-government and independence. In the problematic, vital case of the Central African Federation, both the Kennedy and Eisenhower administrations were less sanguine than the British about the prospects for multi-racialism in the face of African political opposition. Once the British had responded to African demands in Nyasaland and Northern Rhodesia in 1960, the difficulty was changing the form of the Federation to make it acceptable to Africans without alienating white Rhodesians. In February 1961 the Bureau of African Affairs was concluding that there was little chance of this and therefore considering what to do when the Federation broke up rather than if it did.[51] Yet Kennedy's assistant secretary for African Affairs,

G. Mennen Williams, saw what would happen in the Federation as the key to the success of the transition to independence.[52] With the British commitment to a Federation effectively based on its acceptance by an African majority, the US, as in the past, was simply encouraging greater speed in the transfer of responsibilities to Africans.[53]

By then the Congo crisis, an event that the American assessment of the dangers inherent in decolonization had long pointed to, had begun. Even before the crisis broke in July 1960, US Secretary of State Christian Herter was explaining to the French that the new leaders might turn immediately to Russia and that the Americans would be better placed than the colonial powers to help.[54] In fact the Congo soon came to be seen as the make-or-break of US policy on bringing about, through decolonization, a community of independent nations free from Cold War tensions and dedicated to social and economic progress.[55] The lesson drawn by the Americans was that preparations for self-government had to be made and speedily implemented through cooperation between African leaders and the colonial powers.

These goals of the Kennedy administration were more a continuation of the Eisenhower administration's policies than the launch of a radical new African policy. The new administration may indeed have attached more significance to African policy, and Kennedy, while still a senator, sent Averill Harriman on an African tour in August 1960.[56] And it certainly faced more problems in the Congo[57] and Angola, which produced disagreements with the Europeans. Yet the policy was still to seek the best means of reconciling Cold War requirements in Africa with NATO harmony in Europe.

The importance of the rebellion in Angola has been linked to the US base in the Portuguese Azores. Kennedy faced Cold War strategic requirements in Europe and the Azores and the vital Cold War need to woo the newly independent African nations who were increasingly hostile to Portuguese colonialism. How best to respond to the emerging states in Black Africa was the real Cold War challenge, yet it is claimed that the Kennedy administration ultimately betrayed the anticolonial African cause. The US opposition to the ending of Portuguese rule allegedly weakened because of fears of being denied the Azores.[58] Such interpretations fail to appreciate fully the nature of US Cold War concerns and the nature of the African policy inherited from the Eisenhower administration.

In December 1960 the US supported a UN resolution on colonialism which referred to subjugation to alien domination as a denial of human rights and called for immediate steps to be taken for the transfer of power. The Kennedy administration then caused a furore by supporting a more specific resolution on 14 March 1961 calling for Portugal to introduce reforms in Angola for the purpose of permitting the people to exercise the right of self-determination and for a UN committee to report on Angola. Yet Kennedy's policy remained one of support for the principle of self-determination and the promotion of agreement between Europeans and Africans to bring this about. The trouble for Kennedy was that the Portuguese rejected self-determination and independence, and the UN resolutions pertaining to Portuguese colonialism became more and more extreme. As cooperation was thus superseded by confrontation within Angola and at the United Nations, it became more difficult for the forces of moderation, including the US and many of the newly independent African states, to wield influence. The Americans were faced with a choice they wanted to avoid, between Portugal and NATO on the one hand and throwing in their lot with the more radical Africans on the other. This new Cold War dilemma, and the thrust of US policy, would have been the same with or without a US base in the Azores.

The crisis in Angola developed between January and March 1961 with a number of violent protests, which became a more organized rebellion promoted by the Union of Angolan Populations (UPA). Despite the deployment of over 40 000 troops, the Portuguese were unable fully to suppress it.[59] As early as February 1961, the US was aware that, faced with the prospect of reporting on developments in Angola, the Portuguese were issuing veiled threats to leave the UN, withdraw from NATO and reconsider the Azores base agreement, which expired at the end of 1962.[60] The State Department believed that in order to avoid jeopardizing US standing in the UN and with the African states it would be necessary to maintain a position which would be unpalatable to the Portuguese.[61] This remained the Department's view despite the concern over the Azores, which emanated from the Defense Department.

In 1961 it was deemed vital to champion African self-determination even if Portugal denied the US the Azores and withdrew from NATO because of the larger and more important considerations associated with the Cold War and the future of Africa.[62] And Kennedy, while concerned to avoid a complete break with Portugal, and American expulsion from the Azores, did not deviate from the March 1961 stance even though it proved impossible to influence the Portuguese on Angola. In July 1961 the US ambassador in Lisbon, C. Burke Elbrick, reported a conversation with the Portuguese foreign minister, Franco Nogueira. The latter claimed that the communists would take over the whole Iberian peninsula if Portugal lost her African territories, that Angola was much more important than Berlin and that Portugal was prepared to go to the bitter end in Africa and face the prospect of world war.[63] These difficulties influencing the Portuguese were compounded by the problems of convincing African leaders that the US did not support Portuguese African policy.[64]

Whatever the views on the Azores, there was general agreement on the need to get the Portuguese to accept change. The issue was whether the emphasis should be on private remonstrations with the Portuguese or on the pursuit of a vigorous public policy. After 1961 the US continued to maintain a public stance against the continuation of Portuguese colonialism, and the State Department remained committed to this policy. Bowles believed it would be unthinkable to modify African policy to fit in with the eighteenth-century views of Portugal.[65] In the White House it was believed in 1961 that firm opposition to oppression was necessary if Afro-Asian support was to be expected.[66] This became less attractive as African ideas on ending Portuguese rule became more radical and extreme.

Unfortunately, because the Portuguese failed to move significantly closer to the African position, US difficulties increased as the two sides became more confrontational. The general US approach to Angola in the UN became conditioned by attempts to deflect extreme anti-Portuguese resolutions while maintaining a principled stand against colonialism. The hope was that influence could be exerted over the Portuguese if the US abstained on the more extreme resolutions.[67] In 1962 the State Department remained determined not to retreat from the principled stand of March 1961.[68] As an Angolan government in exile was recognized by many African leaders, the Portuguese moved slightly by accepting an ILO mission and indicating a willingness to receive a UN rapporteur. When the UN Committee of 17[69] called for sanctions against Portugal in December 1962, the US argued that this would torpedo any chances of a peaceful settlement and moved to block the resolution.[70] This was not a weakening of a principled position for Cold War military reasons (and indeed the Azores agreement was not renewed although neither were the US military expelled) but a continuation of the attempt, for Cold War reasons, to promote self-determination without violence and upheaval.

Indeed in 1963 the State Department argued for a more vigorous anti-colonial position while still seeking to prevent a sharp break with Portugal.[71] Kennedy, however, was not keen to increase the risk of being thrown out of the Azores, because of a number of other critical Cold War issues in 1963, most notably the possibility of a Test Ban treaty. Nevertheless while the US abstained on a July resolution[72] against Portugal it supported one in December 1963 which reaffirmed previous UN resolutions calling for self-determination and on states not to provide arms for use in the Portuguese territories. The policy of supporting self-determination, to keep one foot in the African camp, while encouraging the Europeans to respond to African demands without a rupture of relations, had changed very little since the 1950s.

Before that the US stance was less sympathetic to European colonialism in Africa. At the end of the war colonial empires were seen as economically and politically damaging to US interests and the preservation of peace. With the advent of the Cold War the US had rapidly to qualify its anti-colonial stance and seek ways of supporting the principles of self-determination and self-government without damaging relations with the European colonial powers. This proved difficult and the attempt to portray Soviet colonialism, as the real source of oppression did not resolve the US dilemma as the Cold War importance of Africa increased. The problem in the second half of the 1950s was the pace of change as much as the principle of change, particularly when both the French and the British were committed to self-government and self-determination. In addition, as the first African states attained self-government, the Cold War dangers of premature independence were more a matter of concern to those US policy-makers who regarded Africans as primitive peoples incapable of governing themselves. On the other hand there was no retreat from the principle of self-determination and the Americans were more eager than the British that the demands of African nationalists should be promptly met as part of a Cold War strategy of preserving stability. It was still expected that this stability would be secured through cooperation between Americans, Africans and Europeans. The former would provide aid and assistance to help the colonial powers mitigate the consequences of premature independence that was the inevitable consequence of accepting the equally inevitable African demands for political power. The Kennedy administration found it difficult to implement this African strategy in the face of Portuguese non-cooperation. However, the policy was only modified in so much as new measures were tried to retain influence with the Portuguese. There was no backing away from the fundamental principle of self-determination even though this was damaging to US–Portuguese relations. The Cold War continued to demand that every effort should be made to woo African leaders without a fundamental rupture in American relations with their European allies. The Kennedy administration had to deal with this dilemma at a time when Africa and its newly independent states were increasingly radical and more important for US global strategy but there was no real change in American policy.

Notes

1 US National Archives and Records Administration (NA), Record Group (RG) 59, Notter Files Box 66, P minutes, 3 October 1942. Cited in Wm Roger Louis, *Imperialism at Bay 1941–1945* (Oxford, 1977), p. 170.

2 *Foreign Relations of the United States (FRUS)* 1950, vol. V, State Department summary of the informal panel's discussions on African affairs n.d., pp. 1506–9.

3 NA, RG 59, State Department Central Decimal File (SDCDF) 611.70, 1950–1954, Box 2844, consul general Dakar to SD, 23 February 1950.

4 NA, RG 59, SDCDF 611.70, Box 2844, consul-general Salisbury to SD, 8 May 1953.

5 *FRUS 1952–1954*, XI, Statement by consul-general Salisbury to the American Consular Conference, Capetown, 11 March 1952, p. 11.

6 *FRUS 1952–1954*, III, paper by the Colonial Policy Review Sub-Committee of the Committee on Dependent Area Affairs, 26 April 1950, pp. 1077–102.

7 *FRUS 1952–1954*, III, memorandum by R. B. Knight on US policy towards colonial areas and colonial powers, 21 April 1952, pp. 1102–8.

8 *FRUS 1952–1954*, III, memorandum by the Office of Dependent Area Affairs on the issue of colonialism, n.d. pp. 1169–77.

9 *FRUS 1952–1954*, III, memorandum by Mason Sears, 18 August 1953, pp. 1162–6.

10 *FRUS 1952–1954*, XI, address by H. A. Byroade to the World Affairs Council of Northern California, 31 October 1953, pp. 54–65.

11 *FRUS 1952–1954*, III, editorial note, p. 1167.

12 *FRUS 1952–1954*, XI, draft National Security Council policy statement by the Bureau of Near Eastern, South Asian and African Affairs, March 1954, pp. 98–101.

13 *FRUS 1955–1957*, XVIII, memorandum by the assistant secretary, Bureau of Near Eastern, South Asian and African Affairs, to J. F. Dulles, 12 August 1955, pp. 12–23.

14 FO 371/159681, minute by P. Ramsbottom, 13 January 1961.

15 The so-called thaw in the Cold War is based on a conception of the conflict different to that prevailing at the time among western leaders. The latter saw the competition for political influence and the prevention of the spread of communism as crucial, but the Korean War aroused fears that the competition could lead to hot war. The thaw was based on both sides' concern that the Cold War could bring armed conflict unless measures to prevent it were taken. This helped bring about an improvement in Soviet–American rela-

tions designed to avoid hot war while the commitment to the winning of the Cold War intensified.

16 Soviet moves in Africa are listed in FO 371/118676, jackets 4 to 9, February 1956 and FO 371/118677, jacket 19, EIG(56)2, March 1956.
17 CO 936/318/176, 'Pre-General Assembly UK/US talks on colonial questions', 11–12 October 1956 cited in D. Goldsworthy, 'Britain and the International Critics of British Colonialism, 1951–1956' *Journal of Commonwealth and Comparative Politics*, Vol. 29, p. 15; *FRUS 1955–1957*, XVIII, memorandum of Bermuda conversation, 23 March 1957, pp. 53–6.
18 *FRUS 1955–1957*, XVIII, memorandum by the assistant secretary of state for International Organisation Affairs to the deputy under secretary of state, 20 April 1955, pp. 6–7.
19 *FRUS 1955–1957*, XVIII, consul-general Leopoldville to SD, 28 December 1955, pp. 24–30.
20 *FRUS 1955–1957*, XVIII, consul-general Dakar to SD, 6 September 1956, pp. 149–157.
21 *FRUS 1955–1957*, XVIII, consul-general Nairobi to SD, 30 December 1955, pp. 189–195.
22 *FRUS 1955–1957*, XVIII, consul-general Dar es Salaam to SD, 12 March 1957, pp. 195–200.
23 NA, RG 59, SDCDF 611.70, Box 2543, memorandum 'US Problems in Africa' by the Office of African Affairs, 17 February 1956.
24 FO 371/118683, J. E. Coulson (Washington) to FO, 22 August 1956.
25 FO 371/118677, no. 24, Barbara Salt (Washington) to J. H. A. Watson, 11 June 1956.
26 *FRUS 1961–1963*, XXI, record of Kennedy–de Gaulle conversation, 31 May 1961, pp. 292–4.
27 The exchange led to the British establishing an official Africa committee which produced a lengthy paper entitled 'Africa: the Next Ten Years' in May 1959.
28 *FRUS 1955–1957*, XVIII, NSC memorandum 5719/1, 23 August 1957.
29 FO 371/125304 no 11, copy of despatch from West German embassy Washington reporting comments of George Allen, former assistant secretary of Near Eastern, South Asian and African Affairs, 3 May 1957.
30 *FRUS 1955–1957*, XVIII, memorandum of Bermuda conversation, 23 March 1957, pp. 53–6.
31 FO 371/131189, no. 22, D. Williams (colonial attaché, Washington) to W. A. C. Mathieson, 8 July 1958.
32 *FRUS 1958–1960*, XIV, memorandum by special assistant J. Holmes, 6 February 1958, pp. 1–11.
33 FO 371/131189, no. 24, Lord Hood (Washington) to Selwyn Lloyd, 15 July 1958.
34 *FRUS 1958–1960*, XIV, NIE 75-58, 17 June 1958, pp. 17–18.
35 *FRUS 1958–1960*, XIV, record of discussion at 375th NSC meeting, 7 August 1958, pp. 19–22.
36 *FRUS 1958–1960*, XIV, NSC 5818, 29 August 1958, pp. 23–37.
37 FO 371/137949, record of speech by assistant secretary Joseph Satterthwaite referring to Dulles's speech.
38 *FRUS 1958–1960*, XIV, memorandum by Sears, 29 January 1959, pp. 40–2.

39 *FRUS 1958–1960*, XIV, H. Cabot Lodge to SD, 17 March 1959, pp. 43–4.
40 C. Douglas-Home, *Evelyn Baring: the Last Pro-consul* (1978), pp. 283–4, cited in John D. Hargreaves, *Decolonization in Africa* (Harlow, 1996), p. 179.
41 FO 371/137972, memorandum 'Africa: the Next Ten Years', May 1959.
42 *FRUS 1958–1960*, XIV, NIE 76–59, 20 October 1959, pp. 58–68.
43 *FRUS 1958–1960*, XIV, record of 432nd NSC meeting, 14 January 1960, pp. 73–7.
44 *FRUS 1958–1960*, XIV, NSC 6001, 19 January 1960, pp. 79–93.
45 FO 371/137972, no. 26, record of US/UK talks on the future of Africa, 23 November 1959.
46 NA, RG 59, SDCDF 745c.00, 1960–1963, Box 1690, Joint State–USIA–ICA message to consul general Salisbury, 29 January 1960.
47 NA, RG 59, SDCDF 745c.00, 1960–1963, Box 1690, record of talks between C. Vaughan Ferguson (director of Office of South African Affairs) and Kaunda, 9 May 1960.
48 NA, RG 59, SDCDF 745c.00, 1960–1963, Box 1690, consul-general Salisbury to SD, 21 April 1960.
49 NA, RG 59, SDCDF 745c.00, 1960–1963, Box 1690, ambassador London to SD, 20 May 1960.
50 NA, RG 59, SDCDF 745c.00 1960–1963, Box 1690, consul-general Salisbury to SD, 27 May 1960.
51 NA, RG 59, Lot Files Bureau of African Affairs, 1956–1962, Box 2, O. Deming to J. Penfield, 22 February 1961.
52 John F. Kennedy Presidential Library (JFKPL), National Security Files (NSF), Country Series Africa, Box 2, summary of report on Mennen Williams's African tour, 8 August–1 September 1961.
53 *FRUS 1961–1963*, XXI, memorandum by Lucius D. Battle for McGeorge Bundy, 7 May 1962, pp. 516–18.
54 FO 371/146506, no 21, record of Anglo-French–American talks on the future of Africa, 1 June 1960. Couve de Murville, the French foreign minister, predicted that on independence the 'tribes' might begin by killing the whites and then start killing each other.
55 NA, papers of G. Mennen Williams, subject file, Box 18, State Department memorandum, 9 January 1962.
56 FO 371/146495, no 10.
57 On the Congo, see Madeleine G. Kalb, *The Congo Cables: the Cold War in Africa from Eisenhower to Kennedy* (New York, 1982), R. D. Mahoney, *JFK: Ordeal in Africa* (Oxford, 1983) and from a United Nations angle, A. James, *Britain and the Congo Crisis* (Basingstoke, 1996).
58 See, for example, James N. Giglio, *The Presidency of John F. Kennedy* (Lawrence, 1991).
59 It is still not clear whether the troubles in Luanda, the cotton-growing area of Malange and the coffee-growing areas in the north-west were inspired by Holden Roberto's UPA or were spontaneous protests against Portuguese forced labour and the more unfavourable economic conditions which were then exploited by the UPA. See JFKPL, NSF, Country Series Angola, Box 5, Report of Presidential Task Force on Portuguese territories in Africa, 12 June 1961; John Marcum, *The Angolan Revolution*, Vol. 1, *1950–1962* (Baltimore, 1969) chapter 4; NA, RG 59, SDCDF 753n.00, 1960–1963, Box 1821.

60 NA, RG 59, Lot Files Bureau of African Affairs, 1956–1962, Box 2, talking paper on Angola by G. Mennen Williams, 15 February 1961.
61 NA, RG 59, SDCDF 611.41, Box 1236, talking paper for November 1960 talks with the UK on Africa, n.d.
62 *FRUS 1961–1963*, XXI, pp. 545–6, memorandum from Sam Belk (NSC staff) to McGeorge Bundy, 29 June 1961.
63 JFKPL, NSF, Country Series Angola, Box 5, Lisbon to SD, 11 July 1961.
64 NA, RG 59, Lot Files Bureau of African Affairs, 1956–1962, Box 2, Mennen Williams's talking paper on Portuguese Africa, 15 February 1961.
65 JFKPL, NSF Country Series Portugal, memorandum by Chester Bowles for President Kennedy, 4 June 1962.
66 JFKPL, NSF Country Series Angola, Box 5, memorandum by W. Rostow for President Kennedy, 14 July 1961.
67 NA, RG 59, SDCDF 753n.00, 1960–1963, Box 1821, Adlai Stevenson (NY) to SD, 6 June 1961.
68 *FRUS 1961–1963*, XXI, State Department memorandum for President Kennedy, 25 January 1962, pp. 555–6.
69 The Committee of 17, established on 27 November 1961, was the UN Special Committee on the Situation with regard to the Implementation of the Declaration on the Granting of Independence to Colonial Countries and Peoples.
70 *FRUS 1961–1963*, XXI, SD to UN Mission (NY), 8 December 1962, pp. 564–6.
71 *FRUS 1961–1963*, XXI, memorandum by D. Rusk for President Kennedy, 10 July 1963, pp. 568–72.
72 The 31 July 1963 resolution called on states not to offer Portugal any assistance to enable its repression to continue and not to provide any arms or equipment, which was bound to affect Portugal's position in NATO.

9

The United States and Britain's Decolonization of Malaya, 1942–57

A. J. Stockwell

Introduction

'In the six months since the termination of hostilities with Japan it has become clear that the world is going through a colonial crisis unparalleled in history. The great empires built up by the Western European powers during four centuries have been shaken to their foundations. They are crumbling before our eyes.'[1] This situation presented the United States with a dilemma. Were Americans to prop up these sick men of Europe or were they to smooth the pillow of the dying and act as midwife to emergent nations? As it happened, while ideologically committed to anti-colonialism, the United States approached Western dependencies in Southeast Asia in different ways. Transferring power to the Philippines on 4 July 1946, more or less according to a timetable set in 1935, the US held this up as a model for the European colonial powers to follow. None of them did. Impatient with Dutch intransigence in their struggle with the nascent Republic of Indonesia, in 1949 the American administration forced Holland to end its empire by threatening to withdraw Marshall Aid funding. By contrast, interpreting France's war with the Vietminh as part of the world-wide containment of communism, the United States decided to assist the French empire, prolonging its natural life until that cataclysmic collapse at Dien Bien Phu in 1954. There is, however, scarcely any evidence of American interference altering the course of British decolonization in Southeast Asia. So far as Malaya was concerned, this may have been because the country was peripheral to the Americans' principal interests in Asia or because, by and large, they approved of British policies there. What is clear, however, is that the British authorities were very sensitive to actual and likely criticism from the United States and took care at least to present their Malayan policies in ways which would be acceptable in Washington.

American anti-imperialism and British new imperialism, 1942–48

In 1941–42 Britain lost its empire in East and Southeast Asia. In rapid succession, Hong Kong, Malaya, Singapore, northern Borneo and Burma fell to Japan. At the same time Britain gained an ally, or an ally of a kind.[2] With the United States as a belligerent, victory in war was assured but restoration of lost colonies remained doubtful. American opposition to Europe's colonial empires derived from an ideology dating back to 1776 as well as from self-interest. Empire offended their beliefs in self-determination, free trade and international cooperation. European colonies in Southeast Asia, it was held, had exploited indigenous peoples and contributed to the military débâcle of 1941–42. Moreover, they offended the principles underlying America's plans for the Philippines as well as their commitments to the territorial integrity of Chiang Kai-shek's China.[3] President Roosevelt himself frequently expressed his determination that East and Southeast Asia should not return to the *status quo ante bellum* after its liberation from Japan, but, under the umbrella of international trusteeship, should advance as quickly as possible to self-determination. In short, the Pacific War destroyed colonial empires, unleashed nationalism, and introduced a new world order in Southeast Asia. As the US Under-Secretary of State Sumner Welles put it: 'The age of imperialism is dead.'

Churchill, however, had 'not become the King's first minister to preside over the liquidation of the British Empire'. Although the Deputy Prime Minister, Attlee, sympathized with the concepts of international trusteeship[4] and the Colonial Office feared that the Foreign Office might be tempted to make concessions in the East in order to secure American support in the West,[5] on the whole ministers and officials vigorously rejected American criticisms of the colonial empire and their proposals to dismantle it. They argued that the United States was as much to blame as were the British for the military defeats in Southeast Asia, that American strictures arose from ignorance of the colonial record, and that the advocacy of early independence was naïve and impractical.[6] Moreover, the British detected a strong streak of hypocrisy in the rhetoric of Americans, who, they believed, looked forward to supplanting European imperialism in Southeast Asia. The British commitment to return to lost colonies, particularly to Malaya, was strengthened by, firstly, a determination to restore national pride and avenge the humiliating defeats of 1941–42; secondly, their publicly repeated obligations to indigenous or 'protected' peoples; and, thirdly, the valuable contributions which colonial commodities were likely to make to the postwar reconstruction of the British economy. Furthermore, the British government accepted a responsibility to keep the imperial faith with the Dutch government in exile and, up to a point, de Gaulle's Free French.

Anglo-American differences over the record and future of colonial empires, which were only accentuated by attempts to agree a common statement on the subject, soured the special relationship, distorting strategic planning and breeding mistrust in allied commands. Article three of the Atlantic Charter of August 1941, whereby Churchill and Roosevelt acknowledged 'the right of all peoples to choose the form of government under which they will live', was interpreted very differently in London and Washington. Moreover, the exercise in 1942–43 to devise a joint declaration on the future of colonies revealed apparently irreconcilable viewpoints: the British emphasized gradual and paternal development while the Americans insisted on timetables for independence.[7] Since Americans suspected the British of using United States resources to win back lost territory, these differences affected discussions over the relative significance of the western and eastern theatres of war as well as the conduct of military operations in Asia and the Pacific. Towards the end of 1944 the British government judged that 'the overriding problem throughout the Far East was our relations with the United States'. It expressed concern at 'the misconceptions in the United States of our aims and objectives', which it put down to 'wilful misunderstanding and partly to ignorance', but stressed that 'we had to take the fact of their existence into account'.[8]

Nevertheless, the heat went out of the colonial dispute towards the end of the war. Mulish opposition to American views on the part of the British was qualified by a pragmatic acceptance of their dependence upon American resources. They realized that colonial restitution required US acquiescence, if not active assistance, and that the postwar security of Southeast Asia would necessitate US underpinning. Britain's colonial policy-making during the war, especially for Southeast Asia, was conducted in this wider context of Anglo-American relations. The United States government did not directly intervene in the process but there is no doubt that its probable reactions were taken into account during it: for all that colonial policy-makers maintained that the war merely speeded up advance along well-established lines, they took care to present their plans in progressive terms. At the same time, US anti-colonialism moderated. For example, while both the White House and the State Department continued to press Europeans for more explicit commitments to self-government,[9] the thrust of this campaign was reduced by differences between the President and the State Department[10] as well as by a general reluctance in the US administration to weaken the political positions of Churchill and de Gaulle. The death of Roosevelt and the succession of Truman contributed to an allied alignment on the colonial question, which was also assisted by progressive pronouncements on colonial issues from the British, Dutch and French.[11] Moreover, there was a growing American acceptance, at least in some quarters of government, of the uses of empire. Indeed, as the war went on, the US itself assumed an imperial role in the Pacific and accepted the value of European colonies: the Joint Chiefs of Staff recognized the importance of Pacific islands as bases and of colonial structures for the military reoccupation and subsequent rehabilitation of Southeast Asia. Furthermore, because colonial Southeast Asia was marginal to its principal interests in Japan and China, the United States government was willing to assign its reoccupation to Mountbatten's South East Asia Command. When the Allies finalized their plans for the liberation of East and Southeast Asia at the Potsdam Conference (July–August 1945), SEAC was charged with responsibility for most of the Dutch East Indies (Indonesia) and of Vietnam northward to the 16th parallel, in addition to Burma and British Malaya.

By the end of the war the United States administration viewed with mixed feelings the restoration of colonial regimes. This was evident from the State Department's policy paper, produced a few weeks before the Potsdam Conference, which carried out 'An estimate of conditions in Asia and the Pacific at the close of the war in the Far East and the objectives and policies of the United States'.[12] The US regarded colonial restoration as a necessary evil: while in the short term it could assist the rehabilitation of both Southeast Asian countries and the European metropolitan powers, yet, in the longer term, it would delay self-determination and obstruct 'equal economic and commercial opportunity for all nations'.[13] The paper pointed out that "A problem for the United States is to harmonise, so far as possible, its policies in regard to the two objectives: increased political freedom for the Far East and the maintenance of the unity of the leading United Nations in meeting this problem.'[14] In addressing this conundrum, the US government would 'continue to state the political principle which it has frequently announced, that dependent peoples should be given the opportunity, if necessary after an adequate period of preparation, to achieve an increased measure of self-government, but it should avoid any course of action which would seriously impair the unity of the major United Nations'.[15] America's colonial dilemma was particularly acute in the case of its relations with Britain, its principal ally and the major colonial power in Asia: 'British policy in the Far East is in harmony with United States policies in many respects, but in certain other respects it is at variance.'[16] Reconciled to 'a policy of non-interference in any British possession', the State Department still advocated 'a policy which would allow colonial peoples an opportunity to prepare themselves for increased participation in their own government with eventual self-government as the goal'[17] and expressed concern over the 'apparent unwillingness of the British Government to grant to its dependencies as early and as adequate an increase of self-government as is favored by American opinion'.[18] Six months later this line was repeated by John F. Cady (then a young official in the State Department, later a distinguished historian of Southeast Asia): the United States would refrain from challenging European sovereign claims and was, indeed, willing to assist the re-establishment of their authority 'if it can be accomplished by negotiation, and on terms that accord with the wishes of responsible elements of the populations concerned'. Nonetheless, he restated American opposition to a return to the prewar *status quo*, affirmed the principles of the UN Charter committing colonial powers to prepare for self-determination, and held up as an example US plans for the independence of the Philippines.[19]

Although the British did not share this unquestioning faith in the virtues of self-determination, few expected a straightforward return to old practices of colonial control. They calculated that conditions in the region would necessitate a prolonged period of direct rule – a 'new imperialism', so to speak. For all that Mountbatten sympathized with nationalist leaders – negotiating with Aung San in Burma and advocating a similar approach to Sukarno in Indonesia – his Southeast Asia Command lacked a mandate to advance European dependencies to early self-government. SEAC also wanted the means to restore peace and prosperity: such was the unrest which they encountered that commanding officers in Java and southern Vietnam were on occasions obliged to deploy surrendered Japanese personnel on policing duties and were eager to transfer their responsibilities to the Dutch and French as soon as possible.[20] In Malaya, by contrast, the British Military Administration encountered little resistance and was able to prepare for the return to civil government according to plans which had been drawn up during the war.

Britain's policy for postwar Malaya differed radically from prewar arrangements in two respects: the imposition of direct control and the prospect of political advance. Before 1942 British Malaya had consisted of nine Malay states or sultanates (four of which formed the Federated Malay States) and the three Straits Settlements of Singapore, Penang and Malacca. Prewar British Borneo had been composed of Sarawak (ruled by the Brooke rajahs), North Borneo (under a Chartered Company) and the 'protected' sultanate of Brunei. In addition to this administrative fragmentation, ethnic differences, particularly those between Malaya's Malay and Chinese communities, had been reinforced by pro-Malay attitudes, which marginalized non-Malays as transients or 'birds of passage'. Under the new policy, however, indirect rule was to be replaced by direct rule: while Brunei retained its prewar status, Sarawak and North Borneo were to be annexed, the Crown would acquire sovereignty from the Malay rulers, and significant steps would be taken towards the consolidation of Britain's Southeast Asian empire. Cruel to be kind, the British also intended to use their new powers for economic development, social welfare, and the creation of an eventually self-governing, multi-racial nation. After military administration gave way to civil rule in 1946, crown colony government was established in Singapore (April), Sarawak (July) and North Borneo (July), while the Malayan Union was set up in Malaya (April). The Malayan Union abandoned the principles of the sovereignty of the Malay rulers, the autonomy of the Malay states, and the privileged position of the Malays. Regressive in its imposition of direct and centralized British control, the scheme was progressive in its proposals for a common citizenship, which was open to those from any race who regarded Malaya as home.[21]

For all the radicalism of this new policy, however, there is no evidence either of direct American involvement or even of British consultation with US officials during the drafting of the Malayan Union. It is true that, as soon as he sensed the dramatic change of direction taken in Whitehall, Mountbatten strenuously urged maximum publicity in order to allay American criticisms of Britain's prewar role in Southeast Asia and to woo local opinion in advance of the military reoccupation of Malaya.[22] But, though its enlightened aims were calculated to appeal to progressive opinion and though it had been drafted with the wider issues of Anglo-American relations very much in mind, Whitehall policy-makers fought shy even of publicity. They feared that premature advertisement might be 'a double edged weapon'[23], stirring up opposition in Malaya and among 'old Malaya hands' in Britain that could sabotage success. It was not until June 1945 that the caretaker cabinet agreed to the distribution to government agencies and political warfare departments of a general statement on Britain's plans for postwar Malaya.[24] Even then, Americans were kept in ignorance of the details and the US State and War Departments relied on morsels passed on by American officers in the Combined Civil Affairs Organization of SEAC, who said they were keeping their fingers 'on the British pulse'.[25]

With the return to civil government in April 1946, Malayan affairs were monitored by an American consul-general in Singapore and consuls in Kuala Lumpur and Penang who sent fortnightly despatches to the Far Eastern Bureau of the State Department. The consuls in Malaya and embassy officials in London reported, for example, on opposition to the Malayan Union, particularly from the Malays who felt betrayed by British progressivism, since it appeared to presage an eventual take-over by the economically better-established Chinese. In April 1947, while the colonial authorities were negotiating a way out of their impasse with Malay leaders, the US consul-general surveyed the first year of postwar civil government. He commented on a certain amount of scepticism about British claims to be laying the foundations for a new democratic government: 'Many among the local Asiatic leaders are inclined to believe that these protestations are belied by the reluctance of Government to make specific moves toward the goals which it proclaims for itself.'[26] On the other hand, he noted the absence of a nationalist movement comparable with those in Burma, Indonesia or French Indo-China. He explained this in terms of Malaya's 'racial and religious differences' rather than by reference to any British policy of divide-and-rule whose existence, let alone significance, he explicitly discounted. In 1946–47 it was Malay communalism, not Malayan multi-racial nationalism, which forced the British to retreat from the Malayan Union. A replacement constitution, the Federation of Malaya (1948), drastically modified the Union's radicalism, watering down the provisions for centralized government and common citizenship and guaranteeing Malay political paramountcy. Despite this climb-down, however, the British remained committed to the aims of their new imperialism: the consolidation of disparate territories, the nurture of multi-racial nationhood, and the grant of self-government 'when conditions were right'. Included in these conditions, of course, were the country's security and economic viability. While the American consul-general and officials in the State Department bridled at vestiges of the old Adam of unreconstructed colonialism, which lingered in the attitudes and way of life of the European community, they concluded that after the war Britain was pursuing an essentially enlightened policy in Malaya.

Cold War and decolonization, 1948–57

After the Second World War, three historic principles continued to determine American policy towards European colonies: 'sympathy for the political aspirations of the natives, respect for the legal rights of imperial powers and insistence on commercial privileges for the United States equal to those enjoyed by metropolitan colonial powers'. By the spring of 1946, however, these had been joined by a fourth consideration: 'the growing power of Russia'. At the risk of incurring the opposition of Congress and of the American public, as well as of the colonial powers themselves, the State Department proposed the more active deployment of US 'moral prestige and economic might' in the non-European world.[27] As the retreat from empire gathered pace, the administration needed to establish the extent to which it might have to step into the shoes of departing colonial powers. In mid-May 1947, as deadlines for British withdrawal from India and Burma drew near, Secretary of State George Marshall (through Dean Acheson) asked the American Ambassador in London for an assessment of Britain's 'capabilities, intentions and thinking on world problems', and, in particular, British forecasts of 'the future course of Empire defense and of their defense commitments'.[28] In his reply, Ambassador Douglas drew attention to a fundamental Anglo-American solidarity in international affairs in opposition to the power of the Soviet Union and also to what he regarded as Britain's enlightened policy regarding colonial affairs.[29] Lacking the means to pursue an independent line in world affairs, he wrote, 'Britain, it seems, is seeking desperately to cut her cloth to fit her present stature', withdrawing from the indefensible, spreading defence burdens across the Commonwealth, making political concessions in dependent territories, and following the US lead in world affairs.[30] As far as Malaya was concerned, however, the ambassador noted that the British showed no signs of planning an early departure. Because of its strategic position *en route* to Australasia, its valuable rubber and tin, and the political immaturity of its peoples, Malaya was 'the one important area in the Far East which the British evidently have no intention of abandoning'.[31] He pointed out that the colonial authorities aimed to establish an efficient, liberal, and forward-looking administration which would facilitate its retention under British control, which might be held up as a model for the Dutch and

French to emulate, which could assist regional cooperation, and which should prevent communist infiltration. Malaya was emerging as a frontline state in the Cold War.

It has been argued that 'As the cold war intensified from 1947 to 1951, competition between the two superpowers came to the rescue of the Empire.'[32] As Mao Zedong drove the forces of Chiang Kai-shek before him, America's China policy collapsed in ruins and uprisings occurred in Southeast Asia. In 1948 communist insurgencies flared up in Malaya and the Philippines, Ho Chi Minh's Vietminh was reinvigorated in its struggle for independence from the French, and Sukarno's Republic of Indonesia narrowly escaped being overturned by a communist coup at Madiun in Java. The United States now approached Southeast Asian countries with the Cold War as its top priority. There were both specifically regional and widely global dimensions to the problem of confronting communism. Firstly, whether or not they had yet achieved independence from colonial rule, the stability of individual states was crucial for the security of Southeast Asia as a whole, since together they formed a cordon against communist expansion. Secondly, the fate of Southeast Asian colonies had a direct bearing on the defence and economic rehabilitation of western Europe: whether the outcome was defeat or victory for the European powers, colonial subversion and prolonged counter-insurgency would weaken the capacity of Britain, France, and Holland to play their full part in the western alliance. One State Department official warned:

> we must not ride rough-shod over Dutch and French sensibilities. To do so might result in a failure to achieve our objectives not only in SEA [sic] but also in the Atlantic Community. At the same time, we must not be overawed and blackmailed by the threat of our recalcitrant European powers that they would bring the Atlantic Community down around the ears of all of us – a Community in which, it is sometimes forgotten, they have a more real interest than even we.[33]

The American administration turned to propaganda, diplomatic pressure, and economic aid in order to secure and manipulate the countries of Southeast Asia in the containment of communism. As regards the struggle in Indonesia, because the United States concluded that persistent Dutch attempts to defeat the Republic would be counterproductive, both weakening Holland in Europe and providing an opportunity for the communists to seize control of Indonesian nationalism, it forced the Netherlands to come to terms with Sukarno's nationalist movement by the expedient of threatening to withhold economic assistance from Holland.[34] Elsewhere, the United States supported colonial as well as independent states in their campaigns against communism. Thus American missions were despatched to Southeast Asia to survey the requirements of anti-communist regimes for American assistance. The United States consequently subsidized the French war in Indochina,[35] assisted the Filipino government's operations against the Hukbalahap in Central Luzon,[36] and supplied the British with materials and machinery for the campaign against the Malayan Communist Party.

Though the intentions of the Chinese-dominated Malayan Communist Party in 1948 still remain unclear, by mid-June the British were convinced that labour unrest, rural violence, and murders of European rubber-planters signalled the start of an armed uprising directed by the Kremlin.[37] Following the declaration of what turned out to be a 12-year state of emergency, the authorities engaged in a war against communist guerrillas. Britain could not contemplate defeat: Malaya was a principal dollar-earner, occupied a key strategic position, and was central to British prestige, which a repetition of 1941–42 would destroy forever. The campaign against the Malayan communists involved massive military investment and the assumption of unprecedented power by the British. Though they stated and regularly reiterated their prime commitment to the restoration of law and order, the authorities in London and Malaya soon accepted what under General Templer (High Commissioner, 1952–54) would come to be known as a 'hearts and minds' strategy. Countering the claims of world communism to be 'the champion of dependent peoples against their cynical and self-seeking oppressors',[38] the British invested Malayan revenues in welfare programmes, sponsored rural development, and prepared for the transfer of power to responsible local leaders.

From the start of the emergency, the British assiduously cultivated American support, taking American officials into their confidence, wooing the American media, and generally presenting their policies as both progressive and realistic. Concerned that the US might neglect Southeast Asia to concentrate on China, Taiwan, and Japan, the British took steps to involve them in the region. The tasks of impressing the United States with British achievements and intentions and dispelling ignorance over the colonial record, required the careful presentation of British conduct in Malaya. From London, the Foreign Office assisted the colonial authorities in Malaya 'by ensuring that United States opinion is properly informed about events in Malaya and by trying to secure United States material assistance when necessary'.[39] On the spot,

Malcolm MacDonald, the commissioner-general in Southeast Asia 1948–55, took the lead in the charm offensive. MacDonald viewed Malayan problems in the wider contexts of Southeast Asian defence and Anglo-American relations and broke 'the ice at the top' by inviting the US consul-general (along with Australian and New Zealand observers) to meetings of the British Defence Coordination Committee.[40] The consul-general was placed on the distribution list of the Political Intelligence Journals and was also briefed by the federal police and Special Branch officers (such as Claude Fenner). He received copies of security reports and captured communist documents. In addition, the consul-general was told that Loi Tek (secretary-general of the Malayan Communist Party until 1947) was a double agent[41] and the State Department would later be informed of the top-secret talks between the elected Malayan government and communist leaders at Baling in December 1955.[42] Soon after MacDonald's initiatives the consul-general was reporting to the State Department on the 'exceptional warmth' displayed by MacDonald, whose 'personal attitude [set] the tone of the friendly feeling towards the US'.[43] Indeed, MacDonald distanced himself so deliberately from the 'old colonial attitudes' of the British community in British Malaya that the consul-general wondered at his motives.[44] While naturally less affable than MacDonald, General Templer nonetheless insisted that his staff cultivate the goodwill and respect of US officials and the American press.[45] He told the consul-general that 'If I have anyone who can't work with Americans I'll fire him.'[46]

Consultation paid off. Despite the slow progress of counter-insurgency, American observers were largely persuaded that the British were working on the right lines. In September 1950 the vice-consul observed: 'In practice, the government, particularly in Singapore and the Federation, is much more democratic than it would appear from its authoritarian structure.'[47] He welcomed initiatives like the Rural and Industrial Development Authority and the Communities Liaison Committee as 'bold and effective measures' and accepted that 'unquestionably, the British will continue to give a greater measure of self-government to the Malayan people'. The appointment of General Charles F. Baldwin, as consul-general with the rank of minister in December 1951, indicates the significance with which the State Department now invested this posting. It came at a crisis in the emergency when, following the assassination of High Commissioner Gurney in October 1951, the structure and personnel of Malayan government were undergoing a major shake-up. This resulted in the appointment of Templer as supremo of military operations and civil administration. He was given a definite, political directive, the first provision of which stated that 'Malaya should in due course become a fully self-governing nation'.[48] Just before Templer arrived in Malaya the American consul-general provided the State Department with guidance on the formulation of its Malayan policy. He advised that the 'statement shld [sic] not complicate or embarrass Brit [sic] position or encourage over-hasty demands [for] self govt [sic] and opposition to continued Brit [sic] control', and recommended the use of expressions such as 'political development' in preference to 'independence' or 'self-government'.[49] Consequently, Washington accepted 'the present struggle in Malaya as an integral part of the free world's common effort to halt Communist aggression' and supported British endeavours to defeat insurgents and 'build a new nation'.[50] The statement which the National Security Council included in its paper on 'United States Objectives and Courses of Action with Respect to Southeast Asia', and which was subsequently reaffirmed, declared that US policy was to 'support the British in their measures to eradicate communist guerrilla forces and restore order'.[51]

In addition to moral support in the United Nations against the anti-colonial bloc,[52] the British hoped for material help from the United States. Firstly, since Malayan commodities were vital dollar-earners, they were anxious that the US should guarantee purchases of rubber and tin, though Americans grew impatient with exchange controls.[53] Secondly, the British realized that the Commonwealth proposals issued at Colombo in January 1950 for a 'Marshall Plan for Asia' to promote economic development as a safeguard against 'the menace of communism' would succeed only with financial help from the United States.[54] Thirdly, British authorities applied for technical aid and equipment to assist counter-insurgency operations. Two US Aid Survey Missions visited Southeast Asia in 1950: the first was led by R. Allen Griffin in March and was followed, in August, by that of John Melby and Major-General G. Erskine. The Foreign Office was quick to put in a request for police radios, outboard motors, Chinese interpreters, shot-guns, armour plate, and barbed wire.[55] By March 1953, just over a year since Templer's arrival in Malaya, the security situation had so improved that political advance was in the air: two non-communist parties, the United Malays National Organization and the Malayan Chinese Association formed the Alliance (which the Malayan Indian Congress later joined) and the Malayan authorities contemplated the introduction of elections for the Federal Council (which took place for the first time in July 1955).[56] In the same month Consul-General Baldwin sent the following statement to the State Department. It is a ringing endorsement of Britain's position in Malaya and an unequivocal justification for American support.

The strategic situation of Malaya, its economic importance, political significance, and the fact that, despite the recognized decline in British power, there is still no viable, anti-Communist alternative to British control of Malaya, all justify continued United States support of the British policy of protecting Malaya against external attack, restoring law and order, and guiding Malaya in orderly stages of transition to self-government. The United States, by its general economic policies and by furnishing the British with technical and other types of assistance, can contribute positively to the social and economic improvement of Malaya and thus to its political stability. As the 'battle for men's minds' is a very real and critical struggle in Malaya, United States activities in the information field will continue to be of particular importance. Closely coordinated with those of the British, they should be designed to indicate Anglo-American solidarity and positive American interest in the future stability and well-being of Malaya and the rest of Southeast, and should be directed particularly to the Chinese sector of Malaya's population.[57]

Despite fundamental Anglo-American solidarity over the containment of communism, strains nonetheless occurred in the relationship. Britain and America had different agendas and each tried to shape Southeast Asia in its own image. Just as the Americans regarded colonies as proxies in the containment of communism, so the British attempted to conduct imperial policy by proxy. As the foreign secretary argued in June 1952, 'the more gradually and inconspicuously we can transfer the real burdens from our own to American shoulders, the less damage we shall do to our position and influence in the world'.[58] Because of the marked gap between their commitments and capacity as well as between British and American power, the British hoped to draw upon US resources to underwrite their policies for Southeast Asia. In this they were sometimes to be disappointed as, for example, in their attempts to win US financial support for the Colombo Plan for Asian development. Understandably, the American and British governments were on their guard against being drawn too far into each other's commitments. Although the British realized that less than their whole-hearted support for the United States in the East might (as during the Second World War) reduce America's commitment to Britain's position in the West and while the Americans were reluctant to jeopardize the cohesion of NATO by undermining European colonies, London and Washington were each on their guard against being manipulated, even blackmailed, by the other. In the years 1950–54 Britain and the United States differed markedly in their approach to three major international questions in the region: the status of the People's Republic of China (which Britain recognized in January 1950 though the US refused to do so), the conduct of the Korean War (where the British feared that the US might resort to atomic weapons), and Indochina (where the British and Americans fell out in the run-up to and during the course of the Geneva Conference of 1954). In the aftermath of the Geneva Conference MacDonald reported that the 'conduct of American foreign policy towards Asia during recent months has left the Untied States with few friends, many enemies and almost universal critics amongst Asian Governments and peoples'. Because 'American policy is generally regarded as dominating all Western policy towards Asia', Britain's prestige and good relations with Asian states were likely to suffer as a result.[59]

Despite the paramount importance of the Cold War, Anglo-American differences persisted in the field of colonialism. Although anti-colonialism took second place to anti-communism in the United States, it did not completely overwhelm it. On the contrary, the Cold War exacerbated the 'colonial problem' and had the potential to drive a wedge between Britain and America. In August 1948 the US ambassador in Moscow reported on the Communist focus upon 'Anglo-American imperialism' and the claims that America was taking the lead in the 'oppression of colonial peoples' of Southeast Asia.[60] Anxious to distinguish between legitimate nationalism and pernicious communism, the State Department launched a propaganda offensive to counter Soviet influence over colonial peoples and to neutralize the anti-colonial bloc in the United Nations. In so doing, it endeavoured to 'avoid the appearance of being dependent upon the emergent nations but . . . to "put across" the idea that their independence and future prosperity depend solely upon the US', stressing that its 'appeal to emergent nations should be to harp incessantly upon our willingness to assist them to attain national independence to the extent of their capacity therefor, with our record in the Philippines ever in the foreground'.[61] Their association with European colonialism could still embarrass Americans. They grew impatient with Britain's 'colonial mentality', criticized delays in decolonization, and accused the British of clinging to power while preparing for a future of neo-colonialism.[62] Moreover, they looked forward to supplanting British influence in their former colonies and the wider region and they had every confidence that their superior economic, military and moral position would enable them to do so. Though American power and trade in the region overshadowed those of Britain, the British continued to assert, and the Americans to accept, that the United States did not enjoy the same degree of prestige as the United Kingdom.[63] The British claimed success in coming to terms with the 'nationalist spirit' of Asia through their familiarity with non-European societies, their enlightened but pragmatic colonial policy, and their adjustment of the structure and appeal of the Commonwealth. Nonetheless, US officials gained direct access to Malayan politicians without bothering to go through the high commissioner or commissioner-general, and, after the electoral victory of Tunku Abdul Rahman's Alliance in July 1955, they established closer relations with the prospective leaders of independent Malaya.

Conclusion

Ideologically and for reasons of self-interest, the United States favoured self-determination for Europe's colonies in Southeast Asia. During the Pacific War and its immediate aftermath, the American administration rejected colonialism and for a time attempted to prevent the restoration of lost empires. But it did not pursue decolonization to the extent of endangering Britain's position as a member of the Grand Alliance. For their part, the British regarded American views on colonies with suspicion, though some contemplated colonial concessions for the greater good of maintaining Anglo-American solidarity. In the case of their profitable dependency of Malaya, the British embarked on a new, progressive course for the postwar period, but there is no evidence that they did so as a result of US pressure or because of the active involvement of American personnel.

With the advent of the Cold War, the Anglo-American relationship was reinforced. Approaching communism as a global threat, the United States promoted the security of Western Europe and 'gave priority to anti-communism over anti-colonialism' outside Europe.[64] With respect to Malaya, the American administration 'blessed' the British strategy to counter communist insurgency with a combination of military and non-military methods. The claim that the Cold War came to the rescue of Britain's empire, which was increasingly managed by an Anglo-American partnership where Britain played second fiddle, is largely persuasive but not wholly sustainable in the case of Malaya. First of all, the counter-insurgency campaign led to the abbreviation, not prolongation, of colonial control. While, in the short term, the communist insurrection arrested constitutional concessions, in the longer term it accelerated the ending of empire and Britain's transfer of power to noncommunist Malayan leaders on 31 August 1957 – much sooner than British ministers and officials were contemplating even two years before it actually happened. Secondly, the solidarity of the Anglo-American partnership was tempered by differences over major international problems in East and Southeast Asia as well as over the political advance and future of Malaya itself. Thirdly, the manner and timing of Malayan decolonization were not significantly affected by American rhetoric favouring self-determination or by US material assistance in countering insurgency; they were, rather, partly shaped by Britain's wider imperial experience but largely determined by pressures and circumstances in Malaya itself. Finally, as regards the supposed shift in the balance of the Anglo-American partnership, with Britain subsiding to the junior role, the US consul-general observed, four weeks before independence day, that 'The independent Malayan Government has shown signs of desiring to lessen its dependence upon the British and to look toward the United States for guidance.'[65] Yet, neither the expectations of the British to retain influence over Malaya, nor those of the Americans to supersede Britain in Malaya, were altogether borne out by events. Because Malaya was actually of diminishing economic importance to Britain by the late 1950s and because of Britain's declining power in the region, British influence in Malaya turned out to be more apparent than real after the country achieved independence.[66] With respect to American influence in Malaya, on the other hand, it should be noted that, since the British continued to shoulder a considerable defence commitment which the US came to regard as a useful proxy, it turned out to be in America's interests to leave well alone and not to press for the reduction of Britain's presence in post-colonial Malaya.

Notes

1   P. Bagby, State Department, 'United States policy with respect to the decline of Western European Imperialism,' 13 March 1946, National Archive, Washington DC, [NARA] Lot Files, RG 59: Lot54 D190, Box 5.

2   See Christopher Thorne, *Allies of a Kind: the United States, Britain and the War against Japan, 1941–1945* (Oxford, 1978) and Wm Roger Louis, *Imperialism at Bay 1941–1945: the United States and the Decolonization of the British Empire* (Oxford, 1977).

3   See Andrew James Whitfield, 'British Imperial Consensus and the Return to

Hong Kong, 1941–1945', PhD, University of Birmingham, 1998; for postwar policy, see Wm Roger Louis, 'Hong Kong: the Critical Phase, 1945–1949', *American Historical Review*, 104, no. 4 (Oct 1997), pp. 1052–84.

4   S. R. Ashton and S. E. Stockwell (eds), *British Documents on End of Empire [BDEE]: Imperial Policy and Colonial Practice* (London, 1996), I, doc. 32.

5   Ibid., docs 30 and 31.

6   A. J. Stockwell (ed.), *BDEE: Malaya* (London, 1995), I, docs 4–9.

7   For the Atlantic Charter and subsequent discussions, see A. N. Porter and A. J. Stockwell (eds), *British Imperial Policy and Decolonization, 1938–64*, Vol. 1: *1938–51* (Basingstoke, 1987), docs. 8, 9, 15, 17, 18 and 20.

8   Minutes of the War Cabinet (Official) Far East Committee, 15 Nov. 1944, Public Record Office, CAB 96/5.

9   A. L. Moffat (State Department), 'The dependent territories in Southeast Asia', 17 Jan. 1945, RG 59: lot 54 D190, box 5.

10   Thorne, *Allies of a Kind*, p. 456.

11   For example, Queen Wilhelmina's broadcast of Dec. 1942 promising the postwar reorganization of the Dutch empire as a commonwealth and de Gaulle's Brazzaville Declaration of Jan. 1944 which, however, ruled out political development outside the imperial framework. See Thorne, *Allies of a Kind*, pp. 218–19 and 466–7, and Martin Thomas, *The French Empire at War 1940–45* (Manchester, 1998), pp. 249–54.

12   *Foreign Relations of the United States [FRUS]*, 1945 (Washington), VI, policy paper prepared by the Department of State, 22 June 1945, pp. 556–80.

13   Ibid., p. 572.

14   Ibid., p. 557.

15   Ibid., p. 558.

16   Ibid., p. 579.

17   Ibid., p. 572.

18   Ibid., p. 579.

19   J. F. Cady (State Department), 'The importance of the Philippines with respect to United States policy in Southeastern Asia', 2 Jan. 1946, RG 59, lot 54 D190, box 5.

20   See F. S. V. Donnison, *British Military Administration in the Far East* (London, 1956), Peter Dennis, *Troubled Days of Peace: Mountbatten and South East Asia Command, 1945–46* (Manchester, 1987), and John Springhall, ' "Disaster in Surabaya"; the Death of Brigadier Mallaby during the British Occupation of Java, 1945–6', *Journal of Imperial and Commonwealth History [JICH]*, 24, 3 (Sept. 1996), pp. 422–43.

21   For British colonial policy for Malaya, Singapore, and Sarawak, see Albert Lau, *The Malayan Union Controversy 1942–1948* (Singapore, 1991), R. H. W. Reece, *The Name of Brooke: the End of White Rajah Rule in Sarawak* (Kuala Lumpur, 1982), and A. J. Stockwell, *British Policy and Malay Politics during the Malayan Union Experiment, 1942–1948* (Kuala Lumpur, 1979).

22   *BDEE: Malaya*, I, docs 23, 26–30.

23   Ibid., doc 26.

24   Ibid., doc 36.

25   Brigadier T. S. Timberman (SEAC, HQ) to Col. L. J. Lincoln (US War Department), 29 June 1945, enclosing a copy of Mounbatten's letter of 18 June 1945 to Oliver Stanley on the future status of Malaya and Singapore, RG 59: lot 54D 190, box 14.

26 Paul R. Josselyn (Singapore) to Secretary of State, 19 April 1947, NARA, Decimal Files, RG 59: 846E.00/4-1947.

27 Bagby, 'United States policy with respect to the decline of Western European Imperialism', RG 59L lot 54D 190, box 5.

28 Secretary of State to the Embassy in the UK, 17 May 1947, *FRUS 1947*, I, pp. 750–1.

29 Ambassador Douglas to Secretary of State, 11 June 1947, ibid., pp. 751–8.

30 Ibid., p. 757.

31 Ibid., p. 756.

32 Wm Roger Louis and Ronald Robinson, 'The Imperialism of Decolonization', *JICH*, 22, 3 (Sept. 1994), 462–511, quote at p. 467.

33 Paper by J. Davies Jr, 28 Feb. 1949, RG 59: lot 54D 190, box 5.

34 See Robert J. McMahon, *Colonialism and Cold War: the United States and the Struggle for Indonesian Independence, 1945–49* (Ithaca, 1981) and George McT. Kahin, *Intervention* (New York, 1986).

35 See Andrew J. Rotter, *The Path to Vietnam: Origins of the American Commitment to Southeast Asia* (Ithaca, 1987).

36 See Benedict J. Kerkvliet, *The Huk Rebellion: a Study of Peasant Revolution in the Philippines* (Berkeley, 1977; 1979 edn), pp. 203–48.

37 A. J. Stockwell, ' "A widespread and long-concocted plot to overthrow government in Malaya"? The Origins of the Malayan Emergency', *JICH*, 21, 3 (Sept. 1993), pp. 66–88; see also Anthony Short, *The Communist Insurrection in Malaya* (London, 1975) and Richard Stubbs, *Hearts and Minds in Guerrilla Warfare: the Malayan Emergency 1948–1960* (Singapore, 1989).

38 H. T. Bourdillon (Colonial Office), 'Reflections on Colonial Office organisation', 10 May 1948, in Ronald Hyam (ed.), *BDEE: the Labour Government and the End of Empire 1945–1951* (London, 1992), I, doc 70, para 6.

39 R. H. Scott to A. Eden, 31 Oct. 1951, in *BDEE: Malaya*, II, doc 249, para 3.

40 William R. Langdon (consul-general) to secretary of state, 25 April 1949, RG 59: 846E.00/4-2549.

41 Memorandum of a conversation between A. L. Moffat (chief, Division of SE Asian Affairs, State Department) and W. L. Blythe (secretary for Chinese Affairs, Malayan Union), 16 Dec. 1946, RG 59: 846E.00/1-247.

42 State Department to American consul-general, 16 Nov. 1955, RG 59: 797.00/11-1655.

43 Langdon to Secretary of State, 25 April 1949, RG 59: 846E.00/4-2549.

44 Charles F. Baldwin (consul-general), memos of conversations with MacDonald, 11 Jan. 1952, RG 59: 797.00/2-1152, and 4 Feb. 1952, RG 59: 797.00/2-1852.

45 Baldwin to State Department, 20 Feb 1952, RG 59: 797.00/2-1952; 28 Feb. 1952, RG 59: 797.00/2-2852; and 3 March 1952, RG 59: 797.00/3-352.

46 Baldwin to State Department, 15 July 1952, RG 59: 797.00/7-1552. Templer also tried to dampen American enthusiasm for precipitate political advance, see American consul (KL) to State Department, 15 Oct. 1953, RG 59: 797.00/10-1553.

47 Karl E. Sommerlatte (vice-consul), 'Stability of British Malaya', RG 59: 797.00/9-2550.

48 Directive issued by O. Lyttelton to Templer, 1 Feb. 1952, *BDEE: Malaya*, doc 268.

49 Baldwin to Secretary of State, 24 Jan, 1952, RG 59: 797.00/1-2452.

50 State Department to American consuls Malaya and Singapore and US Embassy, London, 4 March 1952, RG 59: 797-00/3-452.

51 NSC 5405, *FRUS, 1952–1954*, XII, pt 1, p. 366.

52 See CO International Relations Department, 'The colonial empire today: summary of our main problems and policies' [May 1950], in *BDEE: the Labour Government*, I, doc 72, especially paras. 75–88.

53 For Anglo-American discussions in 1949–52 on the prices and stockpiling of natural rubber and curbs on the production of synthetic rubber, see RG 59: lot 54D 190, boxes 4 and 14.

54 See 'The United Kingdom in South-East Asia and the Far East', *BDEE: Malaya*, I, 196 para 8; J. Griffiths to M. MacDonald, 7 Apr. 1950, ibid., II, doc 211 para 2; 'Strategy and current defence policy in South-East Asia and the Far East', 2 May 1950, *BDEE: the Labour Government*, III, doc 335, para 65; Final report of the Commonwealth Consultative Committee on South and South-East Asia about cooperative economic development, Oct. 1950, ibid., II, doc 102.

55 British Embassy, Washington, to State Department, 15 Aug. 1950, RG 59: 797.00/8-1550.

56 Sir D. MacGillivray to Sir T. Lloyd, 14 Mar. 1953, in *BDEE: Malaya*, II, doc 294.

57 Baldwin to State Department, 2 March 1953, RG 59: 797.00/3-253.

58 A. Eden, 'British overseas obligations', C(52)202, 18 June 1952, in Porter and Stockwell (eds), II, 1951–64, doc.11.

59 'Note on relations with the United States, China and the Colombo powers', by MacDonald for Sir I. Kirkpatrick, 8 Aug. 1954, in *BDEE: Malaya*, III, doc 336.

60 Ambassador Smith to secretary of State, 21 Aug. 1948, *FRUS 1948*, I, 611–14.

61 Charles S. Reed, Division of SE Asian Affairs, to the director, Far Eastern Affairs, Butterworth, 13 Aug. 1948, ibid., 607–9.

62 Comments on these lines are made throughout the despatches from the consul-general to the State Department, especially until the autumn of 1954 by which time the first federal elections were clearly in the offing.

63 For the consul-general's assessment of US influence in Malaya, see his despatch of 4 June 1953, RG 59: 797.00/6-453.

64 Louis and Robinson, 'The Imperialism of Decolonization', p. 472.

65 John M. Farrior (US consul-general, Kuala Lumpur) to State Department, 1 Aug. 1957, *FRUS 1955–1957*, XXII, 799–805, quote at p. 804.

66 See A. J. Stockwell, 'Malaysia: the Making of a Neo-Colony?', *JICH*, 26, 2 (May 1998), 136–56.

10
Conclusions: the Decolonization Puzzle in US Policy – Promise versus Performance*

Michael H. Hunt

1. The problem of promise versus performance

To the historically uninitiated it might seem that the United States had arrived by the final months of the Second World War at one of those rare moments when a country's fundamental principles were in accord with no less fundamental global trends. Americans had long nurtured a faith in self-determination. Inscribed in popular discourse and enshrined in seminal policy statements, that principle seemed fully in accord with the palpable movement toward decolonization in what postwar observers would come to call the 'Third World'. Countries and peoples with a shared experience of foreign domination and often formal, preponderantly European colonial control were ready to launch a frontal assault on the *status quo*. Indeed, the pronounced movement of countries making strong claims to full independence in the immediate aftermath of the war would turn into a stampede. The rush began in Asia with India, Indonesia, the Philippines and Vietnam leading the way. It would come to a climax in the 1960s with the liberation of much of sub-Saharan Africa. The rise of new states out of collapsing colonial empires dramatically expanded the United Nations – from 51 charter members in 1945 to 127 by 1970 with more waiting in the wings. Seldom would one country's core-values seem so fully aligned with the tide of history.

Yet as the essays in this volume repeatedly suggest, any expectation of a neat postwar fit between American principles and international trends falls wide of the mark. The United States had begun to backpedal on self-determination even as the Second World War was in progress, and thereafter the American reaction to the crescendo of claims for freedom was far from triumphant or congratulatory. The American political elite worried about a Third World moving toward national independence and often responded to specific cases with hostility rather than support. Though the essays here make relatively little of the point, Third World leaders subjected the US position to equally critical scrutiny. Having for a time taken seriously public American professions of support for self-determination, their disappointment was all the greater when the American government in practice betrayed that commitment. Their preference for statist models of development over the liberal course championed by Washington compounded the rift that increasingly characterized US–Third-World relations in the early postwar era. As the United States established itself not as the champion of freedom but as a major obstacle to those seeking genuine independence, a sometimes-intense anti-American sentiment took shape around the globe.

The essays collected here offer strikingly similar stories of Washington's tortured response when confronted by the decolonization question. According to Dennis Merrill, the sympathy Americans should have felt for the independence movement in India was at best 'muted'.[1] Washington's limited, *pro forma* support was shaped to some degree by American doubts about the capacity of 'darker skinned peoples to practise self-government'.[2] But more inhibiting, in Merrill's view, were the exigencies of US global policy. During the war itself President Franklin D. Roosevelt gave priority to preserving the wartime alliance with the British, and thus avoided openly challenging Prime Minister Winston Churchill on the specifics of 'the Indian business'.[3] At Roosevelt's boldest in March 1942, he pressed Churchill to make concessions to the Indian National Congress, but even then he stood on the practical rather than the principled grounds of keeping India a stable base for wartime operations. The administration of Harry S. Truman continued a course marked by platitudes and avoidance. More and more preoccupied with Cold War bloc-building, Washington affirmed its faith in its British ally's good judgement on this colonial issue. That the Congress Party was non-communist (though regrettably non-aligned) removed some of the anxiety that American leaders usually directed toward independence movements.

The American response to Malayan independence painted by A. J. Stockwell closely follows the Indian pattern. Here too Washington followed a hands-off approach, endorsing the British policy of gradual decolonization. The outbreak of communist insurgency in 1948 served to solidify an already sympathetic attitude toward a continuing British presence. As the US representative on the scene, Consul-General Charles

F. Baldwin explained in March 1953 that British control was critical to realizing the chief goals of US policy: a viable, anti-communist government, restoration of 'law and order', and guidance of the colonial peoples 'in orderly stages of transition to self-government'.[4]

Lloyd Gardner's account of US policy toward Vietnam traces an even more dramatic rout of the principle of decolonization. Roosevelt's vocal condemnation of French mismanagement was from the outset joined to an insistence on tutelage for the peoples of Indochina as they moved toward independence. Small, peaceful and dependent (as the president imagined them), these 'children' required outside guidance over several decades so that they could learn to stand on their own. The American president rendered the principle of national self-determination meaningless for all practical purposes when early in 1945 he acquiesced to the return of French administration. Charles de Gaulle as leader of the Free French was adamant and enjoyed Churchill's backing, while Roosevelt for his part had failed to find anyone else willing to assume the role of trustee. Truman took up where Roosevelt left off, taking a vague French pledge of ultimate independence as a fig-leaf to cover this stark violation of self-determination exercised by the Viet Minh in August 1945. As the Cold War took shape, American backing for French control became ever less grudging until early in 1950 the Truman administration formally threw its moral and material support to the embattled French. They seemed the best hope for restoring regional stability, keeping the Chinese communists at bay, and preserving an outlet for a recovering Japanese economy. Sticking to the Roosevelt–Truman path, the Eisenhower administration accompanied the French in their march toward Dien Bien Phu. There one colonial order would die and another, distinctly neo-colonial and reduced to one corner of Indochina, would immediately take its place.

When sub-Saharan Africa (treated by John Kent) became a significant US policy concern during the late Eisenhower and the Kennedy years, solicitude for European allies, coupled with a deep conviction of African political immaturity, made Washington a reluctant advocate of decolonization. American caution was grounded in part in the fear that pressure on European colonial powers would hurt solidarity on the critical NATO front and cost US forces valued bases (especially the Azores, held by that most recalcitrant of the colonial powers, Portugal). American caution was also prompted by an even older, racist view of Africa. Blacks there were, much like their cousins in the United States, 'primitive savages'. In 1942 Sumner Welles counted them 'in the lowest rank of human beings'.[5] Basic attitudes had changed little by 1960 when Vice

President Richard Nixon observed to his colleagues on the National Security Council, 'Some of the people of Africa have been out of the trees for only about fifty years.'[6] If not accommodated on independence, African liberation movements might fall into the arms of the ever-ready communists, thus placing the region in thrall to a colonialism of new, direr form. But if allowed too much freedom, newly independent states were likely to dissolve into political chaos and fiscal irresponsibility that could only facilitate communist penetration.

To meet this difficult situation, according to Kent's account, the United States backed neo-colonial arrangements that constrained emerging African states in a web of economic and political ties to Europe. In the American estimate, the British offered the best model for implementing a responsible neo-colonial transition. By the late 1950s French colonial practice was also getting the American seal of approval. Keeping Africans on a leash held by London and Paris seemed the best way in the short run to frustrate the communists (whether home-grown or sent by Moscow) while also guaranteeing western Europe's access to the continent's natural resources. Strongmen figured prominently in this formula for stability. American policy-makers looked for leaders who could maintain order and profitably cooperate with businessmen and diplomats from the former colonial powers.

Scott Lucas's treatment of the Middle East shows how an abiding sense of solidarity with the British shaped US policy and led to a regional division of labour. While the United States took as its chief concern the northern tier – Greece, Turkey, and Iran – fronting the Soviet Union, Britain was supposed to maintain order behind that front line, especially in Egypt, Iraq and Jordan. Once more American policy-makers mixed familiar praise with equally familiar warnings. Eisenhower thus wrote Churchill in July 1954, 'Should we try to dam [nationalism] up completely, it would, like a mighty river, burst through the barriers and could create havoc.'[7] But if left to their own devices, the politically immature might run amok, creating dangers at Europe's back door. Ambassador to Egypt Jefferson Caffrey, confident in his knowledge of 'the oriental world', concluded after a July 1954 interview with Gamal Abdel Nasser that the United States 'must to a certain extent adopt the attitude of an intelligent parent faced with a "problem child"'. To get the child to accept guidance, he warned, would require parental 'circumspection and finesse'.[8]

Latin America and the Caribbean, treated by Laurie Johnston, were less concerned with formal decolonization than with getting around the constraints on fundamental domestic change imposed by Washington.

Postwar demands for reducing US political and economic control set off alarm-bells in Washington. Nationalists seemed to threaten investment and trade, open the door to communist influence, and encourage the potentially dangerous mobilization of popular forces. As a result, Washington was quick to violate the advice usually applied to other regions about the tactful handling of ill-behaved children. The stronger the nationalist demands for carving out a truly independent course in foreign and domestic policy, the more intense the US resistance. Washington combined support for repressive military regimes, manipulation of intra-elite cleavages, covert operations, and in extremity the dispatch of US forces. Washington set the pattern in Guatemala in 1954. The string of interventions that marked the rest of the Cold War era and even beyond – in Guyana, Cuba, the Dominican Republic, Chile, Nicaragua, El Salvador, Jamaica, Grenada, Panama and Haiti – established a pattern not seen since the Progressive era.

A recurrent theme in virtually all the case-studies contained in this collection is puzzlement over the gap between formal American support for self-determination and the actual handling of particular cases. How could the United States as the century's leading champion of freedom so consistently entertain a paternalistic and racist outlook, embrace neo-colonial practices, and thus defeat its commitment to freedom in the Third World? In accounting for this gap, let me focus on three broad points that collectively take us to the conclusion that the gap between promise and performance may be a problem more apparent than real.

2. Persistent historical patterns

We would be well served to ask at the outset whether the 1940s waffling on decolonization was a new phenomenon or at least took more acute form than during previous periods of US foreign relations. The answer, as Walter LaFeber shows, is that in this the 1940s hardly departed from precedent. The right to self-determination as a general principle may have been as often compromised as observed in US policy.

The pattern was evident from the outset. Haiti stands as an early, telling test of US consistency. The second country in the hemisphere to claim independence, that neighbouring republic evoked nightmares, not approbation, among US observers. They regarded its dark-skinned population as no more capable of steering an independent course than their black slaves, and in consequence the United States withheld diplomatic contact after Haiti's independence in 1804 and maintained that position for half a century. The process of continental expansion and consolidation inexorably encroached on the claims of native peoples to independent standing. Treaties formally at least conceded that claim. But in fact the overriding goal of state and federal policy reflected the American ambition to tame Indians and drive them from all but the most marginal land. Federal fiat at the end of the nineteenth century assimilated treaties with native Americans into domestic law and turned the remnant of ostensibly independent peoples into wards, many on reservations under institutionalized oversight.

The expansionist initiatives of the 1890s illustrate the continuing ingenuity Americans brought to the colonial question. Newly seized lands were not 'colonies' but rather carried other names. Hawaii, won through the machinations of a powerful minority of US settlers, became a 'territory' and so remained for half a century. Puerto Rico evolved from a colony to a 'commonwealth' status, still short of full-fledged statehood. And where, as in Cuba, Americans decided against direct administration, they demonstrated how thoroughly and effectively informal means could create a dependency even while honouring the formal rights of a people to claim independence. Of the turn-of-the-century cases, the Philippines represented the most blatant and troubling violation of self-determination. The McKinley administration's decision to take the entire archipelago and to brush aside Filipino demands for independence sparked not only fighting on the islands but also the most heated debate over the colonial question in American history. The outcome followed lines familiar from the 1940s. Americans could accept colonialism, even for as long as half a century in this case, so long as the enterprise was saved from stain by its benevolent intentions and by a firm commitment to a timely grant of independence.

3. Competing explanations

To say that Americans have long been deeply ambivalent about colonialism is not, however, to explain the promise–performance gap but rather to compound the puzzle. The writers represented in this collection offer three solutions to this broad problem of ambivalence so marked in the 1940s.

One approach is to explain the repeated betrayal of a core value by recourse to a series of simple interpretive binaries that are all too familiar from half a century of writing about US foreign policy. In the accounts here, we see 'rhetoric' set against 'reality', 'ideology' against 'pragmatism', 'altruism' against 'self-interest', and that hoariest of diplomatic history polarities, 'idealism' against 'realism'. In this formulation American policy-makers were caught between powerful poles – between what they wished or professed and what an intractable world required of them. They understandably waffled. These binaries appear so insistently and play such a central interpretive role that one wonders if they are hard-wired into the brain, even of historians.

This resort to familiar binaries recurs in five of the essays here. Gardner's Americans felt a soft paternalism that envisioned independence as the ultimate goal following a period of preparation for the people of Indochina. But that instinct warred with and eventually lost out to a hardheaded *Realpolitik* that made Indochina too strategically vital to let issues of decolonization stand in the way.[9] Merrill sees in the muted American support for Indian independence a 'disjuncture between American principles and American actions'. He concludes that 'the realist' strain in Roosevelt proved stronger than any attachment to 'a proud anticolonial heritage'.[10] Lucas treats US Middle East policy in similar terms – as a contest between an impulse toward embarking on an 'ideological crusade' and its antithesis, pursing a 'practical, step-by-step approach'. A hardheaded pragmatism, so Lucas concludes, repeatedly blunted the urge to ideological eruptions, although this victory of common sense left US policy with a 'hypocritical veneer'.[11] Finally, Paul Orders and Victor Pungong, despite their differences over how seriously to take FDR's anti-colonialism, agree on the nature of the contradiction at the heart of the president's thinking. His opposition to colonialism was a form of 'idealism' whereas his 'actual policy' was shaped by 'more realistic' concerns with keeping the alliance intact during the war and ensuring great-power cooperation afterwards. And so Roosevelt's 'high-minded idealism' often gave way 'to the reality of national interest'.[12]

Side-stepping the binaries, LaFeber and Johnston point to two other ways to explain our decolonization puzzle. In his explanation of why Americans 'easily sacrificed the principles of decolonization for practices of imperial conquest and global hegemony', LaFeber dissolves the tension created by binaries. He does so by converting ideas (usually one interpretive pole) into expressions of the other pole, the real interests that guide the action of all nations. In a formulation that effectively reduces ideas to epiphenomena in thrall to material forces, decolonization appears as 'a device for conquering a continental empire' and as 'an integral part of the nation's most aggressive self-interest'. LaFeber concedes that Americans did flirt with colonialism and finally rejected it. But they did so, he explains, not because of any commitment to self-determination but because they discovered that informal methods of control were cheaper and more effective in advancing US economic interests than direct, formal control.[13]

Johnston's resistance to binaries goes in the other direction, toward a more complex set of explanatory factors that seemingly gives interpretive pride of place to ideology. An essay that begins by characterizing Latin American policy as the product of a melding of economics, ideology and politics goes on to stress US assumptions of superiority and the resulting national claim of the right to dictate and guide countries in the region and to set prudent limits to change.[14] Part of Merrill seems also to want to head in this interpretive direction. To be sure, he concludes by invoking the tried and true binaries. But his opening treatment of the US handling of the India question has him review US policy in terms not of an essential dualism but of a blend of national experience, ideological forces, the personality of leaders, the requirements of day-to-day politics, and national security paradigms.[15]

In offering an alternative to the dominant binary approach and to LaFeber's dismissal of ideas as a force in their own right, Johnston partially attended by Merrill points us in a suggestive direction – toward an ideological interpretation. Might a US foreign policy ideology of the sort that I elaborated over a decade ago help us close the annoying gap between promise and performance on the decolonization issue?[16] As a first step in that direction, we need to identify four prominent features of an ideology as I understand that term.

First, ideology is complex, not simple. Conventionally, ideologies are treated as formal, codified collections of fixed, coherent propositions. Boiling ideas down in this way may reflect what we might wish in ourselves and in our leaders – clarity and consistency. But our everyday human experience tells us the ideas that we harbour about ourselves and our world are in fact muddy, shifting, often contradictory. Our thinking is fluid because the world around us changes, because there are notable internal tensions in our own minds, and because our perceptions of the world keep those tensions constantly in play. The very fact that ideology is a messy intermingling of ideas and assumptions makes it constantly subject to contestation and adjustment as its interpreters reassemble its parts and reinterpret the reconfigured whole depending on time and context.

Second, ideology is robust, not frail, derivative or ephemeral. Those historians attached to binaries see high-sounding ideas locked in a foolhardy contest with a gritty and often unpleasant reality that ideas are bound to lose. Those inclined to a materialistic interpretation make economic systems so hard and fundamental that ideas, lacking an independent existence, can only serve as a mirror. These two approaches would make historical actors into mendicants stripped by a recalcitrant, unforgiving world of their most treasured notions or into magicians whose words divert us from their political sleights of hand. But here again our personal experience reveals, quite to the contrary, that ideology has considerable potency. Societies generate and sustain ideological systems that are as powerful as our need for social order and meaning. As individuals, we grow into these ideologies, we depend on them to make meaning of our world, and we bear them through our lives. They are not like pieces of clothing to be donned or doffed with every passing breeze or personal whim. They may be cynically invoked but effectively only where they still command belief.

Third, ideology is omnipresent, not escapable. It may be tempting, given the pejorative meaning that ideology carries, especially among diplomatic historians, to compare it to a social disease. The well-bred and respectable among our subjects should not suffer from it, and they get our pity, perhaps even censure, if they stumble into fits of idealism. In this popular rendition, ideology is simply something that practical Americans devoted to the pragmatic pursuit of security and welfare should themselves avoid – and usually do. Conversely, we imagine ideology a common affliction among the benighted, especially peoples that we know so poorly that we can get away with reducing their ideas to a few code-words indicative of an outlook that is extremist, unsound, false, emotional or unreasoning. But both anthropological notions of culture and commonsense psychological insights tell us that the assumptions on which this judgmental approach to ideology rests are false. Ideas are not just part of our understanding of the world; they are our world, or at least they embody our individual and collective understanding of the world and limit the possibilities for our acting within it. We cannot live in the world without those interpretations.

Finally, ideology applies to the entire range of emotions and behaviour, not just those impulses that are well intentioned or praiseworthy. Our ideologically grounded constructs can give rise to altruistic but also mean-spirited and even genocidal courses of action. They can inspire sermons on uplift and calls for human rights but also create images that dehumanize other peoples and make possible indiscriminate application of punishing economic sanctions and military force. Ideology is as important in explaining our impulses to humiliate and destroy as to create and succour.

Arguably an ideology possessed of the features described above and rooted in American nationalism has made signal contribution to setting

American leaders' policy agendas and cognitive frameworks.[17] In this nationalist construct, freedom has been the central, pivotal notion. Americans have seen themselves as exemplars and champions of a universal, progressive principle applicable abroad no less than at home. That Americans might repeatedly argue over how to understand that principle and by extension how to give proper expression to their collective identity in domestic and foreign policy does not negate the point about freedom's importance. To the contrary, it indicates that freedom was a central point of reference and that whoever could impose their definition gained the power to mobilize national sentiment and thus to create political support.

Some of the major debates in US foreign policy turned on the question of how freedom was best realized abroad and whether foreign initiatives would invigorate freedom at home or imperil it. The most notable of these foreign policy debates played out in the 1790s, the 1840s and the 1890s. Participants on each occasion charged that a violation of that principle in foreign lands set in doubt the principle at home and thus betrayed American nationhood. This contested faith in freedom was as alive and pertinent to the fundamental direction of policy in the twentieth century as it had been in the nineteenth. For example, Wilson made self-determination central to his conception of the post-First World War settlement; no less than eight of his Fourteen Points applied that principle to specific cases and another four points applied the criteria of freedom to broad matters of trade, travel and international community. Critics of Wilson's approach to peacemaking countered that he had promoted freedom abroad at the cost of foreclosing American choice on such matters as collective security, immigration and the Monroe Doctrine. Debate resumed on the eve of entry into the Second World War with FDR and his interventionist allies arguing that preserving freedom at home depended on stopping its enemies abroad. Charles Lindbergh and an 'isolationist' America First warned against a global crusade on the grounds that it would create a national-security state inimical to democracy.

Freedom was central to the American foreign-policy ideology but it was hardly the totality. At least two other elements – a conception of racial hierarchy and a fear of revolution – need to be admitted if we are to solve the decolonization puzzle. Americans found it easy to distinguish the civilized from the barbarian, the advanced from the backward. They confidently arrayed themselves and other peoples along that continuum according to their estimate of their cultural achievements and its close correlate, skin colour. In their response to political change as much as in their fixation with race, Americans proved a conservative and ethnocentric lot. They erected their own reformist methods and constitutional structures as the touchstones for judging the readiness of others to manage their own affairs. They saw revolutionary outbreaks as a kind of disease that could spread, sickening societies and deranging civilized values associated with the family, private property, religion and individual freedom. These two additional elements bring us closer to the characteristics of ideology noted above. They gave Americans a handle on a complex world while endowing their understanding of that world with inner tensions. Though the configuration of the ideology changed, its key elements proved relatively stable, like the society whose values sustained them.

Why then did Americans in the 1940s honour in the breach a principle so important to their collective sense of identity and thus so central to domestic political discourse? The answer of course is that foreign-policy ideas germane to the problem of decolonization were crosscutting. For one policy-maker, doubts about the maturity of a people of colour might war with a belief in self-determination as a fundamental national right, while for another with weaker racial views, self-determination might prevail over doubts. Yet a third policy-maker might embrace the notion of racial incapacity and still honour self-determination by arguing that the United States should stand aloof from the unseemly affairs of distant and unruly folk. Confronting a revolutionary outbreak could add new wrinkles. It might, for example, reinforce the conviction about foreign incapacity or shake an otherwise firm commitment to self-determination and accordingly either support or undermine the argument that foreign people should be left to their fate. The waffling evident in US decolonization policy, it now becomes clearer, reflects the interaction of the chief constituents of US foreign policy ideology.

4. Guiding foreign policy ideas and the decolonization puzzle

Let's subject the decolonization puzzle to a reading informed by a sensitivity to ideology and consistent with the evidence laid out in the studies here. What we see is that decolonization was for Americans contested ground and that tensions and permutations within the American foreign-policy ideology help explain the notable shifts and evasions in their position.

A commitment to freedom served as the ultimate justification for

American engagement in the Second World War for good reason. This idea, so central to the national self-conception, was important both to orienting the thinking of policy-makers and to rallying the public. In travelling the road to and through the Second World War, policy-makers and public alike needed some justification for the risk and sacrifice that they as individuals and as a nation faced. It was thus important that the Atlantic Charter in August 1941 make a sweeping commitment to political freedom – to 'respect the right of all peoples to choose the form of government under which they will live'. The US declaration on national liberation of March 1943 flatly affirmed that the principles of the Atlantic Charter applied to all people.[18]

But predictably the thinking within the Roosevelt administration was also influenced by considerations of racial differences. The president and his aides were heirs to the view that the distinction between civilized and savage was fundamental, pervasive and persistent. Coming to political maturity at the turn of the century, they had watched with approval as their country had assumed the international burdens of an advanced civilization. It should come as no surprise then that notions of race, long sanctioned by domestic and foreign-policy practice, would in the 1940s influence their response to the claims of Third World people to independence. That response took the familiar form: only advanced peoples could exercise their rights responsibly, and thus virile, civilized peoples had an obligation to carry, even drag their 'little brown brothers' into modernity and responsible independence.

Roosevelt himself offers ample evidence of how a conviction of Third World inferiority helped to gut a meaningful commitment to decolonization. He referred to Asians as a 'yellow peril' to be guarded against and as children to be directed.[19] In contemplating the future of Vietnamese and Koreans, he could imagine them ready for freedom only after 20 to 30 years of foreign guidance. The same logic gave him ample reason to accommodate the British in Africa and India. This faith in the tutelary role, as Pungong usefully notes,[20] placed FDR in the same frame of reference as the European diplomats who gathered in Berlin in 1885 and proclaimed their duty as trustees to attend to the welfare of their colonial charges.

Along with broad, vague convictions about the backwardness of most of the world went a belief in a special relationship with Britain rooted in an Anglophilia that can only be described as ideological. This far-reaching sense of kinship, an overt expression of racial consciousness, placed the British alongside Americans (at least those who dominated policy-making and debate) at the top of the racial hierarchy. This sense of Anglo-American kinship carried critical implications for the American approach to the colonial questions at two levels.

First, Americans had to concede that Britain as a superior country had a justified claim to play the tutelary role that Roosevelt thought essential in colonial areas. The colonial claims of the British deserved a favourable consideration in the face of competing calls for independence issuing from brash, unprepared peoples about whom he knew next to nothing. Even the French, to whom he felt less close culturally, might yet overcome their deficiencies and redeem themselves by attending to long-neglected obligations as tutors in the colonial world. But American observers had no expectation that the French any more than the Belgians, Dutch or Portuguese could rise to the British standard in colonial or any other matters of significance.

Second, an alliance that arose from an Anglo-American community of values, language and tradition became an additional reason for accommodation on the colonial issue. Through the first half of the twentieth century Britain emerged as the American ally *par excellence*. Woodrow Wilson had moved to the British side in meeting the German challenge because above all he felt a kinship with one but not the other. This same sense of kinship prompted Roosevelt's more self-conscious if equally halting shift to a wartime partnership with Britain that he expected to endure into the postwar period. Colonial issues paled by comparison with this collaboration, and so Roosevelt would have accommodated Britain even if he had seen no virtue in trusteeship. One might attribute the president's stance to 'national security' calculations as long as one keeps in mind that those calculations were framed by racial constructs. Without the shared conviction of Anglo-American superiority, it would be impossible to even imagine the durable, functioning partnership that has survived almost a century of testing.

An outlook on the world that combined racial pride and patriarchal condescension with admiration for Britain as a responsible colonial power and close ally does a great deal to explain a wartime record marked by recurrent colonial compromises. Even while proclaiming in the Atlantic Charter a devotion to self-determination, FDR privately assured Churchill that his interest was limited to 'the development of backward countries' and to the elimination of 'backward colonial policies'.[21] FDR's restraint on decolonization became if anything more pronounced as the war drew to a close. At Yalta he explicitly exempted Britain, the leading colonial power, from any formal trusteeship arrangements. The British would be allowed to guide their colonies to independence at a pace and along lines of London's choosing.

FDR's practical retreat from decolonization continued into the Truman and Eisenhower years. Policy-makers still professed a commitment to self-determination while also acting on a sense of superiority over a Third World given to disorder and in need of guidance. This attitude would have existed even without the eruption of a sharp rivalry with the Soviet Union. The coming of the Cold War served to intensify the importance of the sentimental alliance with Britain as a bulwark of containment not only in Europe but also in the Middle East, sub-Saharan Africa and Southeast Asia and hence of the search for common ground on colonial issues. This mix of concerns bedevilled Eisenhower perhaps even more than it had Roosevelt. He insisted privately that 'we must believe in the right of colonial peoples to achieve independence as we had' and bemoaned the American loss of favour in the Third World. But at the same time he expressed the conventional views shaped by racial taxonomy. The Third World was politically immature and prone to run wild. The British were good tutors. The Anglo-American alliance created and sustained by sentimental attachments required US concessions on colonialism. The British qualified even in the midst of the Suez crisis as Ike's 'right arm'.[22]

The coming of the Cold War revived fears suspended during the Second World War of a revolutionary virus issuing from the Soviet Union, and it injected those fears into consideration of the colonial issue. This contagion seemed most fearsome in the Third World, where Americans entertained the most fundamental doubts about the capacity of peoples of colour to manage their own affairs and to make discriminating judgements about the Cold War contest. Those fears mounted in the Khrushchev years as the Soviet Union began backing its verbal support for rapid decolonization with offers of substantial aid. Third World peoples in their political immaturity would not realize their special vulnerability, would fail to take proper precautions against communist blandishments and infiltration, and thus fall easy prey.

This combination of racial attitudes and revolutionary fears produced in the latter half of the 1940s and through the 1950s the low-water-mark for the American commitment to decolonization. The Truman administration signalled from the outset that it regarded independence as a proper claim for all peoples only in the long run. The US delegation made sure that the United Nations Charter in May 1945 went only as far as to stipulate that colonial powers had an obligation to help dependent peoples take 'progressive' steps toward self-government 'according to the particular circumstances of each territory and its peoples and their varying stages of advancement'.[23] A State Department paper prepared the next month for the Potsdam conference candidly conceded that the best course for colonial peoples was their continued subordination while Europeans guided them into freedom and created permanent bonds between them and the West. The United States could not, the paper argued, afford alienating prime European allies.[24] As late as 1957 a National Security Council report characterized Africans as 'still immature and unsophisticated' on the foremost question of the day, the conflict between nationalism and communism. Nineteenth-century colonialism was bad, the report intoned, but premature independence was no better. Washington had to seek a middle way in which colonial powers were to guide their charges into the modern world – away from the 'extremely primitive' outlooks associated with tribal and family loyalties, away from the lure of radical doctrines, and toward responsible self-government.[25] This persistent line of analysis, heavily tinctured by ideas about race and revolution, had by the Eisenhower years shaped a Third World policy of active support for neo-colonial arrangements, for strongmen and military regimes over 'irresponsible' populists, for covert operations to restore 'order', and, where necessary, for the direct use of the US military.

Attitudes toward the Third World arguably began to shift in the 1960s. The seemingly irresistible march of colonies toward independence forced Washington publicly at least to smother its doubts about Third World incapacity. The civil rights movement, with its growing public support in the early 1960s, also left its mark. By challenging the segregationist order, the movement began to alter the domestic discourse on race and reinforced policy-makers' impulse to check their language in public. Finally, the direct challenge to the Cold War consensus that grew out of radical ideas spawned in the late 1950s and early 1960s helped put Washington on the defensive on Third World issues. Critics seized on arguably racist policy positions to delegitimize the prevailing policy orthodoxy and to draw attention to the links between racial attitudes and practices at home and repressive practices abroad. This ideological connection between foreign and domestic affairs played a prominent role, for example, in critiques of US support for a South Africa compromised by apartheid. It also appeared in charges of a doubly racist war in Vietnam where whites were engaged in profligate destruction of an Asian country and used black Americans to do the dirty work. With this attack on racism went a more sympathetic view of revolutionary change. American radicals found much to admire in the revolutionary experiments in such Third World countries as China, Vietnam and Cuba. These domestic developments did not immediately expunge racial conceptions from the minds of policy-makers, whose formative years had schooled them in longstanding patterns of social segregation and the attendant notions of fundamental human difference. But expressions of sympathy (at least in public) for the aspirations of Third World peoples, and especially the new states of sub-Saharan Africa, enjoyed a vogue within officialdom, and explicitly racial language became increasingly impolitic even while well-worn racial imagery continued to flourish in cartoons and in private conversation.

5.   A world in ferment

Our search for explanation needs to go beyond an American foreign policy ideology to take into account a feature of the postwar world easily overlooked in a collection of essays concerned with US policy. Washington in its preoccupation with race and revolution may have applied an ethnocentric reading to the ferment that characterized the postwar Third World. But the challenge that American policy-makers faced was real, not imaginary. It took the form of a worldwide trend favouring fundamental social–political change at odds with the American model of political economy. It was in its impulse every bit as ideological as American policy. It sought to think through what seemed to many people outside the United States to be the prime problems of the day – thirty years of destructive warfare around the globe, civil conflict fed by social injustice and economic want, and closed, autocratic political systems.

The radical impulse was at work in the parts of the developed world most shaken by war. In Japan and throughout Europe – on both sides of what was to become the Iron Curtain – the immediate postwar period brought with it a strong sense of hope. Parties on the left called for focusing national attention and resources on social and political betterment, and blamed the old regime for the upheaval, destruction and lost opportunities that had blighted the earlier decades of this century.[26] Advocates of change, however, ran up against powerful obstacles, including notably superpower constraints. In Japan and Western Europe it was the United States that prevailed in collaboration with conservative elites operating through centre-right parties, while in Eastern Europe, the Soviets exerted their own conservative, stabilizing influence that made genuine self-determination as problematic as in the traditional US sphere of influence in the Americas.

This discontent with the *status quo* was even more powerfully felt in the Third World, driven by visions of national liberation and domestic renovation. Elites saw independence not just as a formal condition easily met once the offending foreigners decamped but rather as one step toward effecting radical change. To achieve genuine liberation required more than ending colonial administration. No less important was promoting economic autonomy and development, transforming a national psychology of dependency, healing social divisions created by long-term foreign influence, fashioning programmes with popular appeal, and constituting a supportive international community of like-minded states. American observers might want to draw a distinction between countries that were formal colonies such as Vietnam, Palestine and Ghana and those that were at least nominally independent, but the Third World admitted no such simple dichotomy.

Already by 1945 the radical impulse in the Third World had developed considerable momentum that Washington was slow to recognize. The first stirrings date back to the early part of the century and the emergence of nationalist or proto-nationalist elites with foreign education and a sense of the broader world. The Moscow-based Communist International had in the interwar years cultivated this narrow but influential stratum, encouraging political organization and providing support in the form of money, advisers and schooling. Moscow thus demonstrated that it alone among the centres of world power was genuinely committed to a new international order. The upheaval of war provided the last major impetus for a radical push. Japanese conquests discredited European mastery in Asia, while Allied propaganda depicted the war as a battle for freedom, and so Third World proponents of a new postwar order gladly saw it.

Three cases illustrate how rising expectations were building in the Third World even as the war drew to a close and how they helped set the stage for the postwar decolonization drive and the vogue of revolution.

The ferment that would for the first time break colonial control in sub-Saharan Africa is evident in the life of Ghana's founding father, Kwame Nkrumah.[27] An adventuresome spirit, Nkrumah had left the British Gold Coast in 1935 for the United States to continue his studies. At first politically somnolent, he experienced during the war years a sharp rise in his political consciousness, a decided shift to the political left, and a marked impatience with the imperialist system gripping not just his own country but also much of the African continent and the black diaspora beyond. He fell under the influence of W. E. B. Du Bois, who left an especially strong mark on his views on pan-African unity. Marxism too attracted him with its claims that a new, non-oppressive order was a historical inevitability and indeed within the reach of those willing to organize and press forward. At the same time he was electrified by the wartime prominence Africa suddenly gained and by the Allied promise of postwar self-determination. He knew that already the peoples of India and Vietnam were demanding independence on the basis of that principle. He anticipated that the colonial powers might want to hang on to their possessions, but a resolute resistance could, he explained in a 1943 talk, defeat them. 'We must take the torch of liberty in our own hands. . . . We cannot get what we want by asking, pleading and arguing. . . . We are in a world of action, not talk. . . . We must rise and throw off the chains. . . . We must unite. . . . Take our future in our own hands.'[28]

In May 1945 the 36-year-old Nkrumah moved to London to hone his political skills and continue his political education among the active West African community there, itself in the grip of independence fever. When he finally returned home in 1947, Nkrumah carried a bold vision of the changes that were necessary and a confidence that he and other black leaders could put them into effect. He imagined freeing Ghana from external control, cooperating closely with neighbouring African states in creating a fresh destiny for the continent, and launching Ghana itself on a rapid, state-directed programme of modernization. The power of the vision acquired during the war did shake British control. It directed Ghana down a promising but ultimately problematic development road. And it made Nkrumah a thorn in the US side. John Kennedy complained that he was 'unnecessarily difficult' despite American patience and economic assistance, while the US ambassador in Accra offered the president a thumbnail sketch of Nkrumah as 'a badly confused and immature person'.[29]

In a China described by a broad spectrum of its politicians as semi-colonial, the Second World War spawned a strikingly similar dream. They agreed on ending the iniquitous old international system that had done such harm to their land, and some among them linked international reform with long-neglected domestic changes. No one entertained brighter or more consequential thoughts of a new day coming than the leader of the Chinese Communist Party, Mao Zedong.[30] It has long been recognized that the Pacific War facilitated the build-up of Communist base areas; the Japanese invaders kept Mao's long-time Nationalist rival distracted. It is less well known that the war engendered in Mao a marked optimism about China's postwar liberation. He was heartened by the Anglo-American meeting in August 1941 that produced the Atlantic Charter commitment to a new world order and expressions of interest in cooperating with the embattled Soviet Union. Mao declared that the conference marked nothing less than 'the opening of a new stage in the history of the world'. America's entry into the war several months later struck him as a guarantee not only of an anti-fascist victory but also of a lasting international alignment favourable to peace and change within China.

By early 1945 Mao was in even higher spirits. He was confidently predicting that the US–Soviet alliance would survive the tensions produced by the last stage of the fighting and would endure well into the postwar period. Popular forces everywhere were gathering strength; the reactionaries were in retreat; and the successful Soviet political and economic system was setting the pattern that other peoples would take as their model. With fascism discredited, with the left stronger than ever all around the world and with even American capitalism in a conciliatory, progressive phase, China could look forward to an era of peace and progress. In this benign national and international environment, Mao expected that he could force the Nationalists to accept a power-sharing arrangement as the first step toward winning political power. The longer-term prospects were even brighter. While the United States seemed for the moment economically vital, Mao held to the orthodox Marxist view that ultimately, within a decade perhaps, that country would find itself in the grip of a shattering crisis. The Soviet Union would come into unchallenged preeminence, and fundamental change within nations and within the global system would be assured. Mao held to this markedly optimistic view well into 1946. Even as he came to terms with the disappointingly reactionary character of the new Truman administration, he was buoyed by the surprise intervention of Soviet forces in the Pacific War, and remained confident in the tide of popular support at home and the early demise of capitalism on the world stage. Guided by these views, Mao's China would move well beyond the American orbit and far away from the American model.

In Latin America as in Africa and East Asia, the close of the war coincided with a rising demand for change. Reformist regimes and populist movements sprouted everywhere, drawing sustenance from Allied propaganda that victory over fascism was but the prelude to building more prosperous and open societies. Reformers wanted to encourage popular political participation, and so they took such steps as expanding the franchise beyond the ranks of propertied males and legalizing labour unions. Reformers also concerned themselves with pressing questions of social justice and redistribution of wealth in societies marked by glaring inequalities. The urban middle class and the working class as well as students and intellectuals were the chief advocates of these changes. As dictators fell and repression lifted, parties on the left (including communist parties) began to play a prominent political role, and unions became more assertive, sought more autonomy, and saw their ranks increase.

These developments stimulated US fears of reform turning radical and Marxist regimes taking power in the American backyard. During the late 1940s and continuing into the 1950s, alarmed leaders in Washington joined indigenous elites in countering this looming threat to class privilege and regional stability. Through their coordinated effort, they managed to cut off the democratic, populist opening, move the region back to more authoritarian rule, and perpetuate the great economic gulf between rich and poor. Washington and local elites outlawed communist parties and other parties on the left and either repressed labour unions or purged them of their radical leaders on the grounds that they were dangerous subversives directed by Moscow. Calls for US development aid comparable to the help given Europe met an unsympathetic response. Truman explained, 'There has been a Marshall Plan for the Western Hemisphere for a century and a half.' He was referring to the Monroe Doctrine. He and other American leaders assigned private capital the leading role in creating prosperity. If states in the region wanted to attract investment from abroad and hold accumulated wealth at home, they had only to follow the liberal development formula. That meant maintaining stability against leftist or populist agitation, limiting state intervention in the economy, and in general respecting the rights of private property.[31]

Guatemala offers an excellent case in point of how optimism fed during the war years died early in the postwar era. A repressive society had embarked in 1944 on an era of moderate reform. Juan José Arévalo and then Jacobo Arbenz saw reform in terms of national integration and political mobilisation but also the assertion of greater independence *vis-à-vis* the United States. No step in their programme was more important than Arbenz's land reform, the controversial effort to close old and deep ethnic and socio-economic divisions that made Guatemala two nations, not one. Expropriation of American (United Fruit) landholdings as part of the land reform, along with legitimization of organized labour, a shift toward greater neutrality in the Cold War, and the prominence of communists among Arbenz advisers, stirred US fears and finally prompted a successful CIA-orchestrated coup. Guatemala became again a repressive society. But the old days were irretrievably gone. Resistance broke out in the early 1960s, spawning a civil war that persisted into the 1990s.[32]

Americans would in any case have harboured strong preferences about the shape of the postwar world. But the intensity of the radical dreams taking shape in Ghana, China and Guatemala and at other points around the postwar world posed a direct challenge to those preferences and served as a catalyst for American fears. Impatient, determined reformers and revolutionaries seemed about to slip free of the civilizing, stabilizing constraints of the West. The resulting American anxieties would have materialized, Cold War or not. The rivalry with the Soviet Union served to intensify those concerns and give impetus to action aimed at checking the radical impulse. Third World dreams of effecting fundamental change would have been hard to realize in the best of circumstances. Once Americans joined what they saw as a global ideological battle, the obstacles in the way of the likes of Nkrumah, Mao, and Arbenz became formidable and in some cases even impassable, with major and lasting consequences for their countries.

6. Conclusion

Our examination of the gap between American promise and performance in mid-twentieth-century US decolonization policy reveals a need to recast the problem. By taking ideas seriously, by seeing them as inescapable and potent, and by following the ways in which they help leaders make sense of a diverse and fluid world, we get a better sense of the multiple currents of thought that combined in various ways to shape the evolving US approach to decolonization. In other words, to understand that approach we need to put aside the notion that it was the product of a simple, one-sided conflict between long-held ideals about self-determination and real security pressures or alternatively that it was a demonstration of the overwhelming power of material interests to tame and subordinate ideas. We should instead look for the sources and dynamic of the US position in something broader and more complex – the conflicts that played out in the minds of individual Americans and among Americans collectively over which of their basic national values should guide their dealings with an often recalcitrant world.

Notes

* I want to thank Matthew Jacobs, Alan McPherson, and David Ryan for offering helpful comments on a draft of this chapter.
1 Merrill, p. 102.
2 Merrill, p. 102.
3 Merrill, p. 113.
4 Stockwell, p. 197.
5 Kent, p. 169.
6 Reference in Kent, 178; quote from US Department of State, *Foreign Relations of the United States [FRUS] 1958–1960*, XIV (Washington, 1992), p. 75.
7 Lucas, p. 147.
8 Lucas, p. 141.
9 Gardner, pp. 122, 130.
10 Merrill, pp. 103, 105, 114.
11 Lucas, pp. 142, 158, 160 for quoted phrases. See also p. 159.
12 Quote from Pungong, pp. 85, 91, 93. See Orders for a similar formulation.
13 LaFeber, pp. 24, 29, for quotes. See also pp. 34, 38.
14 Johnston, pp. 41–2, 57–8.
15 Merrill, 103–4.
16 Michael H. Hunt, *Ideology and U.S. Foreign Policy* (New Haven, 1987); and Hunt, 'Ideology', in 'A Roundtable: Explaining the History of American Foreign Relations', *Journal of American History* 77 (June 1990), 108–115.
17 The literature on nationalism, which has enjoyed a recent resurgence, bears a relevance to the decolonization question. See, for example, Benedict Anderson, *Imagined Communities: Reflections on the Origin and Spread of Nationalism* (London, 1983; rev. edn, 1991); E. J. Hobsbawm, *Nations and Nationalism since 1780: Programme, Myth, Reality* (rev. edn; Cambridge, 1992); and Geoff Eley and Ronald Grigor Suny (eds), *Becoming National: a Reader* (New York, 1996), which provides a good point of entry to the literature.
18 See Wm Roger Louis's classic *Imperialism at Bay: the United States and the Decolonization of the British Empire, 1941–1945* (New York, 1978), pp. 123–4, 231.
19 Gardner, pp. 129–31.
20 Pungong, p. 87.
21 Quote from Orders, p. 69.
22 Quotes from National Security Council meeting of 7 August 1958, in US Department of State, *FRUS 1958–1960*, XIV: 20; and from Hunt, *Ideology and U.S. Foreign Policy*, p. 164.
23 Quote from Louis, *Imperialism at Bay*, p. 533.
24 US Department of State, *FRUS 1945*, VI, 1969, pp. 557–8.
25 National Security Council report of 23 August 1957, in US Department of State, *FRUS 1955–1957*, XVIII, 1989, pp. 79, 84.
26 For stimulating starting-points on Europe and Japan in the immediate aftermath of the war, see Geoff Eley, 'Back to the Beginning: European Labor, US Influence, and the Start of the Cold War', *International Labor and Working-Class History*, no. 40 (Fall 1991): 91–102; and John Dower, *Empire and Aftermath: Yoshida Shigeru and the Japanese Experience, 1878–1954* (Cambridge, 1979).

27 Marika Sherwood, *Kwame Nkrumah: the Years Abroad, 1935–1947* (Accra, 1996).
28 Quoted in Sherwood, *Kwame Nkrumah*, p. 98.
29 US Department of State, *FRUS 1961–1963*, XXI, 1995, pp. 355, 391. This documentation makes clear that the Kennedy administration at least thought about backing Nkrumah's opposition.
30 The treatment that follows draws on my own *The Genesis of Chinese Communist Foreign Policy* (New York, 1996), pp. 150, 155–7.
31 Leslie Bethell and Ian Roxborough, 'Latin America between the Second World War and the Cold War: Some Reflections on the 1945–8 Conjuncture', *Journal of Latin American Studies* 20 (May 1988), pp. 167–89. Truman quote from p. 186.
32 This account rests on Piero Gleijeses' fine *Shattered Hope: the Guatemalan Revolution and the United States, 1944–1954* (Princeton, NJ, 1991).

11
Afterword

Cary Fraser

The essays in this volume reflect the ongoing quest for an understanding of the importance of 'empire' in the shaping of American foreign policy. Whether that 'empire' was achieved by invitation, assertion, or in the proverbial 'fit of absent-mindedness', the motives, ideology, mechanisms, *modus operandi*, and consequences of American imperial expansion are increasingly under examination as scholars attempt to understand how the 13 colonies that made up the original United States of America became the dominant imperial power in the international system. These essays suggest some intriguing ways to think about that transformative impact of 'empire' in the shaping of American history and politics.

In addition, they should lead scholars to explore the ways in which other states and societies influenced and responded to the process of American imperial expansion. One of the questions that continues to intrigue scholars is the precise relationship between the thorny process of British imperial disengagement and the relatively smooth way in which America has 'succeeded John Bull' as a cornerstone of the international order. It is perhaps time to examine the imitative dimensions of the Anglo-American relationship and the collaboration that it fostered in the transfer of power from Britain to the United States. It is striking that the Monroe Doctrine has come to be perceived as an expression of American efforts to create an exclusive sphere of influence in the western hemisphere when it was in fact an Anglo-American creation that continues to shape the policies of the two powers in the region. For those proponents of the view that the Monroe Doctrine is an anachronism, they should look no further than the Falklands War of the 1980s or the resolution of the Peruvian hostage crisis of the 1990s. The Monroe Doctrine has served as a framework of imperial collaboration in the western hemisphere and while the relative weight of the United Kingdom has declined relative to that of its partner, the United States of America, that framework has served as a foundation of the wider Anglo-American alliance that emerged in the twentieth century. In essence, it is possible to argue that the dynamics of Anglo-American collaboration may help to explain the emergence of the United States as an imperial power – both prior to and since 1945. Certainly, the conditions under which the Truman Doctrine was articulated are very suggestive of the politics of Anglo-American collaboration – Britain's crisis of empire in the Balkans and the Mediterranean led to the American adoption of a major role in the region in collaboration with the British. Whether they were Monroe's, Truman's or Eisenhower's, presidential doctrines have often served as a mechanism for legitimating Anglo-American collaboration and 'empire' in various parts of the world.

The second issue to which scholars should pay greater attention is the distinction to be drawn between 'formal' and 'informal' empire in American strategy. Cuba, Puerto Rico, and the Philippines came under the American imperial umbrella at the same time but their political status differed considerably then and now. It would be of considerable interest to establish why America has pursued both 'formal' and 'informal' empire simultaneously. Any explanations would perhaps also help to explain the ways in which the techniques of imperial rule developed in the 'formal' colonies were used to exercise power in the 'informal' colonies or vice versa. In effect, is it possible to explore the ways in which the exercise of American influence in Panama shaped American rule in Hawaii or the Philippines? Alternatively, how did the American counter-insurgency experience in the Philippines after 1898 shape the rules of engagement in the subsequent American occupation of Haiti in 1915?

These questions, while having their own intrinsic importance, also raise a fundamental question about the American response to decolonization after 1945 – to what extent did the American colonial experience shape American attitudes and policies as the process of European imperial disengagement unfolded? American policy-makers held up the process of decolonization in the Philippines as a model for the Europeans to emulate but it has never been evident that any of the colonial powers or the nationalists gave serious consideration to the Filipino model. Alternatively, the decision to incorporate the colonies of Hawaii and Alaska as non-contiguous states in the federal system has interesting parallels to the French and Portuguese efforts to treat their overseas colonies as units closely integrated to the metropolitan centres. Similarly, how did the challenge to the white supremacist ideas underlying colonial rule in the European empires affect American domestic politics and colonial policy where Jim Crow had become entrenched? In brief, how did the European experience in dealing with the challenge to empire influence the choices of American policy-makers in dealing with their own 'colonial dilemmas'?

In effect, 'empire' has been at the nexus of both American domestic and foreign policies in the twentieth century in ways that have to be carefully considered by scholars. In part, the lack of attention to the relationship between the internal and external dimensions of American imperial activity has been a consequence of the fact that the military has borne the major burden of the enterprise. It is also a consequence of the notion that European empires were the products of a coherent strategy while the United States has only suffered the occasional outburst of imperial fervour – as exemplified by 1898. It is time to revisit the conventional wisdom, especially as the dawn of a new millennium has initiated a phase of American 'informal' imperial expansion into Eastern Europe and the Caucasus.

The theme of 'empire' in American historiography has yet to be systematically mined for the nuggets which will help scholars rethink the exceptional saga of American transformation – from colony to empire. These essays will help us to think in greater depth about this contentious issue.

Select Bibliography

Adams, Charles Francis (ed.). *Memoirs of John Quincy Adams*, 12 vols (Philadelphia, PA, 1874–7).

Alin, Erika. *The United States and the 1958 Lebanon Crisis* (New York, 1994).

Anderson, Benedict. *Imagined Communities: Reflections on the Origin and Spread of Nationalism* (London, 1991).

Anderson, David L. *Shadows on the White House: Presidents & the Vietnam War, 1945–1975* (Manhattan, 1993).

Anderson, Terry H. *The United States, Great Britain, and the Cold War, 1944–1947* (Columbia, Missouri, 1981).

Aronson, Geoffrey. *From Sideshow to Center Stage: U.S. Policy toward Egypt. 1946–1956* (Boulder, Colorado, 1986).

Ashton, S. R. & S. E. Stockwell (eds). *British Documents on End of Empire [BDEE]: Imperial Policy and Colonial Practice* (London, 1996).

Bagchi, Amiya Kumar. *The Political Economy of Underdevelopment* (Cambridge, 1982).

Barraclough, Geoffrey. *An Introduction to Contemporary History* (Harmondsworth, 1964).

Bailey, Thomas A. *A Diplomatic History of the American People*, 7th edn (New York, 1964).

Barnett, Edmund C. (ed.). *Letters of Members of the Continental Congress*, 8 vols (Washington, DC, 1921–36).

Bills, Scott L. *Empire and the Cold War: the Roots of US–Third World Antagonism, 1945–1947* (New York, 1990).

Brands, H. W. *India and the United States: the Cold Peace* (Boston, 1990).

Brecher, Michael. *Nehru: a Political Biography* (London, 1959).

Brown, Judith. *Gandhi and Civil Disobedience: the Mahatma in Politics, 1928–34* (Cambridge, 1977).

——. *Modern India: the Origins of an Asian Democracy* (Delhi, 1984).

Butterfield Ryan, Henry. *The Vision of Anglo-America: the U.S.–U.K. Alliance and the Emerging Cold War, 1943–1946* (Cambridge, 1987).

Campbell, David. *Writing National Security: US Foreign Policy and the Politics of Identity* (Minneapolis, 1992).

Chase, James and Caleb Carr, *America Invulnerable* (New York, 1988).

Chomsky, Noam. *Turning the Tide: the US and Latin America* (Montreal, 1987).

——. *On Power and Ideology* (Boston, 1987).

Clark, Ian. *Globalization and Fragmentation: International Relations in the Twentieth Century* (Oxford, 1997).

Clymer, Kenton J. *Quest for Freedom: the United States and India's Independence* (New York, 1995).

Coniff, Michael L. *Panama and the United States* (Athens, GA, 1992).

Dallek, Robert. *Franklin D. Roosevelt and American Foreign Policy, 1932–1945* (New York, 1979).

Darby, Philip. *Three Faces of Imperialism: British and American Approaches to Asia and Africa, 1870–1970* (New Haven, 1987).

Darwin, John. *Britain and Decolonisation: the Retreat from Empire in the Post-War World* (London, 1988).

Dennis, Peter. *Troubled Days of Peace: Mountbatten and South East Asia Command, 1945–46* (Manchester, 1987).

Donnison, F. S. V. *British Military Administration in the Far East* (London, 1956).

Donoghue, Michael K. 'Colonialism', in Bruce W. Jentleson and Thomas G. Paterson (eds). *Encyclopedia of US Foreign Relations*, 4 vols (New York, 1997).

Dower, John. *Empire and Aftermath: Yoshida Shigeru and the Japanese Experience, 1878–1954* (Cambridge, 1979).

Dunkerley, James. *Rebellion in the Veins: Political Struggle in Bolivia, 1952–82* (London: Verso, 1984).

———. *Power in the Isthmus* (London, 1988).

———. *The Pacification of Central America: Political Change in the Isthmus, 1987–1993* (London: Verso, 1994).

Eagleton, Terry. *Ideology: an Introduction* (London, 1991).

Eley, Geoff and Ronald Grigor Suny (eds), *Becoming National: a Reader* (New York, 1996).

Ferro, Marc. *Colonization: a Global History* (London, 1997).

Ford, Worthington C. (ed.). *Writings of John Quincy Adams*, 7 vols (New York, 1913–17).

Fraser, Cary. 'Understanding American Policy towards the Decolonization of European Empires, 1945–64', *Diplomacy and Statecraft*, vol. 3, no. 1 (1992).

Galeano, Eduardo. *Open Veins of Latin America* (New York, 1973).

Gardner, Lloyd C. *Economic Aspects of New Deal Diplomacy* (Madison, 1964).

———. *The Creation of the American Empire*, 2nd edn (Chicago, IL, 1976).

———. *Safe for Democracy* (New York, 1984).

———. *Approaching Vietnam: from World War II through Dienbienphu* (New York, 1988).

———. *Spheres of Influence: the Partition of Europe, from Munich to Yalta* (London, 1993).

Giglio, James N. *The Presidency of John F. Kennedy* (Lawrence, 1991).

Gleijeses, Piero. *The Dominican Crisis: the 1965 Constitutionalist Revolt and American Intervention* (Baltimore, 1978).

———. *Shattered Hope: the Guatemalan Revolution and the United States, 1944–1954* (Princeton, NJ, 1991).

Gopal, Sarvepalli. *Jawaharlal Nehru: a Biography* (Delhi, 1975).

Green, Duncan. *Silent Revolution: the Rise of Market Economics in Latin America* (London, 1995).

Halebsky, Sandor and Richard L. Harris, *Capital, Power and Inequality in Latin America* (Boulder, 1995).

Hargreaves, John D. *Decolonization in Africa* (Harlow, 1996).

Hathaway, Robert M. *Ambiguous Partnership: Britain and America, 1944–1947* (New York, 1981).

Healy, David. *The United States in Cuba, 1898–1903* (Madison, WI, 1963).

———. *Drive to Hegemony: the United States in the Caribbean, 1898–1917* (New York, 1988).

Hess, Gary R. *America Encounters India, 1941–47* (Baltimore, 1971).

——. *The United States's Emergence as a Southeast Asian Power, 1940–1950* (New York, 1987).

——. 'Accomodation amidst Discord: the United States, India, and the Third World', *Diplomatic History*, 16 (Winter, 1992).

Hobsbawm, Eric. *Nations and Nationalism since 1780: Programme, Myth, Reality* (rev. edn; Cambridge, UK, 1992).

——. *The Age of Extremes* (London, 1994).

Hobson, J. A. *Imperialism: a Study* (London, 1902).

Hofstadter, Richard. *The American Political Tradition* (New York, 1954).

Holland, R. F. *European Decolonization 1918–1981: an Introductory Survey* (London, 1985).

Hull, Cordell. *Memoirs* (London, 1948).

Hunt, Michael H. *Ideology and U.S. Foreign Policy* (New Haven, 1987).

——. *The Genesis of Chinese Communist Foreign Policy* (New York, 1996).

Jacobsen, Harold K. 'Mandates', in Jentleson and Paterson (eds). *Encyclopedia of US Foreign Relations* (New York, 1997).

Jagan, Cheddi. *The West on Trial* (London, 1966).

Johnston, Laurie. 'Por la escuela cubana en Cuba Libre: Themes in the History of Primary and Secondary Education in Cuba, 1899–1958', unpublished PhD dissertation, University of London, 1996.

Karnow, Stanley. *In Our Image: America's Empire in the Philippines* (New York, 1989).

Kalb, Madeleine G. *The Congo Cables: the Cold War in Africa from Eisenhower to Kennedy* (New York, 1982).

Kerkvliet, Benedict J. *The Huk Rebellion: a Study of Peasant Revolution in the Philippines* (Berkeley, 1977; 1979 edn).

Kimball, Warren (ed.), *Churchill and Roosevelt: the Complete Correspondence: Volume I: Alliance Emerging* (London, 1984).

——. *The Juggler: Franklin Roosevelt as Wartime Statesman* (Princeton, 1991).

——. *Forged in War: Roosevelt, Churchill and the Second World War* (New York, 1997).

Knock, Thomas J. *To End All Wars* (New York, 1992).

Kolko, Gabriel. *The Politics of the War: the World and United States Foreign Policy, 1943–1945* (New York, 1968).

——. *Confronting the Third World: United States Foreign Policy 1945–1980* (New York, 1988).

LaFeber, Walter. *The New Empire* (New York, 1963).

——. (ed.). *John Quincy Adams and American Continental Empire* (Chicago, IL, 1965).

——. 'Roosevelt, Churchill, and Indochina, 1942–1945', *American Historical Review*, 80 (Fall, 1975).

——. 'An Expansionist's Dilemma', *Constitution*, V (Fall, 1993).

——. *Inevitable Revolutions: the United States in Central America*, 2nd edn (New York, 1993).

——. *The American Search for Opportunity, 1865–1913* (Cambridge, 1993).

Lau, Albert. *The Malayan Union Controversy 1942–1948* (Singapore, 1991).

Lee, Steven Hugh. *Outposts of Empire: Korea, Vietnam, and the Origins of the Cold War in Asia* (Montreal, 1995).

Leech, Margaret. *In the Days of McKinley* (New York, 1959).

Leffler, Melvyn. *A Preponderance of Power: National Security, the Truman Administration and the Cold War* (Stanford, Calif., 1992).

Link, Arthur S. *Wilson*, 5 vols (Princeton, NJ, 1947).

Louis, Wm Roger. *Imperialism at Bay: the United States and the Decolonization of the British Empire, 1941–1945* (Oxford, 1977).

Louis, Wm Roger and Hedley Bull (eds), *The 'Special Relationship': Anglo-American Relations since 1945* (Oxford, 1986).

Louis, Wm Roger and Ronald Robinson, 'The Imperialism of Decolonization', *Journal of Imperial and Commonwealth History* 22, 3 (Sept. 1994).

Louis, William Roger (ed.), *More Adventures with Britannia* (New York, 1998).

Lucas, W. Scott. *Divided We Stand: Britain, the US, and the Suez Crisis* (London, 1991).

——. 'Campaigns of Truth: the Psychological Strategy Board and American Ideology, 1951–1953', *The International History Review* (May 1996).

Mahoney, R. D. *JFK: Ordeal in Africa* (Oxford, 1983).

Marcum, John. *The Angolan Revolution, Volume 1, 1950–1962* (Baltimore, 1969).

Mayer, Arno. *Political Origins of the New Diplomacy, 1917–1918* (New Haven, 1959).

McCormick, Thomas. *China Market* (Chicago, 1967).

——. *America's Half-Century: United States Foreign Policy in the Cold War* (Baltimore, 1989).

McKahin, T. *Intervention* (New York, 1986).

McMahon, Robert J. *Colonialism and Cold War: the United States and the Struggle for Indonesian Independence, 1945–49* (Ithaca, 1981).

——. 'Toward a Post-Colonial Order: Truman Administration Policies toward South and Southeast Asia', in Michael Lacey (ed.). *The Truman Presidency* (Cambridge, 1989).

——. *The Cold War on the Periphery: the United States and South Asia, 1947–1969* (New York, 1994).

Merrill, Dennis. *Bread and the Ballot: the United States and India's Economic Development, 1947–1963* (Chapel Hill, 1990).

Morgan, H. Wayne. *William McKinley and His America* (Syracuse, NY, 1963).

Morison, Elting E. (ed.). *The Letters of Theodore Roosevelt*, 8 vols (Cambridge, MA, 1951).

Munro, Dana G. *Intervention and Dollar Diplomacy in the Caribbean, 1900–1921* (Princeton, 1964).

Natarajan, L. *American Shadow over India* (Delhi, 1956).

Neiss, Frank. *A Hemisphere to Itself: a History of US–Latin American Relations* (London, 1990).

Nicolsen, Harold. *Peacemaking, 1919* (Boston, 1933).

O'Brien, Thomas F. *The Revolutionary Mission: American Enterprise in Latin America, 1900–1945* (New York, 1996).

Orders, Paul. 'Britain, Australia, New Zealand and the Expansion of American Power in the South-West Pacific, 1941–46', unpublished University of Cambridge PhD (1997).

Osterhammel, Jürgen. *Colonialism: a Theoretical Overview* (Princeton, 1997).

Patterson, David S. *Toward a Warless World: the Turmoil of the American Peace Movement, 1887–1914* (Bloomington, 1976).

Perez, Louis A. *Cuba and the United States: Ties of Singular Intimacy* (Athens, Georgia, 1990).

———. *Cuba: between Reform and Revolution*, 2nd edn (New York, 1995).

Porter, A. N. and A. J. Stockwell (eds), *British Imperial Policy and Decolonization, 1938–64, I 1938–51* (Basingstoke, 1987).

Pratt, Julius W. *America's Colonial Experiment: How the US Gained, Governed and in Part Gave Away a Colonial Empire* (New York, 1950).

Pringle, Henry. *Theodore Roosevelt: a Biography* (New York, 1931).

Rajan, M. S. *India in World Affairs* (Bombay, 1964).

Reece, R. H. W. *The Name of Brooke: the End of White Rajah Rule in Sarawak* (Kuala Lumpur, 1982).

Ricard, Serge. 'The Exceptionalist Syndrome in U.S. Continental and Overseas Expansionism', in David K. Adams and Cornelis A. van Minnen (eds), *Reflections on American Exceptionalism* (Keele, 1994).

Richardson, J. D. (ed.). *Messages and Papers of the Presidents*, 10 vols (Washington, DC, 1896).

Roosevelt, Elliot. *As He Saw It* (New York, 1946).

Rosenberg, Emily. *Spreading the American Dream: American Economic and Cultural Expansion, 1890–1945* (New York, 1982).

———. 'Revisiting Dollar Diplomacy: Narratives of Money and Manliness', *Diplomatic History* 22, no. 2 (Spring 1998).

Rotter, Andrew J. *The Path to Vietnam: Origins of the American Commitment to Southeast Asia* (Ithaca, 1987).

Ryan, David. 'US Expansionism: from the Monroe Doctrine to the Open Door', in Philip John Davies (ed.), *Representing and Imagining America* (Keele, 1996).

Safa, Helen I. *The Myth of the Male Breadwinner: Women and Industrialization in the Caribbean* (Boulder: Westview Press, 1995).

Said, Edward. *Culture and Imperialism* (London, 1993).

Sbrega, John. *Anglo-American Relations and Colonialism in East Asia, 1941–45* (New York, 1983).

Schlesinger, Stephen and Stephen Kinzer, *Bitter Fruit* (London, 1982).

Sherwood, Marika. *Kwame Nkrumah: the Years Abroad, 1935–1947* (Accra, Ghana, 1996).

Short, Anthony. *The Communist Insurrection in Malaya* (London, 1975).

Singh, Anita Inder. *The Limits of British Influence: South Asia and the Anglo-American Relationship, 1947–1956* (London, 1993).

Smith, Tony. 'Decolonization', in Joel Krieger (ed.), *The Oxford Companion to Politics of the World* (New York, 1993).

———. *America's Mission: the United States and the Worldwide Struggle for Democracy in the Twentieth Century* (Princeton, 1994).

Stanley, Peter W. *A Nation in the Making: the Philippines and the United States, 1899–1921* (Cambridge, MA, 1974).

Stephanson, Anders. *Kennan and the Art of Foreign Policy* (Cambridge, MA, 1989).

———. *Manifest Destiny: American Expansionism and the Empire of Right* (New York, 1995).

Stockwell, A. J. *British Policy and Malay Politics during the Malayan Union Experiment, 1942–1948* (Kuala Lumpur, 1979).

———. ' "A widespread and long-concocted plot to overthrow government in

Malaya?" The Origins of the Malayan Emergency', *Journal of Imperial and Commonwealth History* 21, 3 (Sept. 1993).

———. (ed.), *British Documents on End of Empire: Malaya* (London, 1995).

———. 'Malaysia: the Making of a Neo-Colony?', *JICH*, 26, 2 (May 1998).

Stubbs, Richard. *Hearts and Minds in Guerrilla Warfare: the Malayan Emergency 1948–1960* (Singapore, 1989).

Thomas, Martin. *The French Empire at War 1940–45* (Manchester, 1998).

Thorne, Christopher. 'Indochina and Anglo-American Relations, 1942–45', *Pacific Historical Review*, 45 (1976).

———. *Allies of a Kind: the United States, Britain, and the War against Japan, 1941–1945* (New York, 1978).

Thullen, G. *Problems of the Trusteeship System: a Study of Political Behaviour in the United Nations* (Geneva, 1964).

Tomlinson, B. R. *The Political Economy of the Raj, 1914–1947: the Economics of Decolonization in India* (London, 1979).

van Minnen, Cornelius A. and John F. Sears (eds), *FDR and His Contemporaries: Foreign Perceptions of an American President* (New York, 1992).

Venkataramani, M. S. and B. K. Shrivastava, *Roosevelt, Churchill, and Gandhi* (Delhi, 1983).

Wahab Sayed-Ahmed, M. A. *Nasser and American Foreign Policy 1952–1956* (London, 1989).

Wallerstein, Immanuel. *The Capitalist World Economy: Essays* (New York, 1979).

Williams, Walter L. 'US Indian Policy and the Debate over Philippine Annexation', *Journal of American History*, LXVI (March 1980).

Williams, William Appleman. *The Tragedy of American Diplomacy* (Cleveland, OH, 1959).

———. *et al.* (eds), *America in Vietnam: a Documentary History* (New York, 1985).

Wood, Robert E. 'From The Marshall Plan to the Third World', in Melvyn Leffler and David Painter (eds). *Origins of the Cold War: an International History* (London, 1994).

Index

DATE DUE